TREATING THE OTHER THIRD

TREATING THE OTHER THIRD

Vicissitudes of Adolescent Development and Therapy

H. Spencer Bloch

KARNAC

First published in 2015 by
Karnac Books Ltd
118 Finchley Road, London NW3 5HT

British Library Cataloguing in Publication Data

A C.I.P. for this book is available from the British Library

 ISBN 978 1 78220 219 6

Edited, designed and produced by The Studio Publishing Services Ltd
www.publishingservicesuk.co.uk
e-mail: studio@publishingservicesuk.co.uk

Printed in Great Britain

www.karnacbooks.com

CONTENTS

ACKNOWLEDGMENTS

While writing my earlier book (*Adolescent Development, Psychopathology, and Treatment*) in mid-career, the assistance of colleagues benefited me immeasurably, from editing to helping to articulate some ideas. I was also the beneficiary of the generosity of well-known clinician–researchers in the field of adolescence with whom I was not acquainted, but who agreed to write pre-publication reviews for an unknown author. But when writing this book, approaching the end of my career, I decided to do it all by myself.

That is not to say that I proceeded without objects of my appropriate gratitude. Mentors early in my career and patients throughout years in practice certainly deserve acknowledgement for having provided the foundation and scaffolding upon which my professional being evolved. But their contribution to this endeavour seems less salient than gratitude closer to where (as I will subsequently elaborate) all therapeutic roads lead—to home. My wife, Judy, helpmate extraordinaire, always willingly dropped everything to offer a perceptive opinion when I felt uncertain about the best choice of word or phrase, what seemed redundant, or, conversely, needed elaboration. Our son, David, an attorney, clarified intricacies of the case described in Chapter Four. Our daughter-in-law, Tanya Bloch, photographed the requisite likeness of the author for publicity purposes. Our daughter, Laura Jones, and son-in-law, Emery, always responded immediately to my periodic struggles with word processing and computer glitches. The perspective of our daughter, Monica Kaderali, a practitioner of traditional Chinese medicine, on treating physical conditions lent effective support to my persuasion about an aspect of treating psychiatric conditions. And our son-in-law, Karim, always stood ready to respond had I need for his assistance.

Further in the past, diffused imperceptibly and wafting in the background landscape where professional and personal essence intermingle, the influence of my sociologist–criminologist–author father, Herbert A. Bloch, my mother, Adeline, herself a nonpareil helpmate, and my younger sister, Susan Bloch (quoted in the Prologue of my earlier book) enrich much of what I think, feel, and do. Each of them cast long enough shadows in their own right not to need acknowledgement from me, yet none lived to see it in print.

Finally, back to the present, and certainly not least, is my great appreciation, respect, and admiration for Rod Tweedy, Editor, and Constance Govindin, Publicity Manager, at Karnac Books. For, in a day and age when publishers seem wedded to the herd instinct of following only the currently most popular trends, they neither flinched nor hesitated to accept a manuscript that did not—one that went more and less against the grain.

ABOUT THE AUTHOR

H. Spencer Bloch, MD, has devoted the past forty-five years of his career to the psychiatric and psychoanalytic treatment of children, adolescents, and adults in San Rafael, California, including teaching and consulting with therapists and staffs of non-profit agencies and special education schools. Following graduation with honors from Amherst and AΩA from Cornell University Medical College, he completed an internship in internal medicine at Bellevue Hospital in New York City, and then psychiatric residencies in Boston at Harvard's Massachusetts Mental Health Center, Judge Baker Guidance Center, and the Children's Hospital Medical Center, where he served as chief resident in child psychiatry. The latter followed an interruption for military service in Vietnam, where he was awarded the Bronze Star for meritorious service, and duty at Letterman General Hospital in San Francisco. Dr Bloch trained and taught courses on adolescent and oedipal development at the San Francisco Psychoanalytic Institute. He is certified in the psychoanalysis of children and adolescents, and adults, and board-certified in general psychiatry and child and adolescent psychiatry. A distinguished life fellow of both the American Academy of Child and Adolescent Psychiatry and of the American Psychiatric Association, his published articles have appeared in major psychiatric and psychoanalytic journals.

PROLOGUE

Perhaps the most unexpected boon from the maturation of the so-called "evidence-based" revolution in both adult and child/adolescent psychiatry was the paradoxical rediscovery of the value of psychotherapeutic interventions. During the heady youth of this neurobiologically, psychopharmacologically, and epidemiologically driven era, psychotherapy at the least fell by the wayside, and initially seemed destined for the dustbin.[1] But then, as research began providing a more balanced and refined understanding of the efficacy of psychiatric medications, psychotherapeutic treatments also became further studied and compared with medicinal management (see, for example, March, Silva, Vitiello, et al., 2006). To this end, manualized protocols were developed so that psychotherapeutic approaches could be subjected to randomized controlled trials, the "gold standard" of research in the other fields of medicine. And significant positive effects have been demonstrated from variants of cognitive, behavioral, and interpersonal therapy—as stand-alone treatments for some conditions, and as adjuncts or in combination with medicinal management in others. While elements of psychodynamic psychotherapy are embedded in these other psychotherapies (Shedler, 2010), nevertheless, the major casualty of this era seemed to be psychodynamic therapy that originated from psychoanalytic precepts.

Psychoanalytically influenced, psychodynamic psychotherapy itself had for some time been evolving in the direction of greater balance between drive theory, ego psychology, the role of object relations, and the stance of the therapist *vis-à-vis* the patient. But it had not been thought to lend itself as readily to manualized approaches or randomized controlled trials (Milrod, 2009). Yet, it has been observed that the necessary "methodologic rigor" has been achieved (Michels, 2009, p. 1319), and "more and more psychodynamic studies are being published in high-impact, peer-reviewed journals" (Hoffman, 2009, p. 1481). Positive results have been reported from randomized, controlled studies for children and for the mother–preschool child dyad (Lieberman, Ippen, & Van Horn, 2006; Moran, Fonagy, Kurtz, et al., 1991; Muratori, Picchi, Bruni, et al., 2003; Toth, Maughan, Manly et al., 2002; Trowell, Kolvin, Weeramanthri, et al., 2002; Trowell, Rhode, Miles, et al., 2003, the latter summarized in Ritvo, 2006a,b, 2007), and for adults (Bateman & Fonagy, 2009; Clarkin, Levy, Lenzenweger, et al., 2007; Diener, Hilsenroth, & Weinberger, 2007; Leichsenring, Salzer, Jaeger, et al., 2009; McMain, Links, Gnam, et al., 2009; Milrod, Leon, Busch, et al., 2007; also see Moran, 2007 for new therapies which incorporate psychodynamic aspects). These studies are still few compared to those of other psychotherapeutic modalities, and only recently has comparison between psychodynamic and other psychotherapeutic modalities been reported (Driessen, Van, Don, et al., 2013; Leichsenring, Salzer, Jaeger, et al., 2009; Thase, 2013).

Yet, the understandable enthusiasm within the fields of psychiatry and psychology to legitimize psychodynamic and other psychotherapies in this way has, nevertheless, left lingering questions. At base is whether "evidence-based medicine" as currently conceptualized and accepted by the field of child psychiatry is authentically applicable to the mental health and psychological disorders of children and adolescents (Gupta, 2004; Szatmari, 2003, 2004; Waddell & Godderis, 2005). Or, at the least, is the current exclusive subscription to this model effectively hindering rather than promoting knowledge of effective treatments (Brubaker, 2013)?

Psychoanalytically oriented psychodynamic psychotherapy had probably been the most influential treatment model in the USA since the Second World War—as, if not more widely espoused than the other major approach, behavior modification treatment derived from social learning theory. Basically, it traces symptoms and aberrant behaviors to the individual child and adolescent's efforts to resolve normative, internal, developmental conflicts. Unique features of the on-going interaction between each person's endowment and experiences can render these intrapsychic conflicts problematic and their resolution symptomatic. Given that, are the plethora of variables and uniqueness of individual experiences implicit in the foregoing description amenable to this research model (without even considering the vicissitudes and vagaries of the patient–therapist interaction)? And how can essential elements of a paradigm for psychodynamic psychotherapy for children and adolescents be derived (see Milrod, 2009)?

Or, as a recent commentator from outside the field observed, is the mental health field as a whole based on a degree of uncertainty and individual variation that makes it impossible and distracting to attempt such reductionism? Rather, Brooks (2013) characterized mental health practitioners not as heroes of science like those in the other medical specialties, but as heroes of uncertainty. While his appellation as "heroes" is undeservedly flattering, his point is well taken. He noted, "The best psychiatrists are not coming up with abstract rules that homogenize treatments. They are combining an awareness of common patterns with an acute attention to the specific circumstances of a unique human being" (p. A19). Can "common patterns" and "specific circumstances of a unique human being" be conflated into data that can meaningfully be integrated into manualized protocols?

In any event, the developing credibility of this "evidence-based" research model for psychodynamic psychotherapy has in turn created another problem in child/adolescent psychiatry and psychology (see for example, Tynan & Pendley, 2013). The current preoccupation with producing statistically significant studies seems to be shifting research interest away from the importance heretofore accorded the external, interpersonal environmental side of the nurture–nature interaction. The latter refers to separate contributions from endowment and experiences to the individual's final psychological organization (i.e., Freud's complemental series, or the psychosocial dimension of the biopsychosocial model). It appears that is being replaced by greater emphasis on the genetic/neurobiological "environment", effectively moving toward an exclusively biological model of development (e.g., Hoffman, 2014; Petanjek & Kostovic, 2012; Raznahan, Greenstein, Lee, et al., 2012; see also Hyman & Lieberman, 2013). Much will certainly be learned from studying the genetic/neurobiological correlates of an individual's ultimate psychological structure. However, as a lead author of the genome-wide association studies on shared heritability across mental disorders observed,

> ... heritable risks are only a part of the pathophysiology of psychiatric disorders. Disease-triggering environmental factors and gene-environmental interactions remain mostly unknown. Other research methods are needed to clarify the sources of environmental risks. (Yan 2013, p. 22 reporting observations by Kendler)

So, it would be unfortunate if the biomedical/genetic emphasis were to occur at the expense of understanding the manner in which the external experiences of individual children/adolescents become integrated into their psychological development/structure (including their neurobiological environment), and their relevance to treatment from a practical clinical standpoint. This is an area where single case study retains an important role.

Yet, single case study has fallen out of favor except in a few psychoanalytic publications. Neither is it clear how influential these are in both the mainstream of current clinical practice and psychotherapeutic research. And, parenthetically, at least some of these psychoanalytic publications seem hampered by conflicts regarding age-old shibboleths about what constitutes psychoanalysis. This, in turn, compromises acceptance of credible ideas originating from within their own field.

If the trend I am suggesting is accurate, the sobering implications of a recent study should be carefully considered before reducing or eliminating any reasonable sources of data from research: a review of all original studies published between 2001 and 2010 in the *New England Journal of Medicine*, the medical journal with the highest impact rating (and, thus, expected to influence medical practices) found that 146 articles, approximately half of those related to the then current standard of care, reversed those practices (Prasad, Vandross, Toomey, et al., 2013). That is, the existing practices were found to be no better than lesser therapies. An accompanying editorial observed,

> Despite better laboratory science, fascinating technology, and theoretically mature designs after 65 years of randomized trials, ineffective,

harmful, expensive medical practices are being introduced more frequently now than at any other time in the history of medicine. (Ioannidis, 2013, p. 780)

If "evidence-based" research in fields much better suited to the randomized control model is so fallible, can we expect better when applying that model to psychiatry, much less to child and adolescent psychiatry?

At the least, those findings should raise a cautionary note before throwing single case study out with the proverbial bathwater. "Evidence-based research" has become synonymous with the large sample, less intensive, epidemiological perspective, while single case study involves intense scrutiny of the smallest sample size possible. The limitations of each are well recognized: That of the first is epitomized in the adage that "statistics have limited relevance to the individual case", whereas overreaching when extrapolating conclusions is the pitfall of the second. To date, neither can rightfully claim to be the only, or the most accurate, source of ideas or data that may advance our understanding and treatment of adolescents. Thus, seeking insight from both perspectives is reasonable.

Some single case studies should contribute to developing increasingly accurate clinical paradigms for use in protocols of "evidence-based" studies. In others, such insights, paradigms, and techniques developed might have to stand on their own. That is, they will be utilized by practitioners undertaking psychotherapy that can only succeed if it is not time limited (Driessen, Van, Don, et al., 2013; Glass, 2009; Leichsenring & Rabung, 2008). It is also worth remembering that psychodynamically oriented therapy is not only directed toward symptom reversal when treating adolescents. The latter is important and, understandably, the manner in which improvement is measured in "evidence-based" studies. However, centered as it is on how symptom formation relates to psychological development, the sought-for endpoint includes evidence of the resumption of progressive development. Thus, the therapist's on-going assessment should always be considering how he or she anticipates their adolescent patients will be psychologically functioning several years down the road of their lives from that moment in their developmental time when they are being treated.

In an effort to bridge the gap between these two approaches, extensive surveys of the clinical and evidence-based literature that I think would be most potentially useful to clinicians are incorporated in this book. To this end, *Treating the Other Third* refers to one appropriate focus for such study, which is that more than one-third of adolescent patients, for whatever reason, do not respond to psychotropic medication.[2] Specifically, Part I is devoted to the psychotherapeutic treatment of severe psychopathology (suicidal depression, bipolar symptoms, bulimia) that is typically managed with medications. Detailed case descriptions are utilized to explicate both the internal conflicts responsible for symptom formation and the difficulties encountered when trying to maintain treatment in the face of the adolescent's normal developmental imperative to emancipate from relationships with parental-type figures (Chapter One). Chapter Two illustrates the manner in which an adolescent's strivings to complete development can be capitalized upon to lead and advance the treatment. Techniques developed to accommodate both circumstances are elaborated and enumerated.

Parts II and III consider, respectively, unique and collective outcomes of development. Part II focuses on two outlier end points of psychological development with respect to the opposite poles of relatedness—that is, the objects of one's love and sexual desire, and of one's aggression. Chapter Three traces a possible developmental pathway to homosexuality. A specific developmental trajectory is posited, in part clarified by the failure of the therapist to respond to the patient in a certain way. Also, the confounding problems created for practitioners when clinical issues become drawn into political agenda are discussed. The latter refers to the controversy regarding the normality or abnormality of homosexuality. Chapter Four describes a type of developmental experience that led an adolescent to the most serious of aggressive acts, and it posits that a specific psychodynamic factor can instantaneously motivate a shift between homicidal and suicidal inclinations with devastating consequences from either position.

In Part III, the interface between developmental psychology and sociology is examined in one specific respect. Chapter Five addresses the question of how dramatic changes in both normative adolescent practices (risk-taking behavior) and in social institutions (divorce and day care) can occur in one to two generations. A specific contribution from the psychological development of individuals is proposed as a necessary condition for such societal changes to evolve so quickly.

Finally, what is the organizing theme or purpose of this book's three seemingly disparate sections? It is to make a case, at a time when "evidence-based" research on psychodynamic psychotherapy is gaining momentum, for the continuing, fundamental importance of contributions from single case studies for identifying and more accurately defining clinical paradigms as a research tool to deepen our understanding of psychological development, psychopathology, and treatment of adolescents. To this end, distinctive insights from each patient that are likely to be relevant to at least some other adolescents, but probably could not be identified in broader population analyses than individual case study, are illustrated:

1. To understand the development of and to treat severe (and less serious) psychopathology, especially when it does not respond to medication or when medicine is refused.
2. To illustrate and emphasize the profundity of environmental influences on the individual child and adolescent's psychological development during an era when that seems to have been brushed aside in favor of genetic and biochemical formulations.
3. To consider that some remediable roots of recent disadvantageous sociological changes may be traceable to the psychological development of individuals. For, if so, then the focus of therapeutic efforts might appropriately revert to according parents a more central role in, and responsibility for, preventing and, thus, reversing these larger problems than the dispensing of medication implies is necessary.[3] If successful, that approach and emphasis, in addition to being more gratifying to all involved, would be better placed than the alternative expectation that seems to abound today: that the solutions for our psychological ills are to be sought in pills or from larger groups than the nuclear family—when, in fact, "All (therapeutic) roads lead to Home."

PART I
TREATING THE OTHER THIRD

Introduction

S ince epidemiology and psychopharmacology displaced psycho-dynamics from the center stage of child and adolescent psychiatry and psychology, clinicians of all professional disciplines have felt under greater pressure to medicate adolescents—even if on an empirical basis. The result has been sufficiently dramatic that a recent, official "Practice Parameter" published by the American Academy of Child and Adolescent Psychiatry noted that ". . . reports of increased psychotropic medication use has also led to concerns that some children and adolescents are being over-diagnosed with psychiatric disorders and are being treated with medication/s that are not appropriate for them" (American Academy of Child and Adolescent Psychiatry, 2009, p. 962).

Yet, this trend persists, even as the experimental rationale has lost much of its authority on the basis of newer research findings and re-examination of published and unpublished data. For example, half of antidepressant studies (generally of patients eighteen years and older) fail to produce a significant response (Kirsch & Antonuccio, 2002; Kirsch, Moore, Scoboria, et al., 2002; Sloan & Stancavish, 2005). It now remains a matter of controversy whether even severe outpatient depressions respond better to medication than to non-medicinal treatments or placebo (DeRubeis, Gelfand, Tang, et al., 1999; Sloan & Stancavish, 2005). A review of four meta-analyses of antidepressant effectiveness/efficacy studies submitted to the FDA, and an analysis of the largest, and perhaps most carefully conceived and executed study, Sequenced Treatment Alternatives to Relieve Depression (STAR*D), reported antidepressants to be only "marginally efficacious" compared to placebo. Neither antidepressants (nor cognitive therapy) achieved positive results for the majority of patients (Pigott, Levanthal, Alter, et al., 2010).

Regarding youth more specifically, with the possible exception of fluoxetine (see Whittington, Kendall, Fonagy, et al., 2004b; Wohlfarth, Lekkerkerker, & van Zwieten, 2004), the latter recently disputed (Cooper, Callahan, Shintani, et al., 2014), meta-analyses of the risk–benefit ratio of serotonin and serotonin/norepinephrine reuptake inhibitors have unfavorable risk–benefit profiles in 5–18 year-olds, when unpublished, negative outcome studies are included (Whittington, Kendall, Fonagy, et al., 2004a). The NIMH-funded Treatment for Adolescents with Depression (TADS) found statistically greater efficacy of medicine compared to placebo. However, 77% of those treated with medication failed to achieve full remission after the first twelve weeks of treatment (Kennard, Silva, Vitiello, et al., 2006); and 80% of those treated with medication continued to experience significant impairment (Jensen, 2006; Vitiello, Rohde, Silva, et al., 2006). Six to nine months of treatment were required to achieve response rates of 81% for fluoxetine or cognitive–behavioral therapy and 86% for combined treatment. But 30% failed to meet remission criteria during the one-year follow-up (Yan, 2009). And the findings from the longer-term follow-up study are considered less "robust" than those from the initial twelve weeks because of cumulative attrition of one-third of the original cohort of 327 moderate to severely depressed adolescents and lack of a placebo arm during the longer study (March & Vitiello, 2009, p. 1118). Also, it was concluded that about 40% of treated patients do not respond to either monotherapy (March & Vitiello, 2009).

The conclusions from the extended segment of the Treatment of Early-Onset Schizophrenia Spectrum (TEOSS) study are perhaps even more dramatic. To determine the long-term efficacy and safety of antipsychotic medications in adolescents after one year of treatment, strict, double-blind protocols were maintained after the acute phase, eight-week study (Findling, Johnson, McClellan, et al., 2010). (The initial eight-week study had found 50% maximum response and no superiority of second- over first-generation antipsychotics (Sikich, Frazier, McClellan, et al., 2008).) Only 12% of the original 116 participants completed the extended phase. Lack of efficacy and side effects were the most common reasons for discontinuing. In addition to demonstrating the importance of continuing studies past an acute-treatment phase, Findling (2010) pointed out the need to find better, safer treatments for psychoses in adolescents. While the current common wisdom in the field emphasizes that better medicines need to be found and ways of determining which patients will respond, results like these should do nothing to discourage investment in psychotherapeutic approaches, especially for the adolescent population.

The re-assessment of the existing research literature centers on the premise that "Evidence-based medicine is valuable to the extent that the evidence base is complete and unbiased" (Turner, Matthews, Linardatos, et al., 2008, p. 252). The findings—selective publication favoring positive outcome studies, multiple publication of the same study findings, selective reporting in studies sponsored by pharmaceutical companies, positive reporting of studies and reporting greater effect sizes than FDA conclusions about the same data, plus failure to include published or unpublished but available negative ones in meta-analyses (Turner, Matthews, Linardatos, et al., 2008) prompt reflection on the degree to which journal readers have been treated to "evidence b(i)ased medicine" (Melander, Ahlqvist-Rastad, Meijer, et al., 2003).[4] The last-noted lack of access to all existing studies of a medication has called into question the very legitimacy of meta-analyses, the gold standard for authenticating the efficacy of research (Wieseler, McGuaran, & Kaiser, 2010). In fact, the editors of the *British Medical Journal* planned to devote a themed issue to this matter in late 2011, citing that "urgent action is needed to restore the integrity of the medical evidence base" (Godlee & Loder 2010, p. c5641).

Also, the perennial matter of the fallibility of evidential data has been raised. That refers to the degree to which the interpretation of data is influenced by subjectivity emanating from within and/or deriving from outside the individual interpreters of that data. The issue of integrity in scientific inquiry has always hovered at the periphery of ours, as it does all fields. Yet, one wonders if it has moved toward the center in recent years, based on the type of findings outlined above in conjunction with more recent considerations. The latter involve the degree to which current psychiatric practice, which is largely pharma-cologic, has been unduly influenced by the pharmaceutical industry's financial relationship with leaders in our field. Parenthetically, ProPublica, an investigative journalism group, determined that in 2009–2010, more psychiatrists received payments from pharmaceutical companies than practitioners of any other medical specialty (Wood & Lowes, 2010). At issue is whether the prevalence of personal income payments to prominent academic, research, and other psychiatrists has created "a culture of influence" (Insel, 2010, p. 1193). For example, a recent survey of the members of twenty work groups responsible for the American Psychiatric Association guidelines for treatment of schizophrenia, bipolar disorder, and major depressive disorder re-vealed that 90% had undisclosed ties to industry (Cosgrove, Bursztajn, Krimsky, et al., 2009, cited in Insel, 2010). And, a study of published, randomized, placebo-controlled, double-blind clinical trials revealed that those for which there was author conflict of interest were 4.9 times more likely to report drug superiority over placebo (Perlis, Perlis, Wu, et al., 2005). Such findings raise questions about whether these relationships have biased widely promulgated recommendations in favor of more expensive drugs when evidence supports the efficacy of generics. Moreover, proven, non-pharmacologic interventions have been underutilized. Basically, the integrity of our field appears to have been compromised by the public perception and reality of these finan-cial relationships between prominent psychiatrists and drug com-panies (Insel, 2010). While unconscionable if accurate, the sum and substance of all these new disclosures have, one hopes, reduced a kind of field-wide complacency that seemed to have settled in about the use of psychotropic drugs to the exclusion of non-medicinal treatments. Parenthetically, one gets the impression that the editorial leadership of American child psychiatry may have embraced the evidence-based paradigm and psychopharmacology more indiscriminately than have their counterparts in other countries. In any event, the matter of the most effective and safest treatments remains less clear-cut than rank and file practitioners might have been led to believe.

Several other factors complicate efforts to determine the most effective treatments:

1. People are disinclined to use psychiatric medications. While acknowledging their effectiveness, nevertheless only 41% of

almost 1400 Americans interviewed would take antidepressants. Fifty-six percent would take medication if they feared "going crazy" and were experiencing physical symptoms associated with intense fear, and 37% were unlikely to take psychiatric medications under any circumstances (Croghan, Tomlin, Pescosolido, et al., 2003). Moreover, as many as 60% of patients fail to take prescribed antidepressant medications for a recommended six months of treatment (Bowes, 2002). Furthermore, among Americans and Canadians, the adolescent/young adult group, that is, the subjects of this book, is the least likely to adhere to prescribed medicinal regimens (Edlund, Wang, Berglund, et al., 2002; see also Gibbons, Hur, Baumik, et al., 2006). In a recent meta-analysis of studies that examined patient preference for anxiety and depressive disorders, 75% of patients preferred psychological rather than medicinal treatment (McHugh, Whitton, Peckham, et al., 2013).

Especially among Americans surveyed in the 18–34-year-old age range, there was greater willingness to seek mental health treatment and less embarrassment about doing so during the years 2001–2003 than in 1990–1992 (Mojtabai, 2007). Also, 34% of patients recruited for a study of panic disorder refused to take medication while only 0.3% refused to receive psychotherapy (Hofman, Barlow, Papp, et al., 1998). So, the reluctance to take medication does not necessarily reflect unwillingness to seek and expect help for psychiatric problems.

2. The existence of placebo effects is well established. In fact, a survey of internists in the USA, consistent with findings in several other countries, found that about half routinely recommended placebos (Harris, 2008). While 60–70% of mildly and moderately depressed patients and those with generalized anxiety disorder respond to medication, 30–40% of them and up to 50% of those suffering panic attacks respond to placebos (see Brown, 2006; Lipton, 2000). Placebos can produce neurochemical changes in the brain similar to those produced by medications. For example, Parkinson's Disease patients experienced the same increase in dopamine in the damaged nigrostriatal system of the brain that the active medications induce (de la Fuente-Fernández, Ruth, Sossi, et al., 2001). In another study, patients given morphine for pain on two consecutive days experienced a placebo

effect when administered saline solution on the third day (Bene-detti, summarized in Stone, 2006). And activation of at least one endorphin site, the μ-opioid receptor, occurred on the basis of expectation and/or need for relief from pain when placebo was administered to healthy volunteers (Zubieta, Bueller, Jackson, et al., 2005; also summarized in Milne, 2005 and Spittler, 2005). Cognitive expectation and/or behavioral conditioning (which are difficult to differentiate), plus activation of endogenous endorphins and relief of distress are currently thought to account for placebo effects (Brown, 2006). Understanding differences between placebo responders and non-responders is a subject of continuing scrutiny (Stone, 2006).

3. The prevailing theory of therapeutics (developed from medica-tion studies) is that psychotropic medications alter levels of neurotransmitting chemicals in certain parts of the brain. These alterations relieve symptoms by inducing more normal neuro-chemical levels for that individual. Preliminary imaging studies of areas of the brain that are thought to be involved in depressive illness have shown that psychotherapy gives rise to the same kind of normalizing neurochemical alterations in blood flow/cerebral metabolic activity as medications (Brody, Saxena, Stoessel, et al., 2001). Psychodynamic psychotherapy was associated with enhanced, normalizing serotonin uptake in a single case study using radiographic imaging techniques (Viinamäki, Kuikka, Tiihonen, et al., 1998, summarized in Gabbard, 1998). Implications of such findings have been discussed (Gabbard, 1998; Pies, 2004).

4. Prescribing patterns by clinicians can change very quickly. For example, the number of antidepressant prescriptions for patients under eighteen years of age dropped almost 20% in the fifteen months following the Food and Drug Administration's public health advisory warning in March 2004 about the increased risk of suicidality in both children and adults taking these medica-tions (Rosack, 2005). The questions raised include how those patients taken off, or not started on, antidepressants are to be treated (see Pfeffer, 2007). Psychotherapy utilization did not increase (Libby, Brent, Morato, et al., 2007).

The foregoing data prompt reflection on several matters. One is the way clinicians present any form of psychiatric treatment to patients.

In today's prescribing climate, the focus has become one of persuading patients of the value of medication. However, the disinclination to take psychiatric medicines, or continue after having started to do so, and their preference for using non-medicinal treatments bespeaks the desire of people to rely on their own grit, insight, and determination to wrest control over their symptoms. (That may be additional data suggesting that the stigma against psychotherapy is giving way.) The dual findings that medication may not be significantly more efficacious than placebos for some psychiatric conditions, and that placebos and psychotherapy can create the same biochemical changes in the brain as medications, suggest that some realignment of that emphasis with patients is warranted.

Nevertheless, it is not clear what the change from the current prescribing ethos should be. For example, those who emphasize the importance of placebo effect recommend that the prescriber utilize all his/her authority and its trappings to urge the patient to take the medicine and to suggest that he or she will benefit from it (see Brown, 2006; Lipton, 2000). On the other hand, data on placebo compared to medicinal effects, and adolescents' disinclination to take medications, would favor presenting the alternatives without overselling one therapeutic modality. This is especially so since psychotherapy, too, is not free from adverse effects and bad outcomes; the latter, though, are usually less immediately apparent than those from medications. So, thoughtful consideration of alternative treatments that incorporates awareness of the type of data just summarized might be the most judicious and honest way to present psychiatric treatment to adolescent potential patients.

Second, regarding the prevailing theories of therapeutics, more sophisticated refinements than those noted above have been advanced both with respect to the intracellular processes involved in therapeutic change (e.g., Duman, 1998) and the vagaries and malleability of gene expression (Kandel, 1998). However, these, as well as the other postulated mechanisms of the locus of necessary neurochemical changes in the brain, remain theoretical and preliminary (Sackheim, 2001; Thase, 2001). The postulated mechanisms may not be what effect therapeutic change; rather, those measured biochemical changes are the only markers identified to date that correlate with therapeutic improvement. That is, they may be correlational but not causal. In either event, most important are the preliminary findings that similar neurochemical changes can be created by psychotherapy and medication. The sum total of the data just outlined justifies investigating both treatment resources.

Last, there is an additional factor that warrants focusing on psychotherapy for even severe mental disorders. Whether from failure to take prescribed medicine or from non-responsiveness of their psychopathology to available medications, in the aggregate, at least one-third of adolescents treated for serious psychiatric symptoms do not respond to medicine.[5] The following chapter addresses specific issues in the treatment of that sizable minority.

CHAPTER ONE

Treating severe psychopathology*

This chapter is organized around the therapy of a late adolescent who presented with fears that he would suicide impulsively during an immobilizing depression. He went on to develop other serious symptoms during treatment, but he steadfastly refused to take medication, even during the most anxiety-engendering periods of his illness. That refusal never seemed to represent an accession to the despair of his depression. Rather, his rationale for wanting neither medication nor therapist reflected his overriding, normal, developmental imperative to fend for himself—part of his effort to emancipate to a young adult level of psychological autonomy. Issuing an ultimatum to take medicine would have been inappropriate because it was contrary to this developmental prerogative, presumptuous because it was not a sure cure for his symptoms, and fruitless because he would have declined. Refusing to treat him would have been neither professionally responsible at worst nor fitting at best, since none of us has the last word on what makes any treatment effective. So, we worked exclusively psychotherapeutically—as intensively as he would allow.

* An earlier version of this chapter appeared in *The Psychoanalytic Study of the Child*, *66* (2012), and is included here by kind permission of Yale University Press.

The major purpose of this chapter is to elaborate on the integration of the psychodynamic and the developmental, two equally important tasks if his treatment were to succeed. This requires an extended case presentation. One task was identifying and working through a distinctive psychodynamic formulation to relieve his symptoms. The other was managing the perennial problem of retaining adolescents in treatment when this conflicts with their developmental imperatives.

A third purpose is to present a rationale for at times intervening in ways to which we are not typically inclined in conducting psychodynamically oriented treatment of late adolescents and young adults. A fourth is to call attention to some bedrock features of therapy that currently seem in danger of being forgotten, even though they are relevant to any form of treatment of adolescents.

Adolescent development

Instinctual, intersystemic tension between id and the ego–superego constellation is the most frequently described of the intrapsychic conflicts that are the cornerstone of clinical psychoanalysis, the basis of most psychodynamic treatment. This has been particularly so when discussing adolescents, for the upsurge of drives associated with pubertal development has traditionally been understood to initiate the emancipation process of adolescence. Thus, an instinctual conflict becomes the basis for symptoms that arise when adolescent development goes awry.

However, the clinical significance of intrasystemic, intrapsychic conflicts is also well established. These involve the individual's efforts to reconcile different ego motives that have become mutually incompatible. Bibring's (1953) formulation of depression arising "primarily from a tension within the ego itself, from an inner-systemic 'conflict'" (p. 26) is perhaps the best-known example. I have found much adolescent psychopathology better explicated and treated on the basis of intra- or inner systemic conflicts.

* * *

Comprehending my approach to Will requires understanding my ego psychological-oriented conclusions regarding three basic issues of adolescent development (Bloch, 1995): (1) psychological development during adolescence is driven by an inherent, maturational factor which has been characterized as "urges" or "strivings to complete development" (Bibring, 1937; Deutsch, 1944; A. Freud, 1965, 1968; Jones, 1922). But, (2) adolescents must experience a felt sense of confidence that their parents are sponsoring those strivings if they are to achieve a young adult level of psychological independence. Thus, (3) adolescents wish and need to feel they have a basically positive underlying relationship with their parents, despite many seeming expressions to the contrary from their outward behavior.

When adolescents conclude, accurately or not, that what is required to gratify their parents is incompatible with their strivings to move ahead, they experience inner conflict because they are motivated to achieve each of these ego-oriented goals. They typically react to breaches in their relationship with parents or lack of parental sponsorship of their forward movement by experiencing guilt about emancipating. If this emancipatory guilt intensifies to pathological proportions, it becomes akin to the survivor–separation guilt continuum.[6] This type of guilt is invariably accompanied by an "omnipotence complex"; the latter comprises feeling both that one has great power/influence over a troubled parent or sibling, and also responsibility for having caused and/or for rectifying the other's problems (Weiss, 1993; Weiss, Sampson, et al., 1986). (This use of "omnipotence" differs from the historically more typical characterization of "omnipotence" as a postulated feature of the cognitive mindset of two-year-old children as feeling "all powerful".)

Clinically, the latter usually occurs when adolescents conclude that their parents are either weak or hostile, and thus do not (consciously or unconsciously) support their adolescent's forward movement. In response, adolescents tend to sacrifice their own progress. They typically develop signs and symptoms of failing in some equivalent way to the manner in which they perceive their parent(s) to be floundering. Resorting to these defensive identifications appears to be an effort to protect their parents at the expense of their own personal advancement. However, essentially they are trying to reinstate/retain a view of their parents as stronger and more competent than themselves, in the hope that the latter will sponsor their development (Bloch, 1995). This view of adolescent development integrates the intrapsychic and the interpersonal.

Will

Will's mother called to schedule an appointment for her twenty-year-old son, a college junior. She explained that Will was struggling with a lot of things he found difficult to articulate. Three months earlier, his relatively young and healthy father had suffered a severe, paralyzing stroke. He was improving, though gravely disabled with little ability to move. Will had always acted the most insecure of their three children when change occurred. The eldest, his sister, was a rising creative software engineer in a field dominated by men. His brother, Kip, thirteen months older than Will, had a long history of alcohol and drug abuse and was now living at home. Their father, also a successful computer scientist, had been alcoholic, stopping only after she had given him an ultimatum when Will was fifteen.

Will had always refused to get help even though his troubles had been evident for a few years. He was only now willing to see a therapist after he started to "come apart" during finals that spring. He returned home after his father's stroke and was very helpful. His mother characterized him as "a sweet guy with a great heart" who now seemed out of control. For example, he had just lost a job for failing to show up, which was most untypical behavior, since he had always maintained high expectations of himself and others. He now felt life was no longer worth living. We met two days later.

Will was a sad-looking youth whose mild voice and deferential manner seemed incongruous with his imposing physical demeanor. He began by saying, "No offense to you, but I feel that I should and can only work out my problems myself." He had been struggling with depression and "existential anxiety" for a couple of years. He could not foresee making a contribution to the world, or if he were to do so, it would get "washed away to insignificance", that is, not be recognized. He had never felt actively suicidal, but lived with a fear that something was going to happen—that he would suicide without being able to stop himself. Yet, he did not want to hurt his family.

In fact, Will had been resolving his existential dilemma that year in college and planning his future. Then, his father's unexpected illness threw him back into yearning for the closer relationship they had never enjoyed (which Will felt responsible for effecting). Temperamentally, his father had been tight-lipped, explosive, and tended to shame his sons, which Will attributed to drinking. They could play sports together, at which his father was extremely competitive, but whenever Will tried to talk with him, his father was "taciturn" and Will withdrew. He now felt guilty about previously having refused at times to play tennis with his father, who could no longer do such things.

Will thought he was the only one who could heal his family and felt responsible for doing so. To go off and fulfill his own life meant separating from his parents, and Will acted as if he could not tolerate that. While voicing such separation anxiety, which implied dependency, he also feared that fulfilling his potential would be "too much" for other people. His success would occur at the expense of others. That suggested that his avowed separation anxiety warded off awareness of these concerns about overwhelming others. He felt particularly obligated to help Kip, who would otherwise become a derelict or criminal. He also thought his dad's outcome might have been different had Will spoken with him prior to his stroke (i.e., further evidence of an omnipotence complex).

Thus, Will was experiencing emancipatory guilt to survivor guilt proportions, and an omnipotence complex, manifested in feeling responsible for, and able to buoy up, everybody in his family. He was exhibiting defensive identifications, that is, behaviors that were equivalent to the disabilities of his father and Kip. To wit, he would lose his own cogency when talking with his now untypically inarticulate father. And he was imitating his brother in losing the job for being unreliable. Will had used marijuana for years and now drank as well, which he considered the reasons he had drifted off the fast track at college—otherwise he would have surpassed his sister's scholastic achievements.

At our second session, Will waxed poetic about how hard his father had worked and what he had sacrificed for his family. But, in response to questions, he acknowledged harboring a different view: From childhood he had realized that his father's tirades were out of proportion to the provoking stimuli. Yet, Will always felt he himself was terrible and bad, despite his mother's assurances that his actions had not warranted his father's wrath. Will also observed that he would have rather been hit than endure those invectives. Recognizing that a minor action on his part would precipitate a disproportionate reaction from his father enabled Will to consider that he may have sensed that his father was fragile beneath a fearsome exterior.

Will was to contact me after returning from a trip after that second meeting. I sent him this note a week after he was supposed to have called:

Dear Will,

I don't want you to feel as if I'm pursuing you with respect to continuing the work we started, but you indicated when we last met that you'd be in touch with me after the 17th. I'm writing now because in my experience the longer one puts off such matters, the easier it becomes to not follow through. I think that would be a mistake, especially since in the two meetings we had, you yourself identified some very important contributions to your inner turmoil. Those insights hold out the hope and promise of bringing you some well-deserved relief.

So if you have any reservations about resuming from where we left off, please call me without delay so we can address those concerns. For as you realized, the issue of your psychological peace of mind is much too important to let slide any longer. There is no objective reason why you should continue to have to suffer.

I'll look forward to hearing from you.

Will telephoned ten days later, apologized for not having called, and agreed with the substance of my letter.

Engaging Will in treatment

We are usually reluctant to pursue late adolescent patients because it is important to honor their independence and to underscore their responsibility for themselves. But each case must be considered on its own merits. For example, it makes sense to pursue youth who are depressed or discouraged, or think for other reasons that they do not deserve to get better, or have felt rejected by their parents. One attempts to do so in a way that is compelling but still honors their autonomy. Thus, in the note, I was trying to offset resistances by appealing to Will's own perspective. Whether and when to attempt to hold on to him and when to let him go was a continual technical dilemma for the duration of Will's treatment. I will illustrate shortly that we look for cues from adolescent patients to help determine what they need at the moment.

Will's suicidal ideas intensified as he began to realize how irreversible was his father's condition. Will thought that if he himself remained depressed, then his father would somehow be spared the weight of depression, desperation, pessimism, and perhaps the suicidal feelings that Will sensed lurked beneath his father's outwardly good spirits. Although he had no plan, when feeling desperate Will thought he would throw himself from the Golden Gate Bridge. He said he would either call me or put himself in touch with other people at such moments. But he feared the impulse taking him by surprise and having no control over it.

Will's historical difficulty modulating anger and relating to his family

As a child Will would be roused to tears, throwing rocks and knives at his siblings who tormented him. During early adolescence he yelled and cursed at his mother, but feared displaying anger toward his father. So historically Will seemed only able to manage anger by suppressing or impulsively expressing it when frustrated. Also, from a young age he had never felt protected by his parents from merciless teasing by his siblings. This had led him to sense that submission to tormenting (and by inference, acting and feeling helplessly frustrated and hurt) was the price of being accepted as one of the family.

Maintaining treatment as Will analyzes his omnipotence complex and feels better

As we focused on his omnipotence complex, Will wanted to meet less often, for fear of becoming dependent on me, and therapy the central focus of his life. For example, he called on the day of an appointment asking to reschedule. He had awoken feeling better and felt best when he thought he was curing himself, though hastened to add that he did not want to discount the value of our talks. He then canceled the next appointment because he was working with a friend, but called later and we found time to meet that day. In this back and forth of canceling and rescheduling, Will seemed to be testing his fear of dependency and my flexibility. Because he feared being reeled into a relationship of dependency, I attempted to be as accommodating as possible. My motives were to demonstrate that I was not rigid like his father and that I wanted to see him (i.e., was not rejecting). An alternative to offering a corrective ego experience to this transference issue would have been to first explore his reaction were I to offer or not offer him alternative appointments. That would have had the advantage of helping confirm what stance Will truly wanted me to take. But he was just beginning treatment, so I thought he might interpret such an exploration as a veiled criticism. Also, a common technical practice has been to emphasize to such a patient that his therapy had to become the most important thing in his life. You can understand from the approach I am advancing that such a stance would have made it more difficult for Will to continue. Better that he reach his own conclusion about the value of therapy and keep it secret if need be to feel less vulnerable to me.

Will began to exhibit more "observing" than "experiencing" ego. For example, he felt unable to write a paper he had to submit to complete the spring semester and started to sink into depression. But this time he told himself that it had to be done, did it with a sense of relief and pleasure, and now would be a college senior.

Still, his mood fluctuated. He had intrusive thoughts of jumping from the Golden Gate Bridge and realizing in mid-air that he was making a mistake, but it would be too late. That is, he did not want to suicide but feared his impulsivity would preclude warning anybody. Reinforcing the importance of maintaining contact with me (the object relationship) was the way I tried to offset the danger represented by his impulsivity.

On being his brother's keeper

Exploring Will's omnipotence complex with respect to Kip revealed that developing his existential view of the futility of accomplishing anything significant had helped Will accommodate survivor guilt. His achievements risked making unsuccessful Kip look worse to their parents, who had been harder on Kip. Also, while no longer thinking that he had caused Kip's problems, Will still felt responsible for fixing them, and wondered how Kip could have so much influence over his behavior. I suggested that was a reversal that enabled Will to avoid awareness of his even greater fear of having such influence over Kip. Will claimed that was very helpful and agreed to meet twice that week.

Dealing with transference material

Will was now eager to attend sessions. He could put pessimistic ideas out of mind rather than letting them get him down. Yet, because he had nothing on his mind as he drove to a session, he asked about meeting less often. I thought to myself that he did not truly want to meet less frequently since he was starting to make headway on these issues. Under the guise of bespeaking the importance of being independent, he was making a self-defeating offer to pull back before accomplishing his objectives. The risk of acceding to this request was that Will might conclude that I wanted him to settle for less than the best outcome we could achieve. Admittedly this was a supposition on my part. It would have been better to try to analyze his request, but sometimes late adolescent/young adult patients are disinclined to do so. Essentially, then, I just tried to buy some time by recommending that we continue twice weekly appointments for a month and then re-evaluate.

Will wanted to look for a part-time job but feared becoming more depressed. He left that session dissatisfied because we had talked about jobs. He mentioned that during the next hour, but focused on having felt uncomfortable about the abrupt ending of the prior session. I may have ended it with less warning than usual, but I thought it more likely that he feared having offended me with his veiled criticism of our last meeting as job counselling, not psycho-therapy. He was dealing with that by reversal—saying that I had hurt him rather than that he had hurt me. Instead of addressing that criticism (because he seemed so sensitive), in line with principles enunciated by Settlage (1974), I asked if there were anything familiar about a sudden separation. This brought to mind his separation anxiety whenever he leaves his mother. He is a "momma's boy" who would cry inconsolably at age five whenever he had to leave her.

Sensitivity to the environment and externalizing transference attitudes

Despite feeling better (after five months of therapy), Will still considered himself too responsive to his environment. For example, reading in local papers about people who had just jumped from the Bridge would depress and draw him back into suicidal thinking. And all his worries persisted. So he took a leave of absence from college. As he contemplated looking for a job, he voiced fear of disappointing bosses. I asked who came to mind when he thought about disappointing an employer; he responded, "My father," because his father was always critical. So his fear was a compliance with his (accurate or inaccurate) perception that his father wanted to criticize, transferred to employers.

The development of Will's suicidal ideas

As he felt more resilient, he reported taking a stand against the suicidal thoughts that always lingered in the back of his mind—a nagging sense that he was going to kill himself, if not this year, then within the next two to five years. And he recounted the development of his suicidal thoughts and urges. He might have been able to do so at this time because he felt more certain he would not suicide, that is, he felt safer. The urges had begun away from home early in his freshman college year. One late night, while having trouble writing a paper, he called his sister—not for help but for someone with whom to talk, that is, to feel close. She had been off-putting, which left him feeling more alone. I surmised that we needed to understand how feeling alone in a world where people "blasted each other" (i.e., were hostile to each other), led him to conclude that his efforts would be futile, and thus there was no reason to live. Thus, his existential ideas about suiciding because he could not make a significant contribution seemed to represent a displacement from feeling that he could achieve neither recognition from, nor a harmonious relationship with, his family. On that occasion, the displacement was from parents to his sister. (Such material and that which follows suggest that the intensity of his developmental imperative to do everything himself served an additional defensive function of warding off yearnings to have felt closer to, and more protected by, his parents when he was growing up.)

Suicidal thoughts as compliance

The continuing exploration of Will's linked feelings of influence and responsibility, particularly identifying its pervasiveness in his sensibility, led to consideration of Will's relationship with his mother. He had never felt as secure with her as he had sensed was necessary to be able to leave home. He struggled with the same issue with both parents. He had anticipated returning home after graduating from college as the time when he would finally receive the stamp of both parents' approval. He feared feeling shunned by them—neither loved nor wanted. I asked if he ever felt that they truly wanted him out of the way, and he replied "Yes". So, it seemed that his suicidal thoughts were a compliance with what he had accurately or inaccurately perceived his parents wanted; he replied that he had never thought of that.

Will was now actively engaging with friends to feel better and reverse his depressive symptoms, the value of which I underscored. However, he was still not able to sustain a jaunty manner when feeling unfairly blamed at home. His father became inflamed when Will acted indifferent to criticism, and Will would then comply by experiencing the humiliation that he thought he had caused his father to feel. My interpretive efforts during this period were primarily to emphasize that Will should trust his own judgment in dealing with his parents, that is, supporting his autonomous thinking.

The appeal of the familiar

After seven months of treatment, Will returned from a weeklong Christmas vacation feeling better. He had suffered neither depression nor suicidal ideas, and felt more secure within himself and within his family. He asked about meeting only weekly. I suggested that we wait a couple of weeks, but he preferred to start the following week, so I told him to make the decision. Having decided to wait one more semester before returning to college, he elaborated on his earlier observations that difficulty in seeking work related to his father. He subordinated himself to bosses as he did to his father. He was convinced that male bosses wanted him under their thumb and would always be competitive with him. This raised the possibility that Will was basically distrustful, unable to believe that any man truly wanted him to succeed (to not be subordinate). So, I wondered if he sought out the familiar in work situations. For, bad as it was to endure that, it was even more potentially painful to risk trusting an employer who seemed different from his father and might be supportive. For Will's expectation of being disappointed outweighed the hoped-for outcome. Thus, seeking the familiar was an (albeit misguided) self-protective effort.

Reinstatement of the emancipation process

Will summarized how his illness had begun after his father's stroke: At a time when he had been feeling critical and dismissive of his father, Will's confidence about his own view was shaken by the outpouring of positive sentiment from others about what a great guy his father was. Will felt guilty—what kind of son would harbor such sentiments about a father whom everyone else was praising? So, he was drawn back again into seeking a more positive relationship with his dad at a time when he had been invoking this typical adolescent turning-love-into-hate mechanism to aid his emancipation (A. Freud, 1958). He asked if it were wrong, or not good, to harbor such attitudes toward his father. I replied that it was good, because, although these were not the attitudes he expected to hold for the rest of his life, he was currently using them to emancipate, to move forward developmentally. He agreed.

At this juncture, after eight months of therapy, Will wanted to discuss stopping, though added that he was willing to continue if I recommended that. That suggested that he was coaching me. So, while acknowledging his steady progress (more stable mood, greater resiliency from depressed moments, increasing confidence in his perceptions and conclusions), I recommended that we continue as we were for a month or so and then reconsider dropping to weekly sessions.

Anger emerges consequent to reduction of his omnipotence complex and survivor guilt

Not long thereafter, when reporting frustration at his parents' urging him to get a job, Will noted having recently become aware of great anger inside himself, which he was directing toward others. He feared "exploding" whenever someone said something about him or "looked cross-eyed at him". I replied, too glibly, that he had not been a violent person. "But what happens to the anger I've swallowed for such a long time?" Will asked. (We now faced the technical matter of helping a depressed person deal with previously repressed anger which psychoanalytic theory posits is directed toward oneself. To this point, it had been dealt with by guilt associated with his omnipotence complex. In a classical analytic approach, that complex would be understood as a resistance to awareness of instinctual conflicts.)

A serious complication develops

Then, just as Will was overcoming his depression and about to face previously suppressed and repressed anger, something happened. A young woman friend since grade school died in a single car crash after leaving a party where he had seen her, and in circumstances that made it difficult to know whether it was an accident or suicide. Will's immediate reaction was to feel glad that he had not jumped off the Bridge; he had been "inches from doing so", and he cried. We talked directly about the possible impact of this tragedy on his own depression and that he had to take very good care of himself. Will agreed, remarked that he had not been depressed for three weeks, and was using what he had learned about survivor guilt to help friends of the deceased woman who now felt they should suicide. He was pleased and proud that he had never hit an adult, but were he to do so, it would really hurt because he was such a strong person. I wondered to myself if he had been smoking marijuana that day, but it immediately became evident that even if so, much more than that was going on.

He arrived for his next appointment with a skinhead haircut, a much different look, and noted himself how loquacious and ebullient he was, but in control. He was that way from the freeing of his feelings and thoughts, not from drinking. He claimed to be very much in contact with his rage but in control of it. Reading Plutarch had inspired him to write a poem, which he read and offered me a copy. He wasn't sure what it meant. He was grandiose and expansive, at moments tearful, and occasionally contorted his face grotesquely to stifle intense anguish and tears. He claimed to not be suicidal and would call if he became emotionally troubled. He had not felt like driving here this morning, but there was no question in his mind that he would do so to keep working with me, though he preferred not to return for a week. He felt more powerful than ever before in his life. He'll "get an A+" in whatever he decides to do; he'll be on the first team and MVP (most valuable player award), the introducer of the keynote speaker and the keynote speaker as well.

As you realize, Will had now switched into a manic, hypomanic, or mixed manic state. The technical issue was to help him maintain behavioral self-control. He had some awareness of this because he talked about "homeostasis"—keeping things in balance, and maintaining self-control. I observed that he was not responsible for his father's stroke or his friend's death. Will said that he had thought repeatedly about survivor guilt.

That same day his parents called, concerned that Will's drinking and driving were endangering himself and others. His father was angry and inclined to react punitively and rejectingly. I shared my impression that the recent tragedy had reactivated anxieties regarding his father's condition, and that Will was trying to maintain emotional equilibrium. I recommended that they maintain contact with him, show forbearance and underscore their confidence that he could surmount his current state in his own way. I noted his worrisome grandiosity, but his unwillingness to take medicine, and not being suicidal, truly out of control, or frankly psychotic would make it difficult to hospitalize him. I was not necessarily persuaded that medication or, particularly, hospitalization would be best for Will, certainly in the long run. However, medicinal treatment has become the standard of care in most, if not all, communities, and in psychological states such as that which Will was exhibiting, parents often raise the question of medication and/or hospitalization. Thus, it makes most sense to address these matters directly, rather than try to sidestep them.

Dealing with requests to end treatment during a manic phase

Will claimed to have been too high "on the drug of life", but not "over-ebullient." He wondered about meeting less frequently because he was approaching the end of his need for therapy. I agreed, but noted that, as he himself had observed, he was not all the way there yet; I advised him to continue treatment until he was all the way there. (Thus, I agreed with the wisdom of entertaining his request, but found a way of using his own observations to urge him to stay.) He agreed to return in a week.

He claimed and appeared to be more settled at the next session. Unlike five months ago when he just wanted to die the next day, he now had a reasonable plan for his future. But he was still struggling with hypomanic grandiosity—writing to the mayor about the "gentrification" of their town, and the local newspaper about the stupidity of some environmental controversies. He asked about reducing to weekly sessions, but thought I did not want that and would be guided by my views; I should just tell him when I felt we could meet less frequently. (Here again he was coaching me.)

Disparity between Will's observations about himself and those of others

His father called that day very worried. He couldn't recognize Will—Will was not the kid he knew. Will's friends had told him that Will was incoherent, exhibiting strange behavior, and making "off-the-wall" statements. He was verbally abusive to his mother and Kip. At the next session, Will brought up those problems presented by his intensity and acknowledged his grandiosity. He felt that he was "coming down, ratcheting down", but needed to do so even more. But, he said, with his face screwed up to hold back tears, his toes had been stepped on so much that he can't let it pass now when someone looks at him "cross-eyed." And he described chasing down and threatening an old lady who almost hit him going through a stop sign. He also recounted several episodes at a local bookstore/café/hangout where he had been a popular part-time employee in the past. It had begun within days after his friend died with a caustic exchange between Will and a woman manager who became provocative and offended Will. It escalated over the course of several subsequent trips there to the point that the police were now called whenever Will entered the café. I advised him to discuss with me what he called the "controlled burn", his rage, until he felt in better position to deal non-self-defeatingly with people who crossed him.

The issue of medication revisited

His marijuana smoking and drinking were purportedly stable at a significantly reduced level. He would consider stopping both, but for now wanted to use them. I wondered if he were using these drugs to medicate himself, and, if so, should we consider using prescription medicine instead? He was reluctant and expressed appreciation for my having previously accepted his wish to not take medication in favor of helping him wrest control over his feelings himself. We agreed that he was not really going to hit or hurt anyone, and that his threats potentially created significant problems only for himself. So, I suggested we meet more often again to see if we could reverse his symptoms and his marijuana and alcohol consumption. Will's reaction was another face-contorting effort to hold back tears, as if meeting more often represented a setback, but he agreed. (Here we see the poignant struggle of the adolescent to feel the master of his own life and destiny.)

His mother told me he was verbally abusive toward her, though he often apologized when she called him on such behavior. That suggested that he was looking for auxiliary ego assistance to keep his behavior within socially acceptable bounds. I told her to call me whenever she was concerned.

Will claimed to be settling down, but he had gotten into a pushing match playing basketball with an old acquaintance, left, but called him later to apologize, and cried. He had an altercation with Kip, who threatened to kill Will, who reacted with both fury and fright. He was enraged when his mother blamed both of them. He felt she was against him. Suicidal feelings resurged after he decided that his parents were against him.

Managing mixed manic behavior

After several more such episodes in public, I again talked about medication, which he still strongly opposed. He used marijuana to calm himself. I told him that I had confidence that we could get through this but was a little worried. I did not want him to alienate himself from others or get into trouble. Will said he had been going to call me over the weekend to talk and check in, suggesting that he was using me outside of hours to enhance his stability. He asked what he should do if someone cut him off on the road. I said pull over and relax and think about himself not the other person. And if his mother angered him, should he walk away? I said he should, and return only when he could discuss the situation dispassionately. (Patients in states of high agitation need to perceive the therapist's confidence in their ability to master and prevail over their anxiety and intensity in crisis-like situations. So I am disinclined to acknowledge my apprehension. But, I allowed that I was "a little worried" after Will refused any medicinal support. I hoped this would induce him to help me help him out of his hypomanic state. He then offered to contact me more frequently, which I had encouraged him to do from early on.)

Nevertheless, Will began the next session wanting to know where I had trained. I almost never respond directly to such questions. But I did this time because it is probably better to be straightforward than cagey with a paranoid patient. Clearly, where I trained was irrelevant to whether he had confidence in me. After I told him, he acknowledged having asked because I had again raised the issue of medication last time and questioned, as had others, the wisdom of some of his behaviors. He had concluded that I had lost confidence in him; he in turn had lost confidence in me, which motivated him to question my credentials. (I don't know whether his purported loss of confidence reflected my having recommended medication or having acknowledged "a little" worry about him.)

He described yet other confrontations with strangers and friends about which he maintained that his perceptions were accurate. I allowed that may well be, but the intensity of his feelings overwhelmed his social judgment at times and he responded in a "tit for tat" manner. Will did not like being told he was wrong, though could at moments acknowledge the self-defeating aspects of his behavior. I raised the other area of my concern—the messianic, grandiose aspect of his current mindset. For example, his "Contract with America" was to teach all those people a lesson by pointing out their lack of consideration for others. His associations suggested that this righteousness covered his survivor guilt, for he said his problem was that he did not deserve to succeed when other people were suffering. He feared functioning to the best of his ability because that would render him very powerful and successful, and that idea was accompanied by feeling so responsible for helping others that it seemed overwhelming, and he felt suicidal. Though still emotionally labile, he recovered more readily. When I told him that I'd be out of touch for four-hour blocks of time over the weekend he replied that he'd try his hardest not to confront anyone.

At the immediately following sessions, he claimed to be gradually feeling more even-keeled. However, he reported having had a temper tantrum in public, probably like ones he had witnessed his father throw in restaurants in the past. The police were called, which proved very sobering for him, and he had thought of calling me but felt he could wait. He wanted to know my concerns about him, and we discussed his diagnosis—hypomanic, depressed, or a mixed manic picture. He claimed never to have been manic, but when he had been most depressed and searching diagnoses in a psychology book, he had thought he was manic–depressive. (Here we witnessed our inherent tendency to use cognition to master anxiety and mood.) I explained my rationale for recommending medication but felt that he was trying very hard and was succeeding, so we could hold that option in abeyance. Will's expression was frequently pained that day, but he did not seem to be stifling tears.

Anger as defense against guilt, in contrast to earlier use of guilt to ward off anger

Will described reacting with fury and reproach when he thought that his mother paid him no attention. Yet, in exploring these experiences, Will realized that he was invariably warding off feelings that he had done something wrong to cause her to neglect him. Or, when he became angry toward other people and felt paranoid (thinking they were looking at him "cross-eyed"), it was always the same issue— invoking righteousness to avoid feeling guilt associated with the idea that he was at fault. He viewed this present manic mental state as his emergence from feeling squelched by a lifetime of guilt and having accepted getting no respect or positive expressions from his family. He asked if he could call and/or schedule extra appointments if necessary. Yet, he was acting with increasingly greater self-control, and observing how scared he had felt when he found himself acting in that manic way; it was as if he did not even know himself. (Will was bespeaking perhaps the greatest of frights—feeling unable to trust and control oneself.) So, he was returning to a euthymic state; this was about six weeks after becoming manic.

A complication intrudes from the outside world

However, at that juncture he called during a weekend because he was frightened. He had received a summons to appear for a restraining order to stay out of the café. He felt devastated, scared, alone, frustrated by the lies in the charge, and unsupported by his parents, who implied that the café management was right. But they were securing the services of an attorney, which I supported. For I did not think he was a danger to anybody at the café, and hoped he could avoid any criminal record that might compromise future opportunities. Will understood that by continuing to return to the café, he had contributed to this complaint being drawn up. He did not perceive his presence as fearsome, because his motive for repeatedly returning was to try to make things right, to reduce the guilty feeling that he had done something wrong, that he was to blame.

The matter was handled outside of court, and while relieved, he continued to feel disconsolate and unsupported by his parents, which made him feel guilty. He struggled not to believe that he was a bad, helpless, and inept person. He felt unable to leave home, and suicide was the only alternative. But he was now struggling against suicidal thoughts by acting happy even though he realized it was a façade. I said it was still worth that effort. He thought about stopping therapy, but agreed to return the next day. (In offering to leave he was probably testing me to see if I, too, was ashamed of him and did not want to see him.)

Despite these concerns about his parents' reactions to him, the café matter, and his indecision about a career, he was functioning with greater stability. He wondered about stopping and, at his request, we reviewed the year. Will felt buoyed and affirmed by my view, which was congruent with his assessment. Suicidal thoughts were now more abstract—a fantasized exit rather than a likely probability. I raised my preference for terminating after he had embarked on the next step, namely a job or return to college. But Will opted for a few more meetings during which his mood continued to be neutral.

At our last session, Will reflected again on his fear of his parents dying and the futility of life without them, and he began to feel depressed, but almost without realizing it, he restabilized his mood. He noted that it was as if he needed his parents for direction and could not function if they were not there to give him "pats on the back." This seemed related to feeling that he had not received his father's love. I replied that if his activities were all directed toward securing expressions of love from his parents that was one thing and a worrisome one at that, reflecting compulsive, guilt-reducing behavior. If, however, they were undertaken with an element of satisfaction in pleasing them and benefiting from their encouragement (sponsorship) of him, that was a different matter. It seemed to me that he had been grappling with this issue for the past few months and striving to feel more independent of their values and wishes. As such, I saw it as work in progress, and if it bogged down he could contact me. With moist eyes, Will said he would miss this and wondered if he could remain stable without our meetings (i.e., the parental transference), but he had "kind of not felt whole while still coming to counseling", but now would have "no excuses". I told him, that I, too, would miss our time together and had enjoyed working with him very much.

Next phase of treatment

Four months later, his mother called. Will had been non-functional, scared, and unmotivated to look for a job or return to school. Yet, in all other ways he was "perfect and a delight", neither depressed nor hypomanic, and good with his father and herself. She had urged him to see me for a check-up, but he had not wanted to do so. I suggested she tell him that I respected his wish to do this himself, and as was the case when we met before, he had done the work; I had only helped a bit.

A month later, he phoned. He had felt immobilized since stopping his treatment. I told Will that I recognized how important it was for him to do things himself, but he also knew that I would be delighted to have the chance to work on these matters with him. Will was willing to meet "twice or once a week" and I told him that he should decide.

Over the next six months, we worked on several related issues that contributed to his inhibition against moving ahead. His combined feelings of guilt about prevailing where others struggled, and his responsibility for and ability to effect change in them (i.e., his survivor guilt and omnipotence complex) were still at issue. I continued to emphasize that failing to mobilize himself to work or plan his return to school was essentially an effort to protect his father and Kip. I said that when such insight does not allow one to alter the behavior pattern, I have found that the patient harbors a fantasy that to do so would be devastating: that is, his father would die. Will responded that he did think about that. Soon thereafter he took a part-time job in computer work that offered opportunities to learn and advance, and made an appointment to start the process of returning to college.

Work proceeded smoothly, and though Will experienced the anxieties toward supervisors that he had previously described, he functioned well, and asserted himself appropriately. He also became intensely preoccupied with Kip, who was also starting a job. Will vacillated between feeling friendly and angry, fearing that Kip would take advantage of their parents' generosity. In trying to understand this renewed preoccupation, I asked Will about his own job. Following our last session, during which Will had been feeling badly about his position there, his boss gave Will greater responsibility and a raise. I interpreted his survivor guilt: Will feared that his own advancement placed Kip at a disadvantage. So, he turned things around and worried that Kip was taking advantage of their parents, rather than that Will was taking advantage of Kip. Will now understood why he had not told his parents about his promotion.

Will had curtailed his marijuana smoking and drinking significantly and felt in control of both. He registered for his senior college year and seemed eager to return. He was neither socially isolated nor withdrawn. He wondered about stopping after one or two more sessions, which seemed reasonable. At our last meeting, Will reported not experiencing the same nagging anxiety about stopping that he had last summer. He observed that we had a good working relationship and that he could return at any time and said, "Farewell, friend" in parting.

Last contact with Will

Ten years later, Will called a couple of months after his job had been eliminated by out-sourcing. While having felt hurt, poorly used, unappreciated, and then angry toward his employers after having been a good, loyal, nine-year employee, his call was prompted by fear that he was falling back into his old despair and existential anxiety about the futility of life as he struggled to motivate himself to seek work.

On the surface he was successful, having been employed by this same company since graduating from college, and involved in a several-year relationship with a young woman whom he intended to marry. Yet, he was probably under-employed, and frustrated by his reluctance to advance himself because of concern for his immediate superior, and he was reticent to broach with his girlfriend his reservations about some of her behaviors and attitudes, for fear that she would be devastated. Yet, she tended to blame him righteously and never apologized, thus leaving him to defer to her whenever they disagreed, seemingly repeating maladaptive patterns within his family.

Will realized that these guilts and inhibitions were extensions of his earlier worries about his father and Kip. He recalled that the latter issues had still been present when we terminated, but he had felt he could and should move ahead on his own. He now wanted to be able to settle on a more satisfying career direction, and feel less guilty about asserting himself in all areas of his life. He did not present suicidal nor hypomanic symptoms.

Will claimed to feel better just having heard my voice on the phone, and relief from being able to talk to me. We set a fee he could afford and met weekly for five months, focusing on how the current expressions of his old survivor guilt conflicts inhibited him from deciding on a career, much less effecting it, and kept him in a more care-taking than mutual relationship with his girlfriend. I opined that he was not inhibited by lack of self-confidence as he claimed, but, rather, he did not feel he had permission to act upon his own judgments. My interventions were directed toward helping him understand why it was so difficult to assert himself in his own behalf in matters involving work, love, and family—essentially giving him permission to do so.

Within three months, he secured a position in an area of his competence and interest, but about which he continued to express fear of not meeting expectations of managers. His new obligations required training and travel, which made it difficult for us to meet, but the option was left open to do so at any time, and our contact faded in that manner.

Five years later, I learned that Will had extricated himself from the relationship with the unsuitable girl friend and was enrolled in a graduate school MBA (Masters of Business Administration) program. Thus, as he had always wished, he made the big forward steps on his own.

Summary and formulation

Will presented with an immobilizing depression accompanied by fear that he would suicide impulsively. The latter was rendered more worrisome by virtue of his marijuana and alcohol use, which, in addition to impulsivity, are identified risk factors for adolescent suicide (Fitzgerald, 1999; Hoberman & Garfinkel, 1988). Growing up, Will had never felt a sufficiently secure relationship with his parents to emancipate during adolescence with a felt sense of sponsorship from them. Will's compliant response to his father's competitive, aggressive, righteous personality contributed importantly to this persistent, underlying attitude of relative insecurity. Also, during his childhood, the attention of Will's mother had been spread thin caring for her children and their grandparents, and dealing with her husband's drinking, and Kip's problems.

Nevertheless, and despite long-time marijuana use, Will had performed well, even if not to his potential in the academic, athletic, and social spheres of his life. Still, his mother's observations suggested that he had been struggling with the adolescent emancipation process for several years. This had taken the form of more "quiet desperation" than overt symptoms, as Will was unable to settle on a college major and career direction. However, he had been making headway in these matters, in part by resorting to the commonly used mechanism of turning his childhood love and admiration of parents into opposite feelings of disgust and rejection (A. Freud, 1958).

Then, his father's stroke brought him home, ostensibly because his help was needed. But from a developmental and psychodynamic perspective, he was thrown back into a quest for the unrequited closer relationship for which he had long yearned. You will recall that he had previously fantasized returning home to secure this after graduating, but he now feared that his father's life-threatening illness would prevent him from ever achieving it.

Once home, Will felt caught between his normative developmental imperative to emancipate and a sense that without a more secure relationship with his father he would never be able to do so. Thus, his worry about his father's welfare included a developmentally self-serving motive. But, closer to his awareness, Will experienced guilt about emancipating from a parent whom he (accurately or inaccurately) concluded was psychologically fragile and needed to dominate Will—not only to maintain his (father's) emotional equilibrium, but now to insure his (parent's) very survival. This emancipatory guilt quickly burgeoned into pathological survivor guilt and separation guilt. This was manifested and revealed in a defensive identification with his father; he appeared depressed and helpless like the latter. His motive was to buoy up his father (and brother, Kip) by appearing no better than them. In my experience, such circumstances are always attended by an omnipotence complex. The net effect was to immobilize Will from moving forward. In this context he considered suicide as the only alternative. He had originally experienced, or at least expressed, his suicidal intention in existential terms: He could never make a significant, lasting contribution to the world. Exploring this revealed that this wish to impress the world was displaced from an unrequited wish for greater recognition from his parents.

The therapeutic tasks during this phase were keeping Will in treatment and from suiciding by reversing his guilt and despair. He was forever trying to stop or reduce the frequency of our sessions— citing the compelling importance of his autonomy, which was, in fact, his normal developmental imperative. The technical task was to avoid acceding to those mandates without being perceived as controlling like his father, or infantilizing, which would be experienced as encouraging the "momma's boy" regression from which he would also have to flee.

Interpreting the irrationality and the pervasiveness in his life of his separation/survivor guilt and the accompanying omnipotence complex helped reduce his persuasion that he was the only one who could fix the family's problems and was responsible for doing so. His progress toward reversing those convictions was then severely interrupted by the death of his friend, which occurred at a time when he had begun to mobilize repressed anger from his earlier life. Whether in response to, or coincident with, that event, Will slipped over into a manic, hypomanic, or mixed manic state. By his own account, Will was relieved not to have suicided, but now struggled with additional survivor guilt. So although the basic psychodynamic underlying his mood state did not change, his manifest symptoms did. That shift is consistent with the classical psychoanalytic formulation that mania defends against depression. He used reversal/projection to relieve this irrational guilt by finding fault with others (instead of himself). He blamed everybody from family members to friends on the basketball court, old ladies, managers at the book store–café, groups of young girls on the street, women shoppers, men who "looked cross-eyed" at him. This angry, aggressive, paranoid-type stance, especially in a hulking, intimidating, articulate young man, created problems for Will with peers and authorities alike.

The major therapeutic task at that juncture was to help him rein in his anger and outrageous, embarrassing, and problematic behavior. This was again accomplished by trying to walk a fine line between bespeaking/acknowledging the importance of his autonomy and personal responsibility, while not being fooled by his protestations into letting him terminate prematurely. Unconsciously, he needed and wanted to be held on to. The clues for this came both from his history of having felt rejected, his responses when I recommended that he stay, and the common-sense conclusion that he was in trouble with himself, manically careening over the line of self-containment at times, and even when most manic (as when he had been most depressed), adamantly refusing to take medicine.

Once he had regained self-control, I did not try to stop him when he wanted to terminate. At that point, after a year of therapy, he had sufficiently reconciled his ambivalence toward other family members to be able to live amicably with them. However, he was unable to progress with life tasks. Upon returning to treatment four months later, he reported having felt anxious about stopping, but had experienced my not having tried to dissuade him as evidence of my confidence in him. In this last six months of treatment, he started to move ahead. These two periods of treatment separated by a moratorium illustrate a phenomenon of therapeutic tact and tactics that has been reported in the treatment of adolescents. That is, working on the problem of the moment and leaving the rest for another time, when the patient feels motivated to do so (Adatto, 1958, 1966; Elizabeth Makkay, 1966, personal communication).

Will returned ten years later, in the aftermath of summarily losing his long-time job, when he became concerned that his depression was recurring. Although his symptoms were subsyndromal, Will may have a recurring condition, be it a penchant for depression or bipolar illness. (My reasons for still not committing to a diagnosis will be discussed shortly.) As in the past, his symptoms of feeling inhibited and stuck responded to guilt-reducing interpretations, offered in the context of a therapeutic relationship in which Will felt sponsored and able both to assert himself and to bare, share, and thus be helped to bear his emotional pain without feeling criticized. He became more functional and less unhappy and frustrated, but his conflicts were not completely resolved when the treatment faded out.

Will's case and course underscore the dynamic nature of human psychology—old conflicts can reappear. But we anticipate that after successful treatment recurrent symptoms are less intense and/or the patient has better adaptive means for coping with them, and, thus, exhibits greater resiliency. Yet, with respect to the latter, the authors of the thirty-year follow-up of the Brody longitudinal study observed that: "Resilience may be a superficial concept, for, in this series of cases, seemingly adequate coping in formerly mistreated children always came at the price of emotional vulnerability and compromised potential" (Massie & Szajnberg, 2006, p. 471). While it is premature to draw this conclusion about Will, the difficulties he was experiencing in performing closer to his abilities and feeling more generally happy are consistent with that conclusion.

Discussion

I will first discuss Will's treatment, and then consider it in the broader context of current research on adolescent suicide and bipolar symptomatology.

Treatment strategy

The key to dealing with Will's suicidal preoccupations was reducing his irrational survivor guilt by "reality-testing" his omnipotence complex. This was the cognitive, interpretive feature of this process. The symptomatic expression of this conflict took the form of what I have termed defensive identifications with a foundering parent and brother. I tried to get a toehold in the door of his pessimistic psychological mindset by presenting this formulation—he was floundering in an effort to make his father (and brother) appear stronger. Pointing out how this dynamic explained several different experiences rendered this interpretation more compelling to Will. From then until the time when the pervasiveness of this disabling pattern had been so repeatedly identified that Will could invoke his own cognitive facilities to override impulsive, emotional reactions, the technical task was to demonstrate my interest in tiding him over times of despair. This was accomplished by underscoring the importance of staying in touch with me, and reinforcing my availability in person or by phone. So, the strategy was to demonstrate that I had something to offer him (that implicitly held out the hope of a better solution than suicide), and to demonstrate my interest in him.

From what I have just posited, it seemed that, despite his protestations and behaviors which suggested otherwise, Will wanted to be held on to until he felt sufficiently secure in the interest of the therapist to emancipate with confidence. Thus, one aspect of his frequent efforts to "reject" me by reducing the frequency of sessions and terminating reflected something in addition to his normal developmental strivings for autonomy. It was a turning passive into active test of me by Will—specifically to see how I would respond to being rejected, that is, what he had experienced from his father. My reaction of not being deterred by his "rejections" enabled Will in turn to identify with my attitude and feel less devastated by the rejection he had felt. This was a corrective ego experience dimension in the therapy that was achieved more silently through our interactions around this issue than through verbal analysis and mutual acknowledgment. I think it had to occur in the former manner because the conflict between his need to emancipate and his fear of being trapped by me were so intense, immediate, and "real" to him, that he could not verbally analyze this transference.

Thus, the therapeutic approach involved two simple issues, which, in a sense, were mutually contradictory or mutually exclusive. One was to maintain close and constant contact with Will while at the same time affording full cognizance and acceptance of his autonomy. The former was to tie him close enough to me that he could attach his own wish not to suicide to me in an alliance that would enable him to call me or someone else if he felt in any danger of harming himself. The latter was to prevent him from feeling treated like a love-starved child (i.e., the mother transference) or obliged to submit (i.e., the father transference), either of which would have inclined him to bolt. The stance I maintained in trying to promote this was akin to what Gitelson (1948) observed years ago in defining the parameters of treating adolescents: presenting yourself as dependable rather than dependency-engendering.

The key in working with Will's hypomanic or mixed manic symptoms was to help him regain behavioral self-control. There were at least two aspects to this—one intrapsychically oriented and the other interpersonally directed. The former involved conveying both implicitly and explicitly my confidence in his ability to control himself. Rather than simply offering blanket assurances in this regard, I drew on such historical data as the fact that he had never been a violent person, despite harboring intense emotions and having been aggressive on the basketball court. The interpersonally oriented, or, in this instance, environmentally directed part involved my actively participating when he needed outside resources to deal with the serious repercussions of his out-of-control behavior. Examples included involvement with his parents and his attorney, and writing a letter in his behalf for court proceedings. In such a context, this type of help actually constitutes age-appropriate auxiliary ego support from parents. This would be in contrast to letting him "hang out there" by himself with a "you're-almost-adult-and-got-yourself-into-this, so-it-will-be-a-good-lesson-to-get-yourself-out-of-it" attitude.

This matter of the contact I had with Will's parents warrants comment, because, at least historically, we usually consider this inappropriate with parents of late adolescents/young adults. It compromises the very psychological emancipation from childhood dependency that they are striving to consolidate. But, as I noted earlier, the nature of the individual case always takes precedence in treatment decisions. You do whatever is professionally responsible to keep the treatment moving. In cases like that of Will, in which the adolescent is living at home and the parents are supporting the treatment, parents may need guidance that cannot as compellingly be given by another therapist, especially if the parents do not see a need for their own treatment. In this case, Will's parents needed my input in two circumstances: when they were feeling that Will was being irresponsible, freeloading off them and they thought that giving him an ultimatum would help, and when Will was exhibiting frightening, incomprehensible behavior and they needed guidance and support. In both situations, it was in Will's best interest that I share my view with his parents.

Treating adolescents with serious mental symptoms who refuse to take, or who fail to respond to, medication

There were three purposes for presenting Will's case in depth. One was to offer a distinctive formulation of the genesis of manic, hypomanic, or mixed manic symptoms in at least some youth. This formulation had previously been found helpful for understanding suicide and helping relieve depression in adolescents (Bloch, 1995). It centers on survivor/separation guilt burgeoning from more normative emancipatory guilt in the presence of the invariably accompanying omnipotence complex. Clinically, this is usually observed in the form of defensive identifications with a parent or sibling.

A second purpose was to illustrate technical approaches in interpreting and working through these dynamics, which seemed important in reducing Will's suicidal concerns and also contributed to bringing his manic symptoms under greater self-control. Whether these interventions were significant in reversing his symptoms, or whether I was simply able to hold him in a therapeutic relationship until the natural curative forces took hold cannot be answered with rigorous confidence. The fact that Will latched on to my interpretations of survivor guilt and the omnipotence complex, and worked with them outside therapy hours, suggests that they were a curative factor. His spontaneous expressions that this formulation was helpful, and his sanguine attitude toward the therapeutic relationship, suggest that the combination accomplished more than merely tiding him over. But even the latter would have been sufficient, since both suicidal intention and bipolar symptoms often wax and wane.

The importance I attached to maintaining contact with him reflects a principle that is as old as the field of psychotherapy itself. In fact, it is older, going back to the interpersonal roots of the healing arts. It is the fact that psychological development, feelings of safety, and anxiety reduction occur in the context of a relationship (Freud, 1926d, p. 155; Mahler, Pine, & Bergman, 1975). Conveying in word and deed a non-proprietary interest in the adolescent's welfare is indispensable to creating a therapeutic relationship, and contributes to the sense of being sponsored that I have found vital for successful adolescent development. The combined factors of needing to experience sponsorship while striving for autonomy, and the resulting difficulty in analyzing transference often make for termination phases that are much shorter than one typically anticipates in analytic, psychodynamic treatment.

The third major reason for presenting this case was to illustrate the vital interplay between understanding and working with both psychodynamic and developmental factors in treating even those adolescents with serious symptoms when their developmental imperative is to emancipate from significant relationships with adults. I have drawn a dozen precepts from Will's treatment for approaching the seemingly paradoxical tasks of supporting adolescents' autonomy and holding them in treatment. The rationale for such efforts is further supported by reports that suicidal adolescents tend to isolate themselves when stressed (Negron, Piacentini, Graae, et al., 1997), and subsequent suicidal activity is reduced in those who meet with therapeutic personnel (see Shaffer, Garland, Gould, et al., 1988).

Specific technical principles

1. Pique their interest early with a plausible formulation of their difficulties drawn from their associations: That is, make immediate, effective contact with adolescents by showing them something which they either have not thought about or have not allowed themselves to sustain consideration. This can help them to legitimately perceive their circumstances differently from the dire way in which they have been experiencing them, or, at least, it holds out the hope of allowing such a shift in their mindset. Pointing out defensive identifications, survivor guilt, or an omnipotence complex have often proven to be such "hooks".

2. Convince them with their own words, not yours: Try to find and present things they have brought up rather than your formulations as reasons to continue. A general example appears in the letter I sent to Will early on when he did not return after a vacation.

3. Be respectful and don't make them feel trapped: I always acknowledged that the decisions about meeting less frequently or terminating were his.

4. Always hear them out: I listened thoroughly to Will's rationale before making any recommendation.
5. Buy time instead of saying "No": I invariably qualified my recommendations that we continue as we were with a specific time-frame, so Will would not feel I was being dismissive of his wish. For example, "Let's consider this change in a couple of weeks after 'such and such' has occurred."
6. The adolescent can be your best guide: Patients often give cues to their therapists regarding how they wish the latter to respond. Thus, for example, when Will said he wanted to reduce our meetings now, but would accept my recommendation, he was coaching me to override his obligatory request.
7. Communicate expressions of worry about the adolescent with a sense of confidence that together you can master the situation: That is, there was a palpable difference between my acknowledgment of worry and my attitude toward the worrisome situation.
8. Convey as much confidence as you possibly can in the adolescent's ability to surmount his or her distress: When Will was manic and fearful of losing control physically, I pointed out that he had never been violent, so we knew he could control himself. Another example was indicating that he had to trust his own judgment in assessing his parents' view of him, which differed from his own.
9. Credit the adolescent with achievements of the treatment: For example, when Will was reluctant to return four months after stopping the first time, I asked his mother to tell him that he had made the changes. On the other hand, accept adolescents' expressions of appreciation for the collaboration, lest they feel rejected by you.
10. Practice what you preach and be flexible: If you are emphasizing the importance of contact between the two of you, then be available. I always offered and tried to schedule make-up appointments for missed or canceled sessions. In this way, I was demonstrating my interest in seeing him, emphasizing that it was important for us to meet, and communicating that I did not interpret or react to his cancellations as expressions of rejection or hostility toward me. I always apprised him of my availability, especially forewarning him when I would be away from town,

and I urged him to call my answering service when distressed. They would contact me, even if I were away from the area during some weekends. Phone contact proved sufficient on those rare occasions when Will did avail himself of that option. So, whenever possible, I took my own call when away from the office. This is particularly important for adolescents who have felt rejected, which includes most who have serious symptoms. Having concluded that keeping Will close to me was a key to reducing the likelihood of him suiciding, I had to "walk the talk". In a field that relies so much on words, we have to remember that actions still speak louder.

11. Practice makes perfect: It takes the adolescent patient longer to integrate a psychodynamic paradigm than to comprehend it intellectually. Thus, for example, I kept pointing out his survivor guilt and omnipotence complex until he could himself identify their pervasiveness in his sensibility and motivating role in his life. This is part of the working through process in psychodynamically oriented therapy.

12. Keep the big picture in mind: I kept my focus on Will's inner and interpersonal life, in contrast, for example, to taking a strong stand against drug use. The latter would be an effort to eliminate a specific risk factor as opposed to concentrating on the larger picture of what we wished to accomplish, which was to reduce his suicidal tendencies. To have approached Will in a more piecemeal fashion would have run too great a risk of placing us in subtle contention at a time when I was trying to forge a strong alliance between us. You will recall how incensed Will became when I was recommending medicine for his manic symptoms, even though by then we had a long-time working relationship.

The relevance of this approach in the current treatment Zeitgeist

With the ascendance of epidemiologically driven, biological treatments in psychiatry and psychology, one must ask what is the relevance or utility of such a formulation and treatment plan? This is especially so, since it often seems now that failure to recommend medications risks not conforming to community standards for treating conditions like suicidal intention and bipolar symptoms in adolescents. This obtains despite the modest data supporting the efficacy of medicinal treatments, controversy about medications representing risk factors for suicidality (Gibbons, Hur, Baumik, et al., 2006; Simon, 2006; U.S. Food and Drug Administration, 2005), the significant proportion of adolescents who fail either to take prescribed medication or to benefit from it, and findings discussed in the Introduction about the psychological and biological effects of placebos. Non-compliance with medicinal regimens is a frequently quoted explanation for treatment failure, but a specific typology of non-compliant adolescents from personality or demographic data has not yet been isolated (Bernstein, Anderson, Hektner, et al., 2000). So, at the very least, practitioners are still left with the problem of engaging adolescents in whatever form of treatment they are attempting. Typically, late adolescents/young adults are more willing to undertake psychotherapeutic exploration than are early and mid-adolescents. Yet, as Will demonstrated, even a number of the former seem always ready to "cut and run" from therapy as well as to eschew medication.

Contributions of formal research to clinical understanding of adolescent suicide and bipolar disorder

The following overview of recent research on adolescent suicide (which is primarily epidemiological) and adolescent mania (which is largely epidemiological and pharmacological), focuses on findings that seem most relevant to clinical practice:

Adolescent suicide

Public health dimension

The incidence declined and stabilized in the decade prior to 2003 (Shaffer & Greenberg, 2002). The reasons for the subsequent increase through 2005 (which period included the sharpest one-year rise in fifteen years) remain unclear and debated (Yan, 2008). Up or down, adolescent suicide perennially ranks among the three leading causes of death in adolescents, and is considered an increasingly serious public health problem (D. Bloch, 1999). With few exceptions, reflecting ethnic/religious affiliation and places of origin (Kohn, Levav,

Chang, et al., 1997), and with variations related to cultural identity (Yuen, Nahulu, Hishinuma, et al., 2000), the prevalence of adolescent suicide and suicidal behavior in all countries and populations studied steadily increased during the four decades prior to 1990 (Potter, Rosenberg, & Hammond, 1998). Moreover, based on calculations of the years of potential life lost (YPLL), the years of potentially productive life less age at death, the loss to society is much greater than the absolute numbers of suicides would suggest (D. Bloch, 1999). Adolescent suicide has been rigorously studied in the past quarter century—perhaps as much as anything because of the enormous social impact it has on those affected by the suicide of a youth. Our society places little credence in the existential idea of free will (freedom of choice) when it involves regressive actions like suicide compared to the value placed on adolescents' autonomy with respect to developmentally progressive activities.

The difficulties in researching adolescent suicide

Adolescent suicide remains a clinical conundrum. The Group for the Advancement of Psychiatry (1996) identifies two general approaches to its study. While not mutually exclusive, they essentially describe the difference in emphasis of psychodynamic/psychogenetic as opposed to medical/biological views. The former seeks the explanation for suicidal phenomena through comprehending attitudes and affects, specifically despair, hopelessness, helplessness, guilt, anger, panic. The latter looks for diagnosable mental illnesses and co-morbid conditions with an emphasis on biological and genetic factors. Neither approach has isolated pathognomonic (i.e., specific/unequivocal diagnostic) symptoms, signs, psychometric or biological laboratory tests that identify individual adolescents who will attempt or complete suicide.

Neither do experienced researchers consider it likely that any single or constellation of characteristics will be found that accurately predict suicide or suicidal behavior in individual adolescents (Goldston, 1999; Gould, Shaffer, Fisher, et al., 1998; Group for the Advancement of Psychiatry, 1996; Pokorny, 1983; Shaffer, 1996, Shafii, Carrigan, Whittinghill, et al., 1985). One long-time student of adolescent suicide observed: "In even the most troubled patient, suicide is a rare event whose eventuality and precise timing defy accurate prediction" (Shaffer, 1996, p. 172). The reasons for this stem from limitations inherent in studying suicide: As noted, it remains a rare event statistically (Werry, 2007), even among high-risk subgroups of adolescents (Brent, 1987). Only the incidence in children is lower (Shaffer, Garland, Gould, et al., 1988). This factor, plus limitations of the psychological autopsy procedure, the primary method used to study completed suicides, restrict, respectively, the number of cases that can be collected for study and the type of information which can be gleaned about suiciders after the fact. So, problems remain in overcoming the general "disadvantages of focusing on either individual uniqueness or universal inclusiveness" in further identifying those at highest risk within the high-risk groups (Motto, 1979, p. 516). At present, risk factor data has more relevance to public health preventive measures than to individual cases (Shaffer, Garland, Gould, et al., 1988). Clinical judgment remains a crucial element in assessing suicidal adolescents.

Approaches to surmounting the difficulties implicit in researching adolescent suicide

To achieve more compelling databases and to be able to study suicide anterospectively, the field of inquiry was broadened to include all suicidal behavior—those who think about and who attempt, in addition to those who complete suicide (ideators, attempters, completers). This approach is empirically justified because, in the broadest sense, there is "a continuum from contemplation to completion" (Klimes-Dougan & Radke-Yarrow, 2000). That is, more ideators than non-ideators attempt suicide, and more attempters than non-attempters complete suicide. It is important to keep in mind, however, that the vast majority of ideators and attempters do not progress to the next, more serious, level in this continuum.[7] Furthermore, if there is a qualitative, and not solely a quantitative difference between the truly suicidal and the non-suicidal (Seiden, 1971, cited in Shafii, Carrigan, Whittinghill, et al., 1985), then research which proceeds on the basis of this continuum concept may confound rather than elucidate efforts to pinpoint those individuals who suicide (Pinto & Whisman, 1996). Nonetheless, it seems eminently reasonable from a clinical and preventive standpoint to attempt to reduce emotionally painful states characterized by suicidal ideation and attempts, regardless of their relationship to completions.

The voluminous literature comprises psychological autopsies performed on suiciders, clinical studies of hospitalized adolescents and those seen in emergency rooms and outpatient settings for suicidal behavior, epidemiological surveys of ideators and attempters in non-patient community samples, and biochemical studies. Collectively, this research has identified and characterized subpopulations at risk for suicidal behavior. However, all risk factor studies report a frequency of false positives (i.e., those who have the identified risk factors but do not exhibit suicidal behavior) that is invariably greater than the incidence of true positives (Werry, 2007). Also, all studies find significant numbers of false negatives (i.e., those who do not have the risk factors being studied but do exhibit suicidal behavior) (Werry, 2007). Moreover, the inter-study differences between populations studied (e.g., clinical, community, hospitalized), measurements, and methodology (Pinto & Whisman, 1996) make it difficult for any but seasoned, dedicated suicidologists to reconcile and synthesize the multiplicity of sometimes seemingly contradictory findings that have been reported for all but the most general risk factors studied (i.e., age, sex distribution of suicides and attempts). In sum, knowledge of subpopulations of adolescents at higher risk for suicide gained from clinical experience, epidemiological surveys, and psychological autopsy can perhaps moderate the clinician's anxiety when assessing suicidal potential. However, risk factor research has yet to contribute any precision to evaluating or treating individual patients.

Differing conceptualizations of adolescent suicide

Conclusions from different studies lead to alternative conceptualizations of adolescent suicide. For example, studies supporting the continuum concept advance a model which emphasizes the importance of both increasing numbers and intensity of risk factors in the individual (e.g., psychiatric diagnoses, substance abuse, impulsivity) and external factors (stressors) from the adolescent's environmental and family contexts which contribute independently to the adolescent's suicidal behavior (Brown, Cohen, Johnson, et al., 1999; Gould, Fisher, Parides, et al., 1996). This is akin to the old military psychiatry adage that "every man has his breaking point". (Refinements to this continuum association are elaborated in the section entitled "What do studies of ideators and attempters reveal", p. 53)

On the other hand, the high incidence of false positive and false negative results favors the concept that there is something unique about those who suicide which cannot be adequately accounted for by the cumulative risk factor model. This paradigm underscores the heterogeneity of pre-morbid personality characteristics, intrapsychic conflicts, and different responsiveness to common, external risk factors in those who suicide (Robbins & Alessi, 1985; Shaffer, 1996). This heterogeneity applies to attempters as well as completers (Goldston, 1999; Khan, 1987). It is also reported within high-risk subgroups, for example, adolescents diagnosed with major depressive disorder (Myers, McCauley, Calderon, et al., 1991).

Psychological autopsy and other studies have suggested two different profiles of suiciders—a larger group for whom it is the culmination of a longer-standing psychiatric illness, and those for whom it seems to occur without such underpinnings. Thus, those typologies raise the question of whether suicidal behavior is more often the expression of a longer-standing psychiatric trait or of a more transient emotional state. Murphy (1985) observes that the problem of diagnosing suicide results from it being a state, not a trait, phenomenon. This represents a third general conceptualization of adolescent suicide.

Of these three models relating to determinants of adolescent suicide, it is easiest to accumulate epidemiological data for the cumulative trauma (continuum) model, especially in large samples, compared to the idiosyncratic response of an uncommon host to common stressor(s) model, and the psychiatric trait *vs.* psychological state model. So, it stands to reason that the greatest number of published studies relate to the first model. But that fact does not render the other two models less relevant, and the current state of knowledge probably favors a clinical approach that relies on risk factor research only as a general guide, while not excluding any diagnostic or phenomenological group from consideration of suicidal behavior.

Typologies of adolescent suicide

While varying in some particulars, conclusions from psychological autopsy studies converge in the following model: The adolescent suicider is predisposed by an underlying psychiatric condition, is living in an unsupportive environment, and experiences a triggering event which creates some intense negative emotion, at a time and place where the means for suicide are at hand (Hoberman & Garfinkle, 1988; Shaffer, Garland, Gould, et al., 1988; Shaffii, Carrigan, Whittinghill, et al., 1985). Thus, there are contributions to the suicidal act from intrapsychic factors, environmental factors, acute stresses, and happenstance, respectively.

The predisposition or "psychopathological substrate" (Brent, Baugher, Bridge, et al., 1999, p. 1497) is some diagnosable psychiatric disorder—usually an internalizing disorder characterized by hypersensitivity, inhibition, and withdrawal, or its phenomenological opposite, an externalizing behavior disorder; both conditions are often complicated by substance use or a substance abuse disorder. The opposite orientation of these predispositions, that is, depressive/internalizing disorders vs. conduct/antisocial externalizing disorders, plus the role of impulsivity, the prominence of substance abuse in both types of presentation, and the factor of timing in reconstructed suicides, have led to the bifurcation of this model into two prototypes of the adolescent suicider. In one, suicide becomes the planned culmination of a long-time internalizing disorder, usually depression, which occurs in a context of mounting external stressors. In the other paradigm, the suicidal act is a more impulsive response to an immediate stressor in an aggressive individual who may or may not be behaviorally disordered (Apter, Gothelf, Orbach, et al., 1995); in both subtypes, the suicide often occurs under the influence of drugs or alcohol when a means of doing so is at hand (Fitzgerald, 1999). Consensus has not been reached with respect to when (i.e., early or later) during the course of these mood, conduct, or substance abuse disorders adolescents are more likely to suicide (Brent, Perper, Moritz, et al., 1993a; Shaffer, Gould, Fisher, et al., 1996).

In fact, many amplifications can be appended and many qualifications must be attached to each model. For example, with respect to:

1. The underlying predisposition: Depressive illness in adolescence is generally regarded as the primary risk factor for suicidal behavior. With respect to that disorder, two-thirds of a large community-based sample, in whom a major depressive disorder had been diagnosed before age nineteen, experienced a recurrence in a

five-year follow-up (Lewinsohn, Klein, & Seeley, 2000). However, it is important to keep in mind that one-third did not have a recurrent depression or other diagnosable disorder.

Although studies have not consistently identified bipolar disorder (Brent, Perper, Moritz, et al., 1993a; Klimes-Dougan, Free, Ronsaville, 1999; Marttunen, Aro, Henriksson, et al., 1991) or schizophrenia (Shaffer, Garland, Gould, et al., 1988) as predisposing conditions in adolescents, a recent consensus of experts' statement concludes that both are risk factors (American Academy of Child & Adolescent Psychiatry, 2001). Anxiety is less often found to be a risk factor for suicide in adolescents than in adults, especially when it does not coexist with depression, at least in a study encompassing late adolescents and adults (Placidi, Oquendo, Malone, et al., 2000), and when it is a more transient state rather than an internalized/integrated trait, at least in hospitalized adolescents (Ohring, Apter, Ratzoni, et al., 1996). (Having concluded that trait, but not state, anxiety increased the risk for suicidal behavior independent of depression in hospitalized adolescents, the authors of the latter study advise trying to reduce anxiety in potentially suicidal patients.)

Risk factor profiles of adolescents who suicide before *vs.* after age sixteen differ in ways that common sense would anticipate. For example, the younger are less likely to have an identifiable psychiatric illness (primarily substance abuse), to have been intoxicated when they suicided, to have intended to die, and more are likely to have experienced a conflict with parents rather than a girl or boyfriend (Brent, Baugher, Bridge, et al., 1999). Different conclusions have been reached regarding whether these findings reflect merely quantitative differences in numbers of risk factors experienced (Grøholt, Ekeberg, Wichstrom, et al., 1998), or qualitative differences based on a differential in the intention to die (Shaffer, Gould, Fisher et al., 1996).

Regarding sex differences, the long-standing 4–5:1 ratio of completions among older adolescent males : females, and the opposite demographic regarding attempts has yet to be adequately explained. This is especially so since adolescent girls are more prone than boys to depression, the primary identified risk factor.

2.   The environmental context: As noted, features of the adolescent's environment have been identified as risk factors independent of

psychiatric diagnoses in the individual. But from the perspective I have been advancing, it is the adolescent's need to adapt to his or her environment (most importantly the parents' behaviors and attitudes) that gives rise to the problematic symptoms. Thus, from a psychodynamic perspective, it is difficult to so differentiate the intrapsychic from the interpersonal in such phenomena as instability in the adolescent's home (characterized by lack of parental support), depressed mother (Klimes-Dougan, Free, Ronsaville, et al., 1999), hostile father (King, Hovey, Brand, et al., 1997), and lack of a felt sense of cohesiveness in abusive families (Brown, Cohen, Johnson, et al., 1999). Suicidal behavior or psychiatric disturbance in another family member(s), relative(s) or friends/acquaintances have been identified as risk factors (Brent, Kolko, Allan, et al., 1990, Shaffer & Greenberg, 2002). This latter contribution from the family context to attempts and suicide by the adolescent is also consistent with the psychodynamic paradigm I have advanced: defensive identification with important family members.

3.   The precipitating event: This is usually a troubling interpersonal experience (e.g., rejection, failure, or disciplinary event), which activates an intense negative emotion in the adolescent, such as depressive affect, anger, humiliation, or embarrassment (Shaffer, Garland, Gould, et al., 1988; Group for the Advancement of Psychiatry, 1996). Yet, a third of those who made a serious suicide attempt could not identify a precipitating event (Beautrais, Joyce, & Mulder, 1997).

4.   Regarding availability of means of suiciding: Conflicting data exist even with respect to politicized issues such as gun control. Since it has been the most common means of adolescent suicide in both sexes in the USA, reducing the availability of firearms might reduce the prevalence of suicide. This may be particularly relevant for those who suicide with no apparent psychiatric disorder, those who have more risk factors (e.g., prior ideation and psychiatrically ill families) than community controls, and those who are acting impulsively. The availability of a loaded firearm would be less significant for those who are suffering a depressive illness in whom suicidal intent would present greater risk than the ready availability of a lethal means (Brent, Perper, Moritz, et al., 1993c). Yet, in Finland, where the youth suicide rate is the

highest in Europe, and suicide by firearms has increased, the significant correlation was not with greater availability of guns; it was with the popularity of a movie in which suicide from auto-mobile exhaust (carbon monoxide poisoning) was depicted (Ohring et al, 1996). Because of the ready availability of means for killing oneself (especially for the impulsive), attempting to restrict access of adolescents to means of suiciding is not consid-ered a particularly promising measure for reducing suicide/ attempts (Shaffer & Greenberg, 2002). The latter point is sup-ported by reversal of the declining rates of adolescent suicide since 1990, which increased in 2003–2004, particularly among 10–19-year-old females and 15–19-year-old males. And among the females, asphyxiation/strangulation became the most com-mon method (Lubell, Kegler, Crosby, et al., 2007).

The relationship between adult and adolescent suicide

Differences between adolescent and adult suiciders have been iden-tified. For example, the widely accepted idea that the cognitive dimension of hopelessness predicts adult suicide better than do affec-tive measures of depression is less consistently found in adolescents (Pinto & Whisman, 1996), and not in some sub-populations of high-risk adolescents (Rotheram-Borus & Trautman, 1988).[8] Other differ-ences from adults include the relative fluidity of defenses and adaptive mechanisms of the ego (Group for the Advancement of Psychiatry, 1996) and the vacillating tendency of adolescents' emotions (Thompson & Eggert, 1999).

In my experience, depressive symptoms tend to fluctuate more in adolescents than in adults. This factor may contribute to the difference in the relative predictive value of hopelessness, as well as other differ-ences that have been described. For example, adolescent attempts are more frequently of low intent to die and thus of lesser lethality than those of adults (Hawton, Cole, O'Grady, et al., 1982; Pinto & Whisman, 1996; Rodham, Hawton, & Evans, 2005). Adolescent attempts more often occur in reaction to stressful experiences than do those in adults (Berman & Jobes, 1991, cited in Pinto & Whisman, 1996). Repeated attempts are more common in adolescents (Eyman & Smith, 1986, cited in Pinto & Whisman, 1996), and more frequently become ways of coping with stress rather than attempting to end life (which might not be experienced as final in 15–24-year-olds) (Allen, 1987; Pinto & Whisman, 1996).

Clusters of suicides in the immediate geographical area following a local suicide, and suicidal behavior following accounts in the media about a suicide(s) seem to uniquely affect adolescents/young adults and not older adults (Shaffer & Greenberg, 2002). While the research data is difficult to synthesize, the impression conveyed in the overview is that existing psychiatric illness and suicidal behavior among those in the proximity of the suicider confer greater risk of (contagious) suicide than emotional closeness of the peer to the suicider. The closer friends of a suicider are at risk of becoming depressed, but not suicidal in an imitative way (Brent, Perper, Moritz, et al., 1993b). However, other researchers found an association between self-harm in friends and other family members of those who had harmed themselves (Rodham, Hawton, & Evans, 2005). Those who feel they knew and thus might have prevented the suicide experience guilt and are at greater risk for persistent or recurrent symptoms of depression and anxiety (Brent, Moritz, Bridge, et al., 1996).

Will exhibited a number of risk factors (depression, current suicidal ideation, drug use, instability in his family, facing a legal/disciplinary action). Yet, the possibly suicidal death of his friend when he was recovering from depression precipitated him into a manic state. But, by his own account, that event specifically helped reverse his suicidal preoccupations and gave him a stronger desire to live. That notwithstanding, he subsequently struggled again with suicidal urges. My point is that adolescent psychology is very dynamic, and a straight-line correlation between risk factors and subsequent attitudes and behaviors may well not be observed.

Another matter that is unique to adolescents/young adults became politicized in recent memory. It is the question of whether the lyrics/themes of rock/heavy metal popular music incite adolescents to suicide. Authors of a questionnaire study of two Australian community samples of young adolescents had the impression that the minority who felt worse after listening to this music were the more dysfunctional and vulnerable members of the population surveyed (Martin, Clarke, & Pearce, 1993).

A reasonable inference to be drawn from these differences between suicidality in adolescents and adults is that developmental considerations are more important in understanding this behavior in the former. There may be a greater multiplicity of psychological meanings and intents in adolescents' suicidal behavior compared to those among adults. It is to be hoped that these can be capitalized upon when clinically assessing the presence and significance of suicidal tendency in individual adolescents.

What do studies of ideators and attempters reveal?

Some studies support the continuum concept that attempters and ideators have profiles similar to completers compared to each other and compared to those who do not attempt or think about suicide (Fergusson & Lynskey, 1995; Lewinsohn, Rohde, & Seeley, 1993). But the relative importance of cumulative external stressors as opposed to underlying predisposing factors (e.g., depression or behavioral pathology, substance use/abuse, dysfunctional families, maladaptive cognitive traits) in predicting ideators and attempters remains in question despite much instructive research (Garrison, Addy, Jackson, et al., 1991; Gould, King, Greenwald, et al., 1998; McKeown, Garrison, Cuffe, et al., 1998; Spirito, Overholser, & Hart, 1991). And heterogeneity is prominent in the risk profiles of ideators and completers (Gould, King, Greenwald, et al., 1998) and within subgroups of hospitalized attempters (Goldston, Daniel, Reboussin, et al., 1998). As with completers, studies have correlated suicide attempts with tendencies to isolate oneself, hopelessness, and with poor self concept/low self-esteem, but not with sufficient precision to be relied upon prognostically (Negron, Piacentini, Graae, et al., 1997; Overholser, Adams, Lehnert, et al., 1995). Adolescents of depressed mothers (unipolar more so than bipolar) reported significantly more suicidal ideas and attempts (greater in those whose mother had attempted suicide) than did adolescents of non-depressed mothers. Consistent with my ideas about the role of defensive identifications, suicidal thoughts/behaviors correlated with similar behavior in the mothers rather than with the severity of the maternal depression (Klimes-Dougan, Free, Ronsaville, et al., 1999). Twenty percent of a large community sample of older adolescent attempters did not meet criteria for a *DSM-III-R* diagnosis between the time of initial assessment and follow-up a year later (Andrews & Lewinsohn, 1992).

In a fourteen-year longitudinal study of lower socioeconomic/ working-class families, preschool behaviors opposite from norms (aggressive girls, dependent boys), and psychiatric diagnoses by age fourteen were associated with suicidal ideation at age fifteen, subsequent attempts by age eighteen, and compromised functioning in late adolescence. But neither parental death, separation, nor divorce were associated with greater risk for suicidal ideation (nor, presumably, attempts) (Reinherz, Giaconia, Silverman, et al., 1995).

Ideators

Roughly 20% of recent community samples of adolescents report suicidal ideation (Centers for Disease Control and Prevention, 2000, cited in Mufson & Velting, 2002). Although it is thought that suicidal ideation is a product of psychopathology, usually depression, one-quarter of a large sample of 9–17-year-olds exhibited no such pathology (Gould, King, Greenwald, et al., 1998).

In moving from ideation to attempts, suicidal thoughts progressed from being experienced as ego dystonic to ego syntonic in severely guilt-ridden adolescents (Haliburn, 2000). Suicidal adolescents perceive death as more pleasant than do non-suicidal youth (Gothelf, Apter, Brand-Gothelf, et al., 1998). Not knowing how else to escape unbearable emotional pain was cited by half of the adolescents in a Dutch study (Boergers, Spirito, & Donaldson, 1998). At least in single studies, attempters were differentiated from ideators by substance abuse (Gould, King, Greenwald, 1998), by social isolation, and spending more time ideating (Negron, Piacentini, Graae, et al., 1997). Using a screening instrument, depression scores were the best predictor of the next year's suicide scores (Garrison, Addy, Jackson, et al., 1991). And among young adolescents of Mexican origin living in the USA, loneliness correlated with depressive symptoms and suicidal ideation (Roberts & Chen, 1995). Previous attempts and recent life stress were the major correlates of current suicidal ideation (Roberts, Roberts, & Chen, 1998). A recent review concluded that currently little is known about the relevance of such factors as cognitive distortions, behavioral dyscontrol and ease of access to a means of suicide in moving suicidal ideation to suicidal behavior (Shaffer & Greenberg, 2002).

Attempters

Between three and eleven percent of high school students attempt suicide (Negron, Piacentini, Graae, et al., 1997; Wickstrøm, 2000). The female : male ratio is much lower in community than clinical samples (Shaffer & Greenberg, 2002). Hawton and colleagues (1993, cited in Shaffer, 1996) estimated that 90–99% of attempts are not fatal. One-quarter of attempters reveal no evidence of psychopathology (Gould, King, Greenwald, et al., 1998). In at least one study, the severity of attempts made by lower class, black adolescent girls did not necessarily correlate with the severity of symptoms reported by the youth or their parents (Summerville, Abbate, Siegel, et al., 1992). Prior attempts are a risk factor for future attempts (Wichstrøm, 2000) and for completed suicide (Brent, Perper, Moritz, et al., 1993a; Shafii, Carrigan, Whittinghill, et al., 1985). However, less than one-half of completed suiciders were known to make a prior attempt (Negron, Piacentini, Graae, et al., 1997; Shaffer, 1996). Multiple attempters are at greater risk of completion than those who have made a single or few attempts (references cited in Stein, Apter, Ratzoni, et al., 1998). Only aggression differentiates single from multiple attempters (Stein, Apter, Ratzoni, et al., 1998). Multiple attempters have more intense, but not longer-lasting, suicidal crises than single attempters (Joiner, Rudd, Rouleau, et al., 2000). As one might expect, survivors of more potentially lethal attempts are at greater risk to complete than those surviving less dangerous attempts (Motto, 1965).

While the majority of serious attempters experienced breakdowns in relationships, legal, financial, and work problems in the year prior to their attempts, more than one-third could not identify precipitating event(s) (Beautrais, Joyce, & Mulder, 1997).

In both a hospitalized and community sample, adolescents with suicidal thoughts and behavior correlated with low self-esteem independent of depression, suggesting the value of focusing on self-esteem regulation in adolescents. However, since a moderate proportion of subjects who were judged to have high self-esteem reported past suicide attempts, the applicability of these findings to the individual case is limited (Overholser, Adams, Lehnert, et al., 1995).

Neglect, abuse, and particularly sexual abuse are all risk factors for attempts (Brown, Cohen, Johnson, et al., 1999). Contextual factors have been reported to be more important in adolescents than in young adults (Brow, Cohen, Johnson, et al., 1999). Assaultive and/or sexual behavior compounded the risk of suicidal intentions and attempts, which depression accorded young, inner-city, minority adolescents (Walter, Vaughan, Armstrong, et al., 1995).

The frequency of self-mutilation in the prior year correlates with attempts, and affect dysregulation differentiates inpatient ideators from attempters (Zlotnick, Donaldson, Spirito, et al., 1997). Past attempts correlate best with future attempts in adolescents after discharge from psychiatric hospitalization for various reasons; yet, a significant number who had not previously attempted did so. The first 6–12 months post-discharge was reported to be the period of greatest risk (Goldston, Daniel, Reboussin, et al., 1999). It is possible that psychiatric hospitalization enhances suicidal tendency in attempters (Shaffer, Garland, Gould, et al., 1988). Major depression in adolescent girls and a prior suicide attempt in adolescent boys are considered the major risk factors for completed suicide (Shaffer & Greenberg, 2002).

Biological markers

Low urinary ratios of norepinephrine-to-epinephrine (which might not reflect the ratio in the central nervous system), lower levels of serotonin precursors in the spinal fluid, and abnormal dexamethasone suppression test results have each been correlated with suicidal behavior in adults (Ostroff, Giller, Harkness, et al., 1985). But, as with psychosocial risk factors, the numbers of false positives and false negatives limit the utility of these measures for assessing individual cases. That notwithstanding, larger numbers of serotonin nerve receptors have been found in the prefrontal cortices of teenagers who committed suicide compared to those who died from other causes, irrespective of whether they had a psychiatric diagnosis, suggesting that this finding is specific to suicide (Pandey, Dwivedi, Rizavi, et al., 2002). There may also be an excess of serotonin receptors in the blood platelets of people who suicide. If confirmed, this might offer a screening instrument for identifying those at highest risk from the broader category of high-risk individuals.

Identifying suicidal adolescents

Has suicidal inclination been identified by parents and/or come to the attention of health and mental health professionals?

It has been reported that few parents of ideators realize that their children are entertaining suicidal thoughts. In one community study, parents were more likely to identify them as oppositional rather than depressed or anxious (Kashani, Goddard, & Reid, 1989). Parents of attempters are more likely to agree with their adolescent's acknowledgment regarding substance abuse and disruptive disorders than about non-aggressive conduct disorders and major depression (Velting, Shaffer, Gould, et al., 1998). It would appear that these parents do not tend to see past their adolescents' outward behaviors to an empathic sense of their underlying mood states. However, it is not clear how different they are from parents of non-suicidal adolescents in this regard.

Many suicidal adolescents are disturbed for sufficient time to have come to the care of mental health professionals (Marttunen, Aro, & Lönnqvist, 1992). Suicidal adolescents seen in emergency rooms have a poorer rate of keeping follow-up appointments than non-suicidal adolescents (Pfeffer, Peskin, & Siefker, 1992), or at least tend to drop out sooner (Trautman, Stewart, & Morishima, 1993). Those who failed follow-up appointments were more likely to have a parent(s) with untreated psychiatric illness (Trautman, Levin, & Krauskopf, 1987, cited in Pfeffer, Peskin, & Siefker, 1992). This bespeaks the wisdom of actively pursuing adolescents referred from emergency rooms for suicidal behavior (Rotheram-Borus, Piacentini, Van Rossem, et al., 1996).

Completers younger than fifteen years old tended to give fewer warning signs and experience fewer precipitants/stressors than 15–19-year-old completers. The latter were determined to have been exposed to more risk factors rather than being more resilient (Grøholt, Ekeberg, Wichstrom, et al., 1998).

Do adolescent suiciders tell others of their intention?

A significant proportion of adolescent suiciders have bespoken their intent prior to acting, but frequently too late for intervention by others than those peers whom they most often tell. Moreover, a significant proportion actively hide their intent from others, and some suicidologists have reported a tendency among suicidal adolescents to be quite uncommunicative with therapists (Zalsman, Netanel, Fischel, et al., 2000). The influential Group for the Advancement of Psychiatry (1996) observes: "Even with careful assessment and competent psychiatric intervention, it is difficult, if not impossible, to predict the suicidality of an individual" (p. xi).

What are the protective factors against suicide?

The relationship of adolescents to their parents was found to be the most important factor in protecting them from suicide and from the development of suicidal behavior (Grohølt, Ekeberg, Wichstrom, et al., 2000). Perceived family cohesion (McKeown, Garrison, Cuffe, et al., 1998) and particularly support from the mother helped differentiate abused youth who did not attempt suicide from those who did (Kaplan, Pelcovitz, Salzinger, et al., 1997). These findings underscore the importance of the object relationship in offsetting suicidality. That supports the possibility that extra-familial social/emotional support can serve a tempering function on the risk of suicidality.

Once an adolescent has been identified as suicidal, it has been reported that he or she will talk with professionals about it, more often when seen alone rather than together with their parents (King, Hovey, Brand, et al., 1997). This suggests a strategy for approaching adolescents who have already been identified as suicidal, but it does not solve the problem of diagnosing who is suicidal. Will did not present the problem of withholding suicidal urges from me, but, rather, the problems of being unwilling to stay in treatment, and of impulsivity, which will be addressed shortly in discussing risk factor analyses.

How can these research findings help us approach the individual adolescent?

From the standpoint of clinical evaluation, the aggregated research findings are reassuring to the practitioner in only two respects. One is that the vast majority of adolescents who exhibit the major risk factors do not attempt suicide. The other is that all risk factors identified to

date conform to great common clinical sense; none appear to be coun-
terintuitive/counterexperiential, except perhaps the finding that
parental death, separation, or divorce do not seem to have a significant impact on suicidal ideation (Reinherz, Giaconia, Silverman, et al.,
1995), nor parental separation and divorce on adolescent completions,
after factoring out parental psychopathology (Gould, King, Greenwald, et al., 1998). Other studies report a correlation between suicidal
behavior in parents and in their offspring (Brent, Kolko, Allan, et al.,
1990; Spirito, Brown, Overholser, et al., 1989, cited in Gould, King,
Greenwald, et al., 1998). The non-reassuring conclusion from risk
factor research is the heterogeneity among adolescent suiciders. That
is, to date, false positives outnumber true positives and significant
numbers of false negative findings have emerged in all risk factor
analyses.

Given those considerations, the practical question arises regarding
how much one's clinical approach should be influenced by each of the
underlying paradigms (continuum model; idiosyncratic reactor to
common stressors; trait *vs.* state condition) that has been identified in
studies of adolescent suicide.

Basing one's clinical interventions largely on risk factor analyses
predisposes to several clinical problems:

- It can compromise the therapist's efforts to understand the individual adolescent and convey his or her insight to the patient.
  All patients want to be understood, but developmentally it is
  particularly important for adolescents to sense that you are
  approaching them as unique individuals.
- Making false positive diagnoses in adolescents, and, thus, treating them as if they are truly suicidal when they are not, can be
  problematic for their own development as well as for the treatment. It complicates the therapist's efforts to work collaboratively
  on the issue with the patient. A therapist's inaccurate suggestion
  that the adolescent is suicidal tends to undermine the self-confidence of an already uncertain-of-self youth. This, in turn, reduces
  his or her confidence in the therapist at a time when you are
  trying to achieve their trust. At best, this challenges the therapeutic relationship and renders the treatment more rocky. At
  worst, it can predispose the adolescent to misinterpret the therapist's motives. It can prompt a currently non-suicidal attempter to

repeat the act. The latter is common clinical experience. The explanation that has traditionally been offered is that the patient is provoking the therapist. It is as likely that the patient is complying with what he or she has perceived to be the therapist's expectation, albeit not the therapist's wish, of them. It is always important to consider this dynamic when faced with escalating acting-up behavior in an adolescent.

• Helping a suicide-prone adolescent through that crisis can be developmentally important for him or her—both in terms of what they absorb from the therapist's confidence in the adolescent and what they accrue to their own shaky self-esteem regulation when going through such periods.

In sum, it is tempting to rely on risk assessment data—both to manage anxiety engendered in us by suicidal adolescents, and to cover ourselves medico-legally by taking the most conservative approach. But that risks winning the battle and losing the war. So, one must temper any tendency to be overly influenced by the risk factor data. On the other hand, the danger of ignoring the results of risk factor analyses because of the magnitude of false negatives and positives is being insufficiently attuned to a potential suicide. I suppose the purport of the foregoing amounts to an acknowledgment of the fact that it is no fun to be working without a safety net.

Perhaps the best a clinician can hope to glean from the extensive research literature is to be forearmed by being forewarned, without placing too much emphasis on any one or several factors, and without excluding any diagnostic or phenomenological group from consideration of suicidal potential. Rose (2000) offered the following mnemonic, FACED WITH GUILT. At the least, it can remind clinicians of risk factors when thinking about suicide in adolescents, and, thus, contribute to maintaining a sufficiently high index of suspicion:

Firearms: Is there access to firearms?

Alienated. Is the child alienated alone or as a group?

Conflicts. Are there significant conflicts with family, friends, or peers?

Ethanol. Is there current alcohol or drug abuse or a history of drug dependence?

Depression. Is depression or a major mental illness present?

Work/school. Are there significant problems at work or school?

Impulsive. Is the child's behavior impulsive or unpredictable?

Trouble with the law. Is there a recent history of trouble with the law or conduct disorder?

Hopeless or humiliated. Does the child feel intensely hopeless or humiliated?

Gender/gay? Is the child male? Is he or she gay or lesbian? [The latter have not been demonstrated to be a risk factor; see Chapter Three, p. 156].

Utilize supports. Is the child able to utilize supports (family, friends, religion, mentors)?

Idea of death. Is death a solution or escape from suffering?

Losses. Are there recent losses (people, pets) or moves (schools, job, neighborhoods)?

Tried self-harm. Child has tried self-harm (suicide attempts, including cutting)? (Rose, 2000)

Clinical contributions

Contributions to the psychodynamic understanding of adolescent suicidal behavior have been fewer in recent times. Defense mechanisms utilized by subgroups of suicidal adolescents compared to non-suicidal patients and non-patient peers have been reported, albeit with some inconsistent findings (Apter, Gothelf, Offer, et al., 1997; Pfeffer, Hurt, Peskin, et al., 1995). But such psychodynamic studies have considered the developmental process in only the most general way, (e.g., suicidal adolescents use more immature defenses (denial, projection, and regression)). The importance of a developmental perspective has been underscored in formal psychoanalytic research on children (Target & Fonagy, 1994b). Guilt has been described as a motivating factor but not elaborated psychodynamically (Haliburn, 2000). And to my knowledge, no recent work has correlated these phenomena specifically with the developmental process of adolescence.

The Group for the Advancement of Psychiatry (1996) has advanced the formulation that the "core meaning" of every adolescent suicide is an effort to wrest some level of control over a situation experienced as intolerable, which the youth feels helpless to address in better ways. That view embraces the importance of adolescents' efforts to experience themselves as the masters of their life, which, as I have emphasized, is a crucial developmental imperative.

All predictive diagnostic tests developed to date (e.g., human figure drawing (Zalsman, Netanel, Fischel, et al., 2000) or screening measures for subpopulations at risk (e.g., Larzelere, Smith, Batenhorst, et al., 1996)) have limited diagnostic value. This is because the requirement that such rating scales be highly sensitive predisposes to significant false positive results; that is, the specificity suffers. This obtains even with hospitalized, suicidal adolescents (Huth-Bocks, Kerr, Ivey, et al., 2007). A recent review concludes that there are currently "surprisingly few well-established and/or well-examined scales assessing youths' suicidality" (p. 1162), particularly ones developed for adolescents (Winters, Myers, & Proud, 2002). While self-report scales are being utilized for hospitalized suicidal adolescents (Huth-Bocks, Kerr, Ivey, et al., 2007), presently these instruments are probably more relevant for first pass screening of large populations to identify adolescents at risk as part of prevention programs rather than for clinical work. The same applies to such clinical maxims as the observation that suicide runs in families, and is related to depression in parents (Brent, 2000).

The problem represented by the heterogeneity among adolescent completers and attempters has led to focusing research and treatment efforts on individuals experiencing conditions which represent risk factors for suicide, such as depression and impulsivity (Mufson & Velting, 2002; Murphy, 1985; Shaffer, Garland, Gould, et al., 1988). Identification of common psychodynamic paradigms could further refine at-risk populations. For example, findings from one large epidemiological follow-up study of depressed adolescents in the community fit well with the psychodynamic formulation that helped relieve Will's symptoms. Specifically, depression in family members of the adolescents and serious conflict between adolescent girls and their families predicted recurrent depression. However, most psychosocial variables (including self-esteem, social skills, coping, life events, social support, negative cognitions, and elevated depressive symptoms) did not (Lewinsohn, Rohde, Seeley, et al., 2000). That pattern of findings is consistent with the psychodynamic constellation I have found at the base of much depression in adolescence (Bloch, 1995), and which was elaborated in Will's case. That is, the adoption of a defensive identification by the adolescent to protect a troubled parent(s), based on survivor guilt and an omnipotence complex.

Some clinical refinements have been offered for the typologies of suicidal adolescents that have been developed from clinical descriptive, epidemiological, and psychological autopsy studies. Such phenomena as levels of social–cognitive development (Borst & Noam, 1993), inability to cope with intense emotions (Zlotnick, Donaldson, Spirito, et al., 1997), and correlations between diagnostic categories, suicidal and violent behaviors (Apter, Gothelf, Orbach, et al., 1995) have been related to these typologies in subgroups of suicidal adolescents. For example, among adolescent girls who attempted suicide, an "angry–defiant suicidal type" exhibited little tendency for self-reflection and awareness of internal psychological conflict. This group used both externalizing and internalizing symptoms, and was at risk for impulsive suicide attempts compared to a "self-blaming suicidal type". In the latter group, cognizance of the feelings and views of others contributed to internal conflicts, guilt, more obvious depression, and lack of aggression toward others (Borst & Noam, 1993). Those researchers observe that the depressive features of the angry–defiant group are masked by the prominence of their aggressive and problematic conduct. Thus, clinicians are less likely to identify the suicidal potential of this group.

Cognitive, supportive, family therapy, and apparently interpersonal therapy have been shown to reduce suicidal ideation in depressed, outpatient adolescents (Brent, Holder, Kolko, et al., 1997; Mufson & Fairbanks, 1996). Reduction of suicidal ideation in hospitalized adolescents has been correlated with cognitive shifts from a negative to a positive attributional style, which refers to how one explains the causality of events (Wagner, Rouleau, & Joiner, 2000). That study did not establish what caused the shift away from adolescents feeling pessimistic and responsible for bad things that happened. My thesis offers an approach to understanding and treating the negative attributional style of many suicidal adolescents.

Clinical approach to evaluating suicidal intimation in adolescents

When it makes sense to assess this issue, one way to initiate consideration of suicidal potential is to ask the adolescent whether he or she no longer feels like living/would not care if he or she were dead, as opposed to thinking actively about killing oneself. Although it has been reported that this is not a valid differentiation, I find that making this distinction helps the patient and me keep the issue in perspective, especially if he or she fears I will jump to a conclusion about their suicidal inclination. A passive despairing thought is less worrisome than an active wish to harm oneself.

I expand on the issue by asking if the adolescent is or has been worried about hurting him or herself. I frame it that way explicitly to help adolescents perceive suicidal thoughts or intentions as ego alien. If they respond in the negative, then the technical question becomes how much to investigate further before he or she perceives my exploration as carrying an underlying interest on my part in him or her suiciding. If the adolescent responds in the affirmative, then my question is "What should we do about this?" I deliberately phrase it as "we" in an effort to instill the idea that we are working together against this suicidal urge; I am trying to render it ego alien.

If the adolescent feels in danger of harming him or herself, either physically or psychologically, the next questions usually involve determining whether he or she has ever attempted suicide, and can and will they contact me or someone else to prevent acting on such urges. If, like Will, they cannot be sure, then you must rely on clinical judgment to decide whether to bring in the family, try for hospitalization, or do what I did with Will. The latter refers to attempting to maintain regular, close contact, while working toward a promise to contact me or someone else.

If, on the other hand, the adolescent's response to the question, "Are you worried about hurting yourself?" is that he or she does not worry about it, but desires it, then the immediate therapeutic task is to determine what the patient feels the two of you should do to preserve their life until he or she understands as fully as possible their reasons for seeking such drastic recourse. I frame the issue in this manner not to be or sound cavalier. Rather, I am attempting to avoid the manipulative struggles around control of their behavior in which adolescents who are using suicidality as a means of dealing with interpersonal conflicts can engage therapists and friends. In line with research noted above, one can query the adolescent about what he or she anticipates accomplishing internally by self-destructive behavior. This is an effort both to flesh out your comprehension of this individual and to assess the degree to which suicidal symptoms are ego syntonic. If the adolescent has a plan or prior attempts, then other documented risk factors (e.g., number and seriousness of attempts, a formulated plan, estimated intensity of the dysphoric mood) can be helpful in evaluating the seriousness of the individual's intentions. But there is no substitute for careful, clinical assessment. This is especially so since, for example, it has been reported that high school students who entertain suicidal ideas without a plan are as likely to attempt suicide as are those with a plan (Simon & Crosby, 2000).

Will never attempted suicide. And since the heterogeneity paradigm suggests that adolescents who suicide are qualitatively different from those who do not, it is not clear how applicable this case is to engaging an adolescent/young adult who does suicide. Certainly Will's openness in acknowledging his suicidal tendencies to me from the outset, and to experience them as ego-alien, and bespeaking his fear of his own impulsivity were huge factors in favor of my being able to help him overcome them.

Manic depressive illness/bipolar disorder

General considerations (with reference to adults)

Bipolar disorder, previously known as manic depressive disease/reaction, is a clinical diagnosis. Historically it was probably made if the patient exhibited the triadic symptoms of mania, but more accurately could only be established by following the patient over time with a high index of suspicion. The latter has been emphasized in recent years because depression (the more typical presentation) was observed frequently to be misdiagnosed, often as unipolar depression, and treated with antidepressants. That can place the bipolar patient at greater risk for manic episodes or rapid cycling (American Psychiatric Association, 2002). So it has been suggested that considering factors in addition to the clinical course of depressed adults, such as manic-type responses to antidepressant medications, family history, and corroborating information gained from other family members, plus characteristics of the depression (e.g., early onset, brief, recurrent, post-partum, atypical, psychotic) can help establish the diagnosis sooner (Ghaemi, 2006). The value of the latter is that, at least in adults, earlier institution of medication is associated with a less severe clinical course (American Psychiatric Association, 2002).

Will's age and developmental stage placed him in the time frame when the adult form of the disorder is often first manifested. The course of his symptoms was consistent with a diagnosis of bipolar disorder: Euthymia, or perhaps subsyndromal depression, had blossomed into clinical depression when he began treatment. This gave way to (hypo)mania followed by return to euthymia. Then, during the ensuing ten years before he returned with subsyndromal depression, Will apparently experienced periods of euthymia, dysthymia, and subclinical depression. Each clinical episode was preceded by psychologically stressful experiences (father's illness, friend's death, losing his job), which is commonly observed in adult bipolar patients (American Psychiatric Association, 2002). But Will's case and treatment were not typical in several respects. His symptoms seemed more comprehensible (than one typically reads about) on the basis of a psychodynamic formulation that Will felt was important in reversing his symptoms, and psychotherapy was the only treatment modality utilized. More typically, bipolar patients are described as lacking insight, particularly during manic episodes. Plus, the cornerstone of the current standard of treatment is proper medicinal management during acute episodes of both manic and depressive symptoms; that regimen is then continued during periods of remission to prevent recurrences (American Psychiatric Association, 2002).

The role of psychotherapeutic approaches in the treatment of bipolar disorder

Several psychosocial or psychotherapeutic treatments have been introduced for adults. All are manual-based, time-limited interventions intended to augment the effects of medication. These include:

1. Psychoeducation oriented toward understanding the illness, fostering compliance with medicinal management, early detection

of prodroma of recurrences, and establishing lifestyle regularity (Colom, Vieta, Martinez-Arán, et al., 2003).

2. Family-focused therapy, which includes training to enhance communication and problem-solving skills (Miklowitz, George, Richards, et al., 2003).

3. Cognitive therapy based on the assumption that teaching patients to monitor and alter dysfunctional thinking and behavior can positively influence mood states and enhance social functioning (Lam, Hayward, Watkins, et al., 2005; Lam, Watkins, Hayward, et al., 2003).

4. Interpersonal social rhythm therapy, which combines a behavioral component to reduce vulnerability to affective episodes by stabilizing daily routines, and an interpersonal element to manage stressful experiences more effectively (Frank, Kupfer, Thase, et al., 2005).

Each (summarized in American Psychiatric Association, 2002) has been shown to help patients maintain their medicinal regimens and to improve various outcome measures, such as fewer and less severe relapses (probably more effective against depression than mania), less time spent in hospitals, longer remissions, symptom reduction, and better social functioning (see also Benyon, Soares-Weiser, Woolacott, et al., 2008).

Some of these have been adapted for children and adolescents (Miklowitz, George, Axelson, et al., 2004; Pavuluri, Graczyk, Henry, et al., 2004). There is developing evidence for the effectiveness of psychotherapeutic interventions in preventing recurrence in bipolar adolescents (DelBello, Hanseman, Adler, et al., 2007) and in stabilizing mood and behavior with dialectical behavior therapy (Goldstein, Axelson, Birmaher, et al., 2007). Child- and family-focused cognitive behavioral therapy (Pavuluri, Graczyk, Henry, et al., 2004), for example, which incorporates elements of family-focused therapy (Miklowitz, George, Richards, et al., 2003) and cognitive–behavioral therapy, is based on the premise that bipolar disorder in children and young adolescents is a neurobiologically based condition, or diathesis toward emotional reactivity. It is a chronic condition to which patients and their families must adapt. In this model, the affective dysregulation is thought to influence cognitive coping mechanisms (Pavuluri, Graczyk, Henry, et al., 2004).

These psychotherapeutic treatments are typically implemented during the maintenance phase, that is, after the children/adolescents have been stabilized on medication. However, they have also been used adjunctively with medication during the acute treatment phase (West, Henry, & Pavuluri, 2007). Flexibility to meet individual patients' needs is achieved by emphasizing different aspects of the protocols on a case-specific basis. All impress me as basically sound, adaptational, problem-solving approaches based on the venerable concepts that "knowledge is power" (self-control), "forewarned is forearmed" (anticipating symptoms), and "there is strength in numbers" (consolidating external support). Thus, one component of each involves an effort to reduce environmental stressors (both interpersonal and physiological), which are thought to potentiate symptoms, by educating patient, parents, school personnel, and even siblings about the condition. Other features include helping the patient develop adaptive strategies for anticipating and coping with symptoms and accepting the need for medication. Another involves helping the environment communicate with the patient and respond to the patient's symptoms in a collaborative manner that minimizes intensity and repetition. None of these therapies has been represented as a basic tool for reversing the course of the underlying illness. Yet, their preliminary results suggest that significant ego strengthening may be occurring in those child and adolescent patients who respond. One might postulate that this could have significant impact on the illness, especially in the recent generations where less societal emphasis has been placed on self-containment of emotion and behavior.

The use of psychotherapy alone for mania is only recommended by default—when medicinal treatment has been refused, involuntary treatment is not appropriate, and the therapy is crisis-oriented or primarily focused, for example, on resolving ambivalence about taking medication. Psychotherapy alone for bipolar depression finds more favor because it reduces both the risk of antidepressant-induced mania or rapid cycling as well as side effects of medications (American Psychiatric Association, 2002). If Will's condition does prove to be best understood as bipolar, he either achieved clinical remission from psychotherapy, or else the treatment kept him from creating even more trouble for himself until the natural course of the disorder effected remission. Even if it were the latter, a ten-year remission followed by a subsyndromal recurrence that responded to five months of weekly psychotherapy is a respectable outcome by today's standards. As such, does this case offer anything helpful in thinking about diagnosis and treatment?

Will's treatment may provide data bearing on a question identified among future research needs regarding the treatment of bipolar disorder: "What are the elements of psychotherapy that are critical to its efficacy?" (American Psychiatric Association, 2002, p. 37). In general, Will's psychotherapy involved insight-oriented, guilt-reducing interpretations relating to an omnipotence complex. These were provided in the context of a therapeutic relationship in which Will felt that his efforts were being sponsored to accomplish his adolescent developmental imperative to achieve greater psychological autonomy on his way to completing his development. In this process, he felt able both to assert himself and to share and bear his emotional pain without feeling criticized by the therapist. If, however, the treatment functioned more as a holding operation than remission-engendering, then different ones among the twelve technical principles developed from Will's treatment may have been more relevant (p. 40).

Such a case does suggest that something akin to Freud's complemental series is operative in bipolar phenomena. That is, the relative contribution of innate and experiential factors to the genesis of the condition varies amongst patients. As such, those who fulfill diagnostic criteria for this condition may vary in the degree to which their case is comprehensible psychodynamically. In turn, the interepisode course of some may be as well handled with psychotherapy as medication. It has been observed that the natural history of the disorder is characterized by periods of remission, and recent studies find that the oft-prescribed antidepressants are less effective than previously thought. Thus, it is incumbent upon us to ascertain whether perpetual medicinal treatment is more effective than the natural history of the condition (Ghaemi, 2006). I am not recommending therapy as the treatment of choice. Rather, I am pointing out that some individuals may be able to use it effectively. So, it behooves us frequently to reassess the diagnosis and best treatment.

The latter becomes particularly important at this time when so much emphasis is appropriately placed in the opposite direction, that is, not missing this frequently unrecognized and misdiagnosed condition. When research reports:

1. that most patients who screen positively for Bipolar Disorder have been misdiagnosed,
2. that many years usually elapse between initial presentation and accurate diagnosis,
3. that the earlier a proper medicinal regimen is instituted the more benign the course of illness proves to be,
4. that antidepressants often worsen the condition, and
5. that the FDA recommends that depressed patients be screened for bipolar disorder before antidepressant treatment is initiated (U.S. Food and Drug Administration, 2005),

then it is certainly not surprising that bipolar disorder has become the diagnosis *du jour*.

But "there lies the rub." For, in a paradoxical way, such data and its reasonable emphasis give rise to the opposite problem of over-diagnosing the condition. So, although one can give a trial of mood stabilizing medication, the danger is in coming too quickly to the diagnosis, particularly in adolescents. The adolescent patient may respond to medication with diminishing intensity of symptoms on a physiological or placebo basis. This response becomes further compli-cated by the fact that, at least in my experience, some adolescents tolerate these medications well. This combination of effects is under-standably interpreted as confirmatory evidence of the bipolar diagno-sis, for it increasingly appears that the diagnosis, perhaps especially for younger patients, is essentially confirmed as much as anything by response to medication. That, in turn, becomes grounds for consider-ing a lifetime of mood stabilizers (and psychoeducation to live with a "biochemically caused" illness), which, in fact, may not be accurate or necessary. An example follows.

In the aftermath of a couple of sports-related concussions at age fifteen, a youth developed puzzling, quasi-dissociative, "spacey" spells characterized by visual illusions, and anxiety associated with increases and changes in the quality of pre-existing, severe headaches, which had kept him from studying. This constellation was eventually diagnosed as a migraine syndrome that recurred every few months. At age eighteen, in the context of comprehensible disappointment and frustration related to the latter, he experienced a six- to eight-month period of irritability. Almost anything could prompt ego-dystonic anger toward everyone, which he apparently had some difficulty controlling. This culminated in a seventy-two-hour psychiatric hospitalization when his family thought he was going to harm his brother. His family history included relatives with depression and bipolar disorder. He had experienced chronic insomnia associated with racing thoughts during childhood, and had used alcohol and drugs during adolescence. A bipolar diagnosis was made at that time and medications begun. At age twenty, he reported periods of greater anxiety to a mental health practitioner as he transferred to another college. He also noted that he alternately experienced periods lasting a day or two of feeling energetic, confidently happy that he could accomplish anything, and other periods lasting a couple of weeks during which he felt depressed (but without significant impairment of his academic performance or social activities). The bipolar disorder diagnosis was affirmed by psychiatrists and neurologists who evaluated and treated him in different geographic areas where he attended colleges. Various combinations of mood stabilizers, antipsychotics, antianxiety agents, and antidepressants were prescribed to effect tolerable and effective regimens.

At age twenty-four, he moved to another part of the country to begin a job. He had been asymptomatic (except for the periodic dissociative-type symptoms and migraine headaches) on a well-tolerated regimen for three years. When he consulted a psychiatrist there for medicinal management, he expressed a strong desire not to have to take medicine. He thought he was outgrowing his symptoms. They commenced weekly psychotherapy oriented toward dealing with difficulties in his current life in the classical areas of love and work; this included identifying roots of current interpersonal conflicts in his earlier family relationships. Concomitantly, they were developing a therapeutic relationship of mutual trust and confidence, so that the patient did not have to withhold important data regarding bipolar symptoms, and the psychiatrist could feel more certain of his assessment of the other's level of functioning. After six months, Inderal, which had been primarily prescribed for the migraine symptoms, was tapered. Then Gabapentin was tapered over thirteen months, followed by Lamotrigene over the next eight months. Psychotherapy was reduced to monthly appointments and continued for another two and a half years, during which time Clonazepam was tapered from 2 mg to 1 mg daily. Prescription of Clonazepam was then undertaken by an ear, nose, and throat specialist because, by that point, it was no longer needed to reduce anxiety; it was serving only to relieve tinnitus, hyperacusis, and ear and neck pain, which he had developed at age twenty-one. He had been essentially symptom-free from possible bipolar symptoms for the 4½ years of that treatment, and was functioning successfully in the professional and personal aspects of his life when they terminated.

This young man might have bipolar disorder. His symptoms were consistent, though with more of an admixture of those described in young adolescents and children than adults. Having a family history, plus insomnia with racing thoughts in childhood, prior drug use, and possibly co-morbid anxiety and migraine headaches strengthen the case to be made for that diagnosis. But he might instead have experienced symptoms of a post-concussion syndrome that were eventually interpreted as bipolar phenomena. Or, he might have experienced a period of intense adolescent turmoil aggravated by anxiety and helpless frustration engendered by his strange neurologic symptoms and the way in which they hampered his life in mid- and late adolescence. The latter reduced his tolerance for disagreeable aspects of his home life; together, these conditions intensified his normative developmental imperative to emancipate to greater psychological autonomy. If he is bipolar, statistically he is likely to experience a future recurrence of symptoms. But even if so, he could be someone whose symptoms can be managed psychotherapeutically. Again, my point is that we should always be reassessing the treatment regimen for individuals diagnosed as bipolar during adolescence.

Moreover, although active medication has proven statistically superior to placebo in a number of studies of both manic and depressive phases in adults, the difference between the two effects is not great, in the order of 20% (Ketter, 2006; Petty, 2006). Thus, there is reason for clinicians continually to reconsider which effect is operative, especially in adolescent patients whose psychological development is still in a state of flux. Moreover, emerging findings from a large National Institutes of Mental Health (NIMH)-funded treatment study of bipolar I (mania), II (hypomania), Not Otherwise Specified, and cyclothymia patients, based on protocols developed by expert consensus and published research, have shown modest rates of recovery (58%) and half of those relapse in two years (Perlis, Ostacher, Patel, et al., 2006). Also, recent medication studies raise doubt about the significance of distinguishing bipolar I from bipolar II (The Carlat Psychiatry Report, 2006).

So, here we have a couple of counterpoints to the research findings about delayed diagnosis predisposing to a more severe clinical course, and another dilemma of adolescent diagnosis and treatment. One counterpoint is how long to wait before confirming the diagnosis, and whether and when to taper medication once symptomatic relief has been achieved. In Will's case, this point was moot because he refused any medicinal treatment. The other counterpoint is the danger of saddling the adolescent and his or her family with both the immeasurable, disheartening worry and stigma associated with a serious but inaccurate diagnosis, with chronic medicinal regimens and their side effects. In general, particularly with adolescents who can change dramatically and who are notorious for not taking maintenance medication, it makes sense always to resist the temptation to approach and treat every adolescent who exhibits bipolar-type symptoms in the same way. That is why I consider it premature to diagnose Will with bipolar disorder.

Difficulties in diagnosing bipolar disorder in youth (and children)

If the validity of distinctive subtypes of bipolar disorder in adults is less clear-cut than we had thought, the situation is even more ambiguous for children and early adolescents (American Academy of Child & Adolescent Psychiatry, 2007; Kowatch, Fristad, Birmaher, et al., 2005). As noted, the original and best-known description of manic depressive disease is of a periodic illness characterized by discrete episodes of depression and mania that interrupt periods of normal emotional equilibrium. Kraeplin described a few cases of childhood onset, but it was historically considered that this disorder did not occur before late adolescence. Yet, variants of the condition, some bearing little resemblance to the classical description, have been reported in the psychiatric literature at least since the nineteenth century. Most notably are cases in which irritability is much more pronounced than elation, cases in which periodic illness interspersed with normality is much less evident than chronic switching between states of depression and aggressive irritability or hypomania, and mixed states in which the person evinces features of both simultaneously. More recently, significant numbers of adult manic-depressives have reported the onset of their symptoms during adolescence and some in childhood (Pavuluri, Birmaher, & Naylor, 2005). This has led students of the disease to conclude that children can experience the diagnostic symptoms. In turn, that has prompted efforts to establish the diagnosis as early as possible for the reasons noted previously of reducing the severity of the course of the illness.

Still, controversy remains about whether it is a viable diagnosis (Harris, 2005; McClellan, 2005). This dilemma was well expressed in an introductory statement to a comprehensive literature review of research on pediatric bipolar disorder covering the ten years prior to 2005: "Despite the dramatic increase in our knowledge of pediatric BD [bipolar disorder], there is considerable controversy about the clinical presentation, particularly its core symptoms, and hence the prevalence" (Pavuluri, Birmaher, & Naylor, 2005, p. 846). There seems to be consensus among experts that the condition exists, but not what it comprises. Currently, the latter controversy centers on the degree to which diagnostic criteria should approximate those of the adult condition as opposed to encompassing more undifferentiated states characterized by affective dysregulation. At the least, the disorder in children and youth is described as having a much more variegated and changeable course than it typically takes in adults (Birmaher, Axelson, Strober, et al., 2006). Also, it has been reported that the symptomatically more diffuse, childhood-onset form is associated with greater levels of psychopathology of several sorts in the immediate families compared to those with adolescent-onset bipolar disorder that more closely approximates the adult form (Rende, Birmaher, Axelson, et al., 2007).

Although the onset of almost 20% (American Academy of Child & Adolescent Psychiatry, 1997b) or 27% (American Psychiatric Association, 2002) of bipolar cases occurs in adolescence (between ages 15–19), and despite the increasing popularity of this diagnosis, bipolar disorder, like suicide, is very uncommon in children and adolescents (see Carlson, 2002). Thus, here too, the problem of accumulating sufficient numbers of cases hinders formal research efforts (Murphy, 1985; Nottelmann & Jensen, 1995; Weller, Weller, & Fristad, 1995). This contributes to the dilemma just noted and to the fact that contradictory results have been reported for practically all findings on bipolar disorder in children and adolescents (Strober, Schmidt-Lackner, Freeman, et al., 1995).[9]

Currently, it would appear that the smallest fraction of pediatric patients diagnosed bipolar have experienced a bona fide manic episode rather than these variations, and the majority of adolescent and young adult onset cases are of the latter forms (Carlson, 2002). These observations make it difficult to know how to interpret reports that the average age of onset of bipolar disease has been decreasing since 1970 (Botteron, Vannier, Geller, et al., 1995; McClellan 2005). For it is not clear whether we are dealing with one condition, which bears some relation to the classic descriptions of the adult disorder or several different conditions.

The major justification for calling these variants bipolar disorder would be finding either a common psychological dynamic, or neuro-anatomical irregularities (Botteron, Vannier, Geller, et al., 1995), or response to the same pharmacological agent. The former two have not yet been identified (Pavuluri, Birmaher, & Naylor, 2005), though Will's case has raised some possibilities of common psychodynamics. There is some evidence that this group responds best to mood stabilizing medications alone or in conjunction with antipsychotics (Pavuluri, Birmaher, & Naylor, 2005), though the response to the variants is generally less than for classical manic depressive disease (e.g., Kafantaris, 1995; Kafantaris, Coletti, Dicker, et al., 2001).

A longitudinal community study found that few adolescents who had exhibited the behaviorally disruptive symptoms thought to characterize juvenile bipolar disorder develop the adult disorder; they had psychological problems and psychiatric diagnoses as adults, but not bipolar disorder (Lewinsohn, Rohde, Seeley, et al., 2000). In a relatively small sample, parents of juveniles with the mood dysregulation symptoms/pattern had rates of bipolar disorder similar to the general population (3%); by contrast, parents of youth with the more classical adult form had a higher rate of bipolar diagnoses (33%) (Brotman, Kassem, Reising, et al., 2007). Those differential responses to medications, and findings in long-term outcomes and in family aggregation, might not be sufficient to justify diagnosing the variants as different conditions. Progress is being made in sorting out the relationship between the classical presentation and those symptom patterns in juveniles characterized more prominently by behavioral dysregulation (Carlson, 2007). But the possibility remains that these are more complicated conditions, which may warrant reconsideration of the diagnostic approach to these illnesses.[10]

Establishing diagnostic criteria for children and young adolescents presents a conundrum. For adult diagnostic criteria must be modified in more ways than common sense equivalences would dictate (e.g., school function instead of work function). This has contributed to a confounding overlap of symptoms with other childhood disorders. That so-called co-morbidity renders it difficult to determine which youngsters who exhibit ADHD, conduct, or externalizing behavior disorders, substance abuse, or psychotic symptoms are, or will go on to become, bipolar. Consensus has not yet been reached regarding whether these common atypical presentations are:

1. forms of adult bipolar disorder expressed in developmentally mediated ways reflecting limitations of the child and adolescent's ego resources (Nottelmann & Jensen, 1995);
2. precursors of the adult condition (Strober, Schmidt-Lackner, Freeman, et al., 1995);
3. specific subpopulations of bipolar disorder (Biederman, 1998);
4. misdiagnoses (Klein, Pine, & Klein, 1998);
5. reflections of severity rather than specificity of psychopathology (Carlson, 1995), or
6. artifacts of the current nosological system (McClellan, 2005).

The other problem is making the diagnosis incorrectly and instituting long-term treatment that has shown only modest success in children and younger adolescents.

The difficulty that has historically attended making the bipolar diagnosis in adolescents and pre-adolescents has led to the recommendation that a "developmental, age-specific viewpoint needs to be considered" (Geller & Luby, 1997). While addressed to pre-pubertal and young adolescents, that observation can probably be applied to older ones as well, since adolescence is protracted in current society. A long-term follow-up study found that adolescent-onset bipolar patients had more often been initially diagnosed as schizoaffective than their adult counterparts; they seemed sicker at index admission but had a better long-term outcome than the adults (McGlashan, 1988). It is reasonable to infer from these findings that the defensive and adaptive mechanisms of adolescents' egos are more fluid than those of adult bipolar patients. This is often attributed to immaturity, and equated with relative weakness of the adolescent ego, which predisposes to more severe symptoms (McGlashan, 1988). That factor may contribute to the diagnostic challenges presented by pre-pubertal children (Biederman, 1998; Carlson, 1995; Klein, Pine, & Klein, 1998) and adolescents (Kovacs & Pollock, 1995; McElroy, Strakowski, West, et al., 1997). However, that same fluidity affords the adolescent ego greater resiliency and flexibility in adapting. This is a boon for psychodynamically oriented clinicians by virtue of offering the greatest opportunity for effective psychotherapeutic intervention (Settlage, 1974).

The importance of capitalizing on adolescents' ego resources becomes particularly relevant when we consider two prominent facts related to the treatment of adolescent bipolar patients: As noted, to date, research data establishing the efficacy of medicinal treatments of adolescent manics are not compelling. The relatively few reported pharmacological studies of bipolar adolescents and children are not considered definitive by the research community (Kafantaris, 1995; Kowatch, Fristad, Birmaher, et al., 2005; Pavuluri, Birmaher, & Naylor, 2005). And while open label studies have identified the efficacy of medicinal regimens (Kafantaris, Coletti, Dicker, et al., 2001, 2003; Kowatch, Fristad, Birmaher, et al., 2005; Pavuluri, Birmaher, & Naylor, 2005), the first controlled study of lithium for adolescent mania did not support a significant effect (Kafantaris, Coletti, Dicker, 2004). Yet, on the basis of limited studies, the combination of mood stabilizers and newer antipsychotics are considered effective for acute treatment of cases diagnosed with pediatric bipolar symptoms, and mood stabilizers and stimulants for those with ADHD as well (Pavuluri, Birmaher, & Naylor, 2005). But, justification continues to be largely derived from medication studies of adults (American Academy of Child & Adolescent Psychiatry, 1997b). Similar extrapolations from adult major depressive disorder (Geller & Luby, 1997) and adult suicide (Pinto & Whishart, 1996) have not proven particularly useful.

My point is not to gainsay the practice of medicating adolescents on an empirical basis; that must continue. Rather, I am sharing my impression that in the current era, medicinal treatment enjoys the imprimatur of greater "evidence-based" justification than is legitimately warranted. The second and more important factor from the perspective of my thesis is that even granting the prophylactic value of medicine for adolescent bipolar patients, this group is even less inclined than their adult counterparts to take medication (Colom, Vieta, Martinez-Arán, et al., 2000). This justifies efforts to find complementary or alternative therapeutic interventions for them. And while the importance of psychosocial factors in the genesis of the condition and in treatment seems widely acknowledged, studies of psychotherapeutic interventions are still preliminary (Pavuluri, Birmaher, & Naylor, 2005).

Will developed manic symptoms after we had established a working relationship. This afforded me the distinct advantage of having a degree of influence with him that is rarely, if ever, enjoyed by a clinician who first encounters an adolescent in the throes of a manic state. Yet, Will still refused medication, but was willing to continue meeting with me. So, it is my hope that features of the technical approach that I enunciated might help others to forge more collaborative working relationships with at least some adolescents with suicidal and/or bipolar symptoms that can tide them over acute phases of illness when medication is refused.

Implications of a psychodynamic/developmental approach in contrast to a "medical"/symptom-oriented, diagnostic syndrome model

The "medical", symptom-based model has the advantage of diagnostic precision, which we hope will ultimately translate into specific medicinal treatments. Since adopting this approach, a frequently used strategy to overcome adolescents' resistance to taking medication has been to explain the condition as an illness which has attacked them. Thus, by implication, they have no control over it, and, by analogy to the prevailing view of serious, adult psychiatric conditions and other medical diseases, medicine is necessary for cure. I find several problems with that approach. One was noted above—that analogy might not be accurate. A number of authors have suggested differences in disease conditions among the still psychologically developing adolescent compared to the more fully psychologically developed adult (Ambrosini, Bianchi, Rabinovich, et al., 1993; Emslie, Rush, Weinberg, et al., 1997b; Geller, Todd, Luby, et al., 1996; Kye, Waterman, Ryan, et al., 1996; Pinto & Whisman, 1996; Strober, Schmidt-Lackner, Freeman, et al., 1995). Access to different coping styles may afford adolescents greater potential for reversing symptoms than adults who lack this resiliency.

In addition to the difficulty determining which adolescents are experiencing the typical adult form of the illness, so as to be truthful with the patient, there is another problem with this approach. Telling adolescents that their illness is essentially out of their control may be a well-intentioned effort to reduce shame, embarrassment, and guilt about their condition, as well as to render them receptive to medication. But that message flies in the face of their developmental thrust to master challenges and move ahead. So, from the standpoint of the psychological motivating factors that potentiate better outcomes in all illnesses, the patient's attitude, I question the value as well as the virtue of this strategy. Over and above being developmentally and motivationally inappropriate, and perhaps inaccurate, a third problem with this-type rendering of the "medical model" approach is that it does not persuade all adolescents. Last, there is a spectrum of severity among all psychiatric disorders, and, consequently, varying levels of urgency to prescribe powerful maintenance medications, and, thus, different timetables for doing so (Sobo, 1999). With the current pressure to treat many patients, we have to be particularly careful not to adopt a "one size fits all" approach to even severe psychiatric symptoms in adolescents.

By contrast, the psychodynamic, developmental model, at least in my hands, lacks the diagnostic precision of the "medical" model, by virtue of focusing on the relative flexibility of the adolescent ego through which we work to help the patient. Endorsing this model basically refers to capitalizing on adolescents' strivings to complete their development, which motivate them to overcome impediments to their forward movement. This is the prime factor that justifies our cautious optimism, and is our main ally against the ravages of whatever psychiatric symptoms our patients experience. Operationally, this means dovetailing our interventions with the ego's own maturational efforts to master. That endorsement, plus our sponsorship of their autonomy, are the therapist's main contributions toward establishing whatever therapeutic *détente* or alliance is possible with any individual adolescent (Bloch, 1981).

Communicating a non-patronizing sense of appreciation for these attributes of the adolescent patient helps establish a positive relationship. A positive transference is a more effective position from which to work with most adolescents than a negative transference. This is particularly the case with suicidal adolescents, for whom maladaptive relationships with parents have been identified as a risk factor for suicide (Hollis, 1996). Adolescents are prone to experience transference toward therapists, but less inclined to analyze it than to bolt treatment or draw the therapist into a repetition of the problematic relationships at home. These factors (working from a positive transference and their disinclination to analyze the transference) are reasons why the termination phase of the treatment of adolescents is often relatively short.

Conclusions

1. In this chapter, I have illustrated the vital interplay between understanding and working with both psychodynamic and developmental factors in treating a depressed adolescent who was fearful of suiciding impulsively, who became manic during treatment, and who steadfastly refused medication.

2. With respect to the psychodynamic formulation, data were presented which suggest that survival guilt and omnipotence complex dynamics underlie some cases of adolescent mania, as well as suicide and depression.

3. Twelve technical precepts utilized to retain the adolescent in treatment (which he experienced as incompatible with his normal developmental imperative to emancipate) have been enumerated.

4. Some features I have recommended might be considered new provisos for establishing a therapeutic relationship with adolescents who have serious symptoms and fear replicating the parental relationship. One example is trying to forge a connection quickly, so that adolescents perceive that this therapeutic encounter holds out the promise of being useful. Finding in their material evidences of emancipatory, survivor, or separation guilt, that is, apprising them of the degree to which their symptoms reflect a severance conflict involving a need to protect parents, often seems novel to adolescents.

5. Other features I have enunciated are no more than great clinical common sense. These include such general guiding precepts as if you come upon someone hanging off the edge of a cliff, they

probably want your help so you should stick around, despite their protestations to the contrary. That relates to the role of the object relationship in treatment. Another is a variation of the old military psychiatry adage of "Treating 'em where they lie". That is, do what is needed to stabilize a critical situation immediately—in Will's case, intervening with parents despite his age.

6. In this day of fiscal prudence, it makes sense to include the expenditure of time and costs of Will's treatment: He had seventy-two biweekly and weekly sessions during the first phase of his treatment, which lasted one year and cost $7470. Then, following the four-month break, we had twenty-one weekly meetings over a period of six months, which cost $1890. The total cost was $9360, or $390 a month when averaged over the total two-year period of my initial involvement with him. Or, if one includes the $1400 for the later five months of psychotherapy, then costs would average about $900 a year, or $75 per month over the twelve-year period.

Appendix

The Introduction to this chapter considers in some detail controversies regarding recent outcome studies. This Appendix lists the results of studies that are generally consistent with a clinical axiom among experienced psychopharmacologists that two-thirds of (adult) patients respond to antidepressant medications and to the atypical antipsychotics. Generally, if anything, children and adolescents are less, or less consistently, responsive to psychotropic medication than adults.

Symptoms of 56% of children and adolescents treated with fluoxetine and 22% of those treated with placebo for non-psychotic, major depressive disorder were rated "much" or "very much" improved (Emslie, Rush, Weinberg, et al., 1997a). Two-thirds of depressed adolescent patients responded to both fluoxetine and placebo, and at mean follow-up interval of twenty-four months, 33% of responders and 50% on non-responders exhibited poor psychosocial adaptation and mood disturbance (Simeon, Dinicola, Ferguson, et al., 1990). Approximately two-thirds of a multi-center study of adolescents with major depressive disorder improved after treatment for eight weeks with Paroxetine, compared to one-half of those treated with Imipramine or placebo (Keller, Ryan, Strober, et al., 2001). The collaborative TADS (Treatment for Adolescents with Depression) study found that 61% of adolescents diagnosed with major depressive disorder responded to Fluoxetine and 35% to placebo after twelve weeks of treatment (March, Silva, Vitiello, et al., 2006). Approximately 60–66% of adolescents with moderately severe major depressive disorder responded to Sertraline and 46–50% responded to placebo depending on the assessment instrument used (Donnelly, Wagner, Rynn, et al., 2006). In another study comparing sertraline and cognitive–behavioral therapy in outpatient adolescents, one-third with major depressive disorder achieved partial remission (Melvin, Tonge, King, et al., 2006). Results from combining a total of four trials involving either Sertraline, Venlafaxine, or Fluoxetine indicated a modest effect size of 0.42 (Safer, 2006).

Approximately two-thirds of children and adolescents treated for bipolar disorder responded to medication and 35% were no longer compliant with medications after eighteen months (Kafantaris, 1995). A year after initial hospitalization for a manic or mixed episode, 39% of adolescents had achieved symptomatic and functional recovery, and only 35% reported being fully compliant with their medicinal regimen (DelBello, Hanseman, Adler, et al., 2007). Response rates of adolescents with acute mania have been reported at 42% (Frazier, Biederman, Tohen, et al., 2001), 63% or 55% depending on criteria (Kafantaris, Coletti, Dicker, et al., 2003), and 38–53% (Kowatch, Suppes, Carmody, et al., 2000) in open-label studies with different medications. A two-year prospective study of bipolar children and adolescents (mean age of thirteen years) found that 70% recovered from the index episode but half of them experienced recurrences, and the clinical course was typically symptomatic (Birmaher, Axelson, Strober, et al., 2006). Lithium is not effective in 20–40% of cases of acute mania in adults (Hopkins & Gelenberg, 2001); it is thought to be even less so in adolescents. Forty-eight percent of adolescents responded in an open-label, small sample study of lithium for bipolar depression (Patel, DelBello, Bryan, et al., 2006). A similar study with lamotrigine reported 84% and 63% responders depending upon the assessment instrument utilized (Chang, Saxena, & Howe, 2006). Retrospective chart review and open-label studies have suggested higher rates of response to the newer antipsychotics (roughly 60–80%) than to mood stabilizers (cited in DelBello, Kowatch, Adler, et al., 2006). Forty percent of euthymic bipolar patients had mild or poor compliance with medicinal regimens, with fifteen to twenty-five year olds more likely to exhibit poor compliance (Colom, Vieta, Martinez-Arán, et al., 2000).

Ten to thirty percent of schizophrenic patients are refractory to antipsychotics, 40–60% are partial responders, and 40–50% have discontinued medications six months after hospital discharge (Menza, 2001).

Depending on who is rating improvement, small cohort studies of benzodiazepines have reported from one-half to eighty-two percent improvement in children and adolescents treated for anxiety disorders (American Academy of Child & Adolescent Psychiatry, 1997a). A meta-analysis of all randomized, controlled, medication (primarily SSRI) studies of anxiety disorders in children and adolescents contained in the Cochrane Database found 58.1% response to medication and 31.5% to placebo (Ipser, Stein, Hawkridge, et al., 2009).

Twenty-five to thirty-five percent of ADHD patients are not benefited by stimulants because of insufficient symptom relief, side effects, and other non-adherence (Wilens & Spencer, 2000).

CHAPTER TWO

Bulimia in adolescents

B ulimia (literally "ox hunger"), long recognized as a symptom of anorexia nervosa, was identified as a distinct eating disorder relatively recently. The original diagnostic criteria for bulimia nervosa were an irresistible urge to overeat followed by self-induced vomiting or purging, and a morbid fear of becoming fat (Russell, 1979). A number of bulimics have previously been anorexic (Robinson & Holden, 1986; Russell, 1979), and it is not clear whether preoccupation with and/or distortion of body image are greater in bulimia or anorexia nervosa. Bulimics (who may be overweight, normal weight, or underweight) do not starve themselves. Rather, they eliminate the caloric intake after binge eating by so-called compensatory behaviors. These run a gamut from strict dieting and fasting, through vigorous exercise and use of diet medicines to "purging" activities, including diuretics, laxatives, enemas, and self-induced vomiting (Fairburn & Belgin, 1990). In the most recent American Psychiatric Association's *Diagnostic and Statistical Manual of Mental Disorders DSM-5*, binge eating disorder (Pope, Lalonde, Pindyck, et al., 2006) is identified as a separate diagnosis, distinguished from bulimia nervosa by the absence of compensatory activities (American Psychiatric Association, 2013).

A spectrum disorder

Each of these compensatory behaviors except purging is commonly practiced in the general population. So, bulimia nervosa is considered a spectrum disorder rather than a discrete, circumscribed illness (Drewnowski, Yee, Kurth, et al., 1994; Fairburn & Belgin, 1990). That is, symptoms exist on a continuum from the psychopathology of everyday life, or mild abnormality, through increasing severity to clinical significance. Thus, the diagnosis is based on arbitrarily defined severity criteria, which in turn influence prevalence statistics (Garfinkel, Lin, Goering, et al., 1995).

The importance of studying bulimic adolescents separately from adults has been emphasized (e.g., Attie & Brooks-Gunn, 1989). But this has rarely been done (leGrange, quoted in DeAngelis, 2002; Steiner & Lock, 1998), ostensibly because bulimia is uncommon in adolescents. Yet, clinicians experienced with adolescents consider bulimic symptoms quite common (R. King, 2010, personal communication). This difference in the epidemiological and clinical perspectives may in part reflect the spectrum aspect of this disorder and/or adolescents' disinclination to seek treatment. In any event, such pooled studies complicate efforts to understand features of adolescence that may predispose to bulimia, features of the condition that may be unique to adolescents, and features of the normal adolescent developmental process that could influence the treatment approach for adolescent bulimics. This may be particularly relevant since it has been reported that "a substantial number" of bulimics may experience remission of pathological eating and weight stabilization during their later teens and early twenties (Kaye, 2009, p. 1310)

Prevalence

Bulimia nervosa was originally considered to be a "culture bound" syndrome, largely confined to middle- and upper-class, achievement-oriented western families. It is now being increasingly reported from many western nations and in the youth of developing countries as well (Al-Adawi, Dorvlo, Burke, et al., 2002; Pate, Pumariega, Hester, et al., 1992).

Differing definitions of specific symptoms, severity criteria, qualifications of interviewers, and a legion of other confounding variables complicate efforts to compare epidemiological studies among both clinical populations and community samples (Fairburn & Delgin, 1990; Pope & Hudson, 1992). The point prevalence and lifetime prevalence of eating disorders, generally quoted at 1–3%, are lower when derived from community samples than when extrapolated from treatment-seeking cohorts, and when established by interview rather than by questionnaire (Fairburn & Belgin, 1990; Garfinkel, Lin, Goering, et al., 1995; Kendler, MacLean, Neale, et al., 1991). Cohort effects (e.g., age of onset, decades in which population is sampled) also significantly influence prevalence statistics (Bushnell, Wells, Hornblow, et al. 1990; Heatherton, Mahamedi, Striepe, et al., 1997). Cases identified in community samples are generally less severe, experience waxing and waning symptoms, and do not seek treatment. A small minority runs a more chronic and severe course similar to clinical populations (Fairburn & Belgin, 1990).

Partial vs. full syndrome bulimia nervosa

The severity of the symptom complex (i.e., the frequency of binge eating and/or purging activity) is typically used to differentiate full from partial syndromes. Many fewer individuals meet full diagnostic criteria than experience milder forms, termed subthreshold, subsyndromal, or partial syndromes. The more dramatic compensatory behaviors, which are self-induced vomiting and frequent recourse to laxatives and enemas, are much less frequently reported in community than in clinical samples, though much of the data on which these conclusions are based are derived from study populations extending through early middle age (Fairburn & Belgin 1990; Garfinkel, Lin, Goering, et al., 1995).

With this background in mind, an adolescent bulimic will be presented, primarily to illustrate an approach to her treatment that may be especially relevant to adolescents. Specifically, this case is presented to illustrate how adolescents' normative "strivings to complete development" can be capitalized upon in the process and technique of therapy. Behaviors that adolescents typically use to promote their own development, and to deal with subclinical symptoms arising in their personal struggles to mature psychologically, can be enlisted to overcome severe symptoms. It becomes important in the curative process to recognize, understand, and facilitate (even if only by acknowledging to adolescent patients) evidences of these inner strivings. The combination of Sydney's response to the treatment approach and her spontaneous insights may shed further light on the bases of this psychopathology in at least some adolescent bulimics, even though several of her own psychodynamic insights have been identified previously (see Crowther, Wolf, & Sherwood, 1992). Precepts that seemed effective in responding to her repeated falling off and climbing back on the non-purging wagon will be discussed.

Sydney and I met for thirty-four sessions during 5½ months and her parents and I had three appointments. Total cost was $4625, or $660 per month, averaged over seven months.

Sydney

Referral

Sydney was just fourteen when her parents called after reading entries in her diary indicating that she had been vomiting after every meal for four months. Upon speaking with her about this, Sydney had acted shattered, depressed, withdrew into a fetal position in her room, and did no homework that weekend.

During our initial telephone contact, her parents noted that Sydney had developed a "severely nasty" personality at age eleven. The latter was characterized by "a very sharp tongue"—saying rude, hurtful things, and cursing her parents. But that contumely was not beyond their ability to help her contain. Her tempestuous manner subsided after several months of therapy. From age eleven, however, she gained considerable weight (an issue with which each parent had grappled successfully). Now, three years later, she had recently returned from summer work as a junior camp counselor having lost thirty pounds and looking svelte.

Sydney had just started her freshman high school year in honors classes but was already exhibiting a long-standing problem of inconsistent academic performance. She was an accomplished artist and a good athlete. Despite no history of drug or alcohol use, or compulsive binge eating, her parents feared she might have addictive tendencies.

Family history

Her father, a chef, had instilled in Sydney and her brother a love and appreciation of fine food. He enjoyed nothing more than preparing for his own family the same rich meals that he did for patrons of his popular restaurant at which they often dined. He himself was slightly overweight. Her mother, a former pastry chef, was now very trim.

Sydney's parents each offered an insightful assessment: Sydney's mother and her sister had experienced eating problems. Her mother had mastered overeating as an adult, losing fifty pounds with the assistance of a group to which she still belonged. Her sister had been bulimic during adolescence, and Sydney's current eating pattern was reminiscent of that aunt's behavior. Her mother also thought that Sydney had been depressed since entering adolescence. And she herself had not been helpful to her daughter because she put more pressure on Sydney to perform academically, artistically, and athletically. Also, her mother liked to work outside the home. In fifth grade, Sydney had urged her mother to return to work because she seemed miserable at home. We were not able to establish whether that experience or puberty correlated with Sydney's weight gain and the period when she became nasty toward her parents. She had probably become pubertal in fifth or sixth grades, and her growth spurt and menarche occurred in seventh grade.

Last, her mother's description of Sydney growing up was characteristic of histories one hears, which currently are compatible with several symptom-based diagnoses. To wit, she was bright, but always underachieved because of difficulty concentrating and tendencies to procrastinate doing assignments. She had received help from learning specialists until fifth grade. From second grade, Sydney's interactions with other children had been problematic. She never seemed to respond to social cues from peers with any degree of sensitivity, and appeared absorbed by her own interests. She did not exhibit empathy, and came across as more self-assertive or callous than did other children. She tended to be domineering with peers, a quality her parents observed in themselves. As a result, she had difficulty sustaining friendships and had become more socially isolated. She was depressed by her own failure to perform closer to her potential. And she tended to "bury" and, thus, to not know her feelings, that is, her affects were isolated.

Thus, her mother was bespeaking symptoms that might have earned Sydney diagnoses of depression, attention deficit disorder, non-verbal learning disability, and obsessive compulsive disorder. I mention this not to dispute the value of symptom-based diagnosis, but to emphasize that children and adolescents are rarely specimens of developmental perfection. Transient symptoms and less than peak performance in every area of their lives are more the rule than the exception. To diagnose them on the basis of a symptom checklist often fails to give due credit to their adaptive tendencies. That is, making symptom-based diagnoses is easy. Doing so accurately is difficult because it requires assessing the adaptive, developmental use of seemingly symptomatic behaviors by the adolescent. In planning treatment, we are always in the position of weighing the potential detriment of any symptom against an estimate of the adolescent's self-righting tendencies.

The perspective of Sydney's father was also of interest. A survivor of multiple stepmothers growing up, he, too, had struggled with weight problems, and felt that Sydney ate impulsively to deal with underlying unhappiness. The latter related to being unpopular with peers, owing in part to what her mother had described, and in part to feeling that her peers did not appreciate her artistic bent.

Development

Following the birth of her brother when she was two and a half years old, Sydney had reverted from early toilet training to regressive oral, motor (crawling), and toileting behaviors. Her maternal grandmother became very ill at that time, requiring her mother to spend much time traveling to her own mother's home in a nearby city. Sydney became more clinging and reluctant to leave home. Otherwise, she was an "easy", delightful, non-rivalrous child with her sibling, who would be crushed by a harsh word—until her 180° turn around at age ten or eleven (fifth grade). From that time on, her parents could neither say, threaten, nor do anything to influence her. They always retained au pair, even though her mother's work enabled her to often be at home. Her brother, who shared the family's pleasure in eating well and occasionally spatted with Sydney, was not otherwise in her life or thoughts.

In the diary she had left around, Sydney had written about wanting to try marijuana and sexual intercourse in addition to her bulimia;

the latter seemed to be the most distressing to both her parents and herself. Each parent had found therapy helpful, were supportive of Sydney being treated, and preferably without medication.

Initial contacts with Sydney

Sydney was a tall, attractive, normally proportioned, pubertal adolescent whose self-possessed manner seemed at odds with her embarrassed complaints about losing her thoughts during our initial meeting. Thus, while looking like a young adolescent, she exuded the forthright and, therefore, seemingly mature manner of an older adolescent.

Until her parents had confronted her about purging she had "kind of been in denial" about being bulimic. Everything had felt perfect this freshman year—making new friends, and developing interest in, and getting attention from, boys at a new school.

Earlier, in fifth grade, she would go through the refrigerator after school, and then have dinner at her father's restaurant. Her parents would observe gently to her that she was eating a lot without ever making allusions to her weight. She would respond by calling her father a hypocrite. In fact, their family particularly enjoyed eating.

Psychotherapy during fifth grade had addressed her unhappiness. Her state of mind and feelings had improved, but her eating pattern had not been discussed. She recalled having been struggling with issues of regulating her behavior as well as her mood. In sixth and seventh grades she joined Weight Watchers, lost fifteen pounds, and then gained twenty. Later, during her last semester in eighth grade, she began to induce vomiting occasionally after consuming large meals. This gradually progressed during the next few months to "a bad habit" in which she engaged after every meal. She claimed to now be retaining only 300 calories a day, though looked remarkably robust for that to be accurate.

Sydney disclaimed any dental or medical symptoms related to chronic purging. The only current manifestation was feeling so full and uncomfortable whenever she tried to keep down a regular meal that she was unable to concentrate on homework or anything else.

Her peer relationships were difficult to assess. She talked of best friends who seemed to shift in a fashion not untypical of early adolescents, but she gave no indication of previously having had a best friend of long standing. Recently, she had mentioned being bulimic to her best friend in a casual, cursory manner. Sydney also had a good male friend (not a boyfriend), to whom she could confide "everything".

Initial insights

Regarding her emotional state and symptoms, Sydney observed during our initial sessions that when she is alone in her room she starts to worry, but when she is out with friends or other people she can "kind of deny the problem" (her bulimia). On the one hand, what she was describing could simply reflect the commonplace ability of human beings to distract themselves from sources of anxiety. However, in noting that peer relationships freed her from inner preoccupations, Sydney was raising the possibility that bulimic symptoms were associated with feeling alone, and, thus, a reflection of adolescent development. Dealing with loneliness, the proverbial "common plight of man", is one of the emotional tasks of adolescence (in addition to integrating adult sexual function and the capacity for more serious expression of aggression).

Several of her observations about herself were synthesized from personal experience and reading: She was a "unique" bulimic, because she did not binge, she just purged. She had felt unable to view her figure dispassionately for the past year. She perceived herself as an "elephant", an image that had not changed since junior high school. The only way she could tell she weighed less was the fact that her clothes fit more loosely and she needed a belt. She assessed her relative weight daily by the appearance of her cheekbones. Any weight gain, even a pound, was reason to purge.

Efforts at self-cure

From the beginning of treatment, Sydney tried in her own fashion to deal with her purging. She ate little for breakfast, and experienced fewer urges to vomit, but the problem resurfaced upon returning from school and after dinner. Within days after indicating that she was doing better, she was admonishing me that, "We've got to get down to the serious stuff", because she had started vomiting again after weighing and "panicking" herself with the idea that she would become bloated.

Observations about her bulimia were interspersed with reflections on other matters of immediate concern. The latter included many normative adolescent conflicts, as well as greater sensitivity to the feelings of others than her own and her parents' characterizations had suggested her capable. For example, when a boy with whom she "just wanted to be friends" asked her for a date, she feared that he would feel rejected if she declined. She elaborated on how difficult it is for her to say "no" if she feels that doing so will "hurt" the other person. This was based "on knowing what it was like to be on the other end", an experience with which she claimed great familiarity. She soon added that she gets over it quickly, suggesting the experience of being told "no" was not so devastating, and therefore by inference, she could acquire the ability to say "no" to others with relative ease.

Additional evidence of observing ego, ego dystonicity of symptoms, and how this influences the treatment approach

Sydney exhibited observing ego capacities in noting that it was "lame" that she should live in such a beautiful area, and have so much going for her, and yet be engaged in this kind of behavior (i.e., purging). That suggested that her bulimic activity was, or could be, rendered ego dystonic relatively easily. So I told her to try as best she could to control the urge. In doing so, I was simply supporting her own ego's efforts to master. Had there been more evidence that her symptom was overtly ego syntonic and necessary for regulating her self-esteem, then I might not so soon have taken a stand on the side of trying to stop vomiting, lest she feel in contention with me about resolving her symptoms.

She was soon perceiving her body image as even more distorted—considering herself to have "chipmunk cheeks" and a protuberant abdomen. That attitude worried her, again suggesting that she experienced these distorted perceptions as ego dystonic. She was also feeling angry and tense, though did not know about what or why. Previously, when feeling this way, she would explode in her friends' faces, which "did not work". Now she found partial discharge in her sports practice. She had witnessed her father acting similarly explosively and would try to mollify him. From these associations, it seemed quite possible that a factor in her volatility was a defensive identification with his behaviors, despite her assurances that the latter had not been traumatically unsettling for her.

She went on to say that she had started biting her fingernails again to relieve her tension and anger—something she had stopped doing a few months earlier for the first time since she was two or three years old. I chose to focus on this because it was more immediate and less theoretical than the possible defensive identification with her father. I observed that in stopping a decade-long habit, she had demonstrated to herself that she can exercise great self control. She responded that after having acknowledged that it was a problem, she was able to control vomiting, and was now doing so only after school and dinner, and not every day. She no longer experienced the sensation of being full after eating, which had compelled her to vomit, and for this reason felt she was improving and did not need twice-weekly sessions. I agreed that her awareness of feeling less full was important.

She added that her "self-image problem" made her feel crazy. But, before leaving, she told me that it had not been as bad a week as she had suggested. It was not clear whether, in the latter statement, she was trying to recoup her defenses or was coaching me to not worry about her. She realized she had to stay focused on not vomiting. She would try to do so by thinking about those parts of her body that she liked and about which she did not have a "distorted image". Yet, within days, she concluded that we should meet a second time each week because she was not progressing, despite talking openly about her experiences and fantasies associated with body image and eating. She frankly assessed her various physical attributes. And she described having become inured to being teased as fat in junior high school. She had become vegetarian for a few months at that time, after becoming "freaked out" thinking about the equivalent part of the human body to that of the animal she was eating. She disclaimed awareness of other cannibalistic-type fantasies.

When she told me that she did not think about purging, she just did it, I responded that she should think about it. Shortly thereafter she began to describe consuming decent-sized meals without gaining weight, feeling tense when she had the urge to vomit, but finding other ways to relax. She noted that the latter amounted to distracting herself with some other activity, such as taking a long bath or shower, or a nap, or jogging or walking. I asked how she had accomplished that. She replied, "by paying attention" to her eating.

Bulimic symptoms as a displacement from other sources of anxiety

Sydney also recognized that she experienced tension from several sources other than her bulimia—many related to school and completing assignments. Perhaps, she observed, focusing on this physical tension distracted her from the psychological ones. Thus, Sydney was suggesting that her bulimic symptoms could represent a displacement from other conflicts. She was now successfully battling her tendency to procrastinate doing homework, and as a result was getting more sleep.

Sydney spent a weekend with friends, one of whom took LSD, and had acted in the same intellectually superior and arrogant way that Sydney recognized herself to have felt on those few occasions when she had smoked marijuana. Yet, what emerged from her friend's mouth was silly; this caused Sydney to reconsider her own drug-influenced attitudes. And she claimed to have "social worries". By this, she meant that because her father said she is arrogant, self-centered, and spent all her time talking about herself, she had to think about those with whom she interacts. When friends point out these same tendencies to her, Sydney now "self-corrects" and has to remain aware of what she says and how her friends are reacting. In these examples, Sydney was exhibiting "observing ego" functioning where she was implying that previously "experiencing ego" had prevailed.

People now frequently complimented her appearance. In the past, others' opinions had been irrelevant, but she was now letting her peers' comments moderate her image of herself. Also, she was currently sitting in the front of the class, because she has "mild ADD" and daydreams a lot. So, we were witnessing further efforts on Sydney's part to help herself. In these examples, she capitalized on her developing self-reflective tendencies to reassess her own prior behavior. She was turning to the outside world for assistance in modulating what she had concluded was an unrealistic appraisal of her body. And she was taking initiative to reduce her distractibility.

She asked me if therapy would end when she stopped purging or when she had achieved a more reasonable body image. She thought the latter, and I agreed, but mentioned that first it was important to develop confidence in her ability to regulate herself in several arenas of her life. Because she had told me that she felt her thoughts and expressions were too random and unrelated during our sessions, I reviewed the changes that she had recently elaborated. Sydney felt this helped her to organize her thinking.

First, she had realized and accepted that she had a significant problem.

Next, she focused her attention on her symptoms and bodily sensations rather than trying to avoid thinking about them. She realized that she felt full after meals, which activated her fear of gaining weight and became the immediate impetus to induce vomiting. The following week she had experimented with eating less, which reduced her post-prandial feeling of fullness, and thus reassured herself that she could control her input and consequently her weight.

Third, this self-reflective thinking about her urge to purge rather than simply doing so enabled Sydney to realize that she felt tense after some meals. So, she actively sought other ways than vomiting to relieve that tension. She found several developmentally adaptive means of doing so in such divergent practices as physical activity and napping, self-soothing distractions such as bathing, and sublimations such as sculpting.

Fourth, continuing to concentrate her attention on why she felt tense on specific occasions led Sydney to recognize that purging had become a way of relieving psychological tensions that originated from different sources than feeling stuffed. Tensions associated with other issues were displaced from their true sources on to her fear of gaining weight, which she dealt with by vomiting.

Last, concurrently she was accepting her peers' compliments about her appearance to offset what she characterized as her distorted body image. This helped her appraise her appearance more realistically, accept her body, and more often like her reflection in the mirror.

But, as she became less compulsive about purging, then, as we might expect, she began to exhibit more doing and undoing of that behavior. That is, compulsive adherence to one pole of her conflict (purging *vs.* not purging) enabled her to avoid obsessing about this activity. When that rigidity was relaxed, she began to exhibit the behavioral equivalent of obsessing: alternating purging and not purging as she attempted to resolve her conflicts and consolidate self-control. In this process of so testing herself, she would feel tense, purge again, and then become angry and disappointed in herself. This indicated that she was increasingly experiencing her symptoms as ego dystonic.

Shortly thereafter she thought she had overeaten, felt full and experienced the urge, but did not vomit. Her explanation was that she had felt too lazy to get up and do so. I observed that the urge was losing its compulsive nature. Perhaps she had challenged herself in this way or allowed herself to be challenged in order to resist the urge. I was implying that she was exerting more active control over her behavior than was suggested by her own passive explanation of sloth.

At this juncture (after six weeks of therapy) Sydney asked about reducing to weekly meetings. I recommended waiting a couple of weeks to be sure she did not fall back, to which she readily agreed. She was feeling greater self-control, eating well, and not purging at all. I said that she would be our most important guide, and we should meet weekly when she felt confident that purging would not be a problem. By emphasizing the importance of her data (specifically confidence in self) in making this decision, I was trying to minimize the likelihood that she would experience us as being in conflict regarding frequency of sessions. She noted that her father was questioning her about eating and purging, which angered her. In that observation, I thought that she was coaching me not to so question her.

Not long thereafter, she arrived chagrined after having purged for the first time in two weeks. She did not know why. She was feeling "compulsive" that day, "well, not really—tense, well not really—wigged—physiologically not psychologically." She could not explain it, and had not felt less tense after purging. After more self-doubting, self-deprecation, and emphasizing that we should meet twice weekly, I told her not to be too hard on herself. Overall, she had done well to this point and could continue to do so.

She arrived at the next session implying that she had gone all the way back. She had not purged on the last day she had seen me, but the next day became "compulsive", which was at times her wont, and is experienced as having to do something "right now". She was feeling "weird" and quickly ate a full meal on returning from school. This left her "a little uncomfortable", and she immediately started to induce vomiting but stopped herself part way through the act. While still a little worried about getting fat, she does not now perceive herself as overweight, and her feelings about her body are changing positively. She did not purge the following day, and hoped not to today. I observed that at the beginning of this session she had presented her situation as worse than it seemed to be. Given that, how had she thought I would react to what she had told me? She had not thought much about it, but suspected I would not be happy. She was just angry with herself for succumbing. She went on to talk about having accompanied her father, uncle, and brother to a rock concert, and how weird it was to observe contemporaries of her father stoned. She did not say whether her father or uncle had used marijuana.

You will notice that she exhibited little interest in my invitation to explore the transference aspect of her presentation that hour. Although her response was quite typical, I think it is still often wise to raise the transference issue (i.e., her thoughts about my reaction), because doing so demonstrates your neutrality around these issues. And in her albeit perfunctory reaction, that I would not be happy, we had a possible clue about what she might be trying to reassure herself. That is, she did not want me to be upset, discouraged, or angered by her actions.

At her next session, she reported not having purged for several days; she was not even thinking about it, and had been enjoying exercising and running. She felt less concerned about gaining weight and liked that idea for the first time. Her view of her body just seemed to be changing—she liked her face, and even liked having a slightly protuberant rather than a scaphoid abdomen, and did not want "a six-pack" (i.e., well-defined abdominal muscles). Her friends were helping to alter her view of herself by reinforcing that she looked good when she asked them. She observed that the longer she goes without vomiting, the more confidence she develops in being able to control herself.

But she arrived at the next session chagrined and petulant, feeling ashamed and guilty for having purged on three successive days. It was even worse, because she had also used marijuana, and felt like a hypocrite after having told me that she did not like it and would not use it again. She immediately went on to say that her mother was angry at her—crying yesterday, screaming at her today, and threatening to send her to a boarding school if she continued to procrastinate in doing her schoolwork. (That association to her mother's emotional and critical reaction was a further cue to me that Sydney did not want me to respond in an intense, critical, or worried manner.) She then mentioned that her brother, too, was not doing well in school.

At the next session she reported doing well, not having "puked". She had even walked into the bathroom, told herself she did not want to vomit and was not going to, then rushed out, grabbed her sketch-ing materials, and began to draw. In the next breath she told me that on a dare she had tried to go through the whole school day without talking—but was "tickled out of it" by friends. She also expressed perplexity about why she can motivate herself to do some things and not others, adding that she does some things for her parents. This may have been a clue to explain that dilemma, which is experiencing the adolescent emancipatory conflict regarding pleasing her parents as opposed to herself (i.e., autonomy).

She went on to observe that her mother is always critical, even when Sydney tells her about good things she has done. Her mother's response is, "Fine, but I wish you could be doing as well in (some other areas)." It was not clear that Sydney had developed the idea that her mother derived satisfaction from criticizing. But Sydney later noted that she had been doing make-up schoolwork since second grade. She also recalled having been very clinging to her mother when she was in fifth and sixth grades (the period when her parents repor-ted her to have become so rejecting of them). That suggested some apprehension and/or ambivalence in relation to her mother. She currently preferred her father, who was more convivial and encour-aging. Her mother just made her "mad".

These last several sessions afford the opportunity to comment upon the interplay of possible interpersonal and intrapsychic dynam-ics in this condition, their relationship to features of normative adoles-cent development in the process of curing her illness, the transference, and technical considerations:

Sydney seemed to be lurching back and forth between purging and controlling the urge—pendulum swings in which the therapist might get caught up. Or, at the least, the therapist might be inclined to suspect that the patient was being manipulative for some reason. But, as noted, Sydney's immediate and subsequent associations (to her mother's upset and tendency to be critical and implacable and the earlier similar sequence with her father) were interpreted by me as an admonition that I not respond in a way that replicated her mother's intense or critical attitude. It was not certain that her bulimic symp-toms were persisting in an effort to gratify what she perceived, accu-rately or not, to be her mother's need to scold, criticize, or feel superior. But I think she was looking for a corrective ego experience to offset her tendency to comply with what she perceived as her parents' wishes to criticize. For within a couple of sessions after my positive response to such setbacks, she would do better. But her associations during these hours suggested that in addition to compliance with what she perceived to be her mother's need to criticize (i.e., giving her mother reason to criticize), Sydney also exhibited defensive identifications with her father's and brother's maladaptive behaviors. To wit, she felt mortified telling me she had used marijuana, which in itself was probably related to her father's or uncle's behavior at the concert, and she had also noted her brother's flagging academic performance.

These associations in the face of her own failures to stop purging consistently conform to the survivor guilt dynamics I have emphasized in the psychology of adolescent psychopathology (Bloch, 1995). But, even if accurate, that only accounts for the generic mechanism of needing to protect a sibling or parent by exhibiting similar/equivalent behaviors. It does not explain symptom choice, which is a more family or case specific matter. In this regard, Sydney's parents had successfully struggled with challenges in the areas of eating and academic accomplishments, making it likely that they would subtly or overtly focus their attention on these areas of their child's development. Their child, in turn, would be likely to perceive this consciously or unconsciously. You will recall that among Sydney's diary entries about trying sex, drugs, and bulimia, the latter was of greatest concern to all three of them.

A question from the standpoint of technique was whether to raise these compliance/survivor guilt issues to help Sydney understand her perplexity and embarrassment. I did not for a couple of reasons. This dynamic was more speculative, and when I had raised it she did not react in a way that suggested that it struck a respondent chord in her. Rather, she focused exclusively on the purging itself. And she was reporting phenomena that sounded as if she were capitalizing on features of the normative developmental process to help herself. Specifically, she challenged herself by going into the bathroom and then leaving; she also experimented in another venue, not talking for a day at school, which involved the same issue of holding things in. Thus, it seemed most prudent to underscore and support that adaptive, self-curative effort.

So, I told Sydney that I was impressed that she was proving to herself that she can control purging, even to the degree of going right to the brink of doing so, and then aborting the act. In emphasizing her efforts to utilize such behaviors in the service of mastery, I was under scoring both her desire and her capacity to do so. The danger of taking this stance is that Sydney could experience me as Pollyanna-ish, downplaying or making light of the seriousness of the matter, and thus being unable myself to face the severity of her struggle. Or, she might react as if I were giving her more credit than was legitimately due to her. Such a perception on her part could cause Sydney to lose confidence in me. But, since the form of those activities is a common way that adolescents challenge themselves to determine and enhance the limits of their abilities to contain and control themselves, it would be clarifying for her to understand how these fit into her efforts to cure herself. That clarification would be easier for her to perceive and integrate than an interpretation of her efforts to protect parents and sibling via the survivor guilt dynamic suggested by her associations to father, brother, and mother.

At that juncture, Sydney's parents requested to meet. Her mother observed that Sydney seemed to need external assistance to regulate herself. She had become furious with Sydney, but recognized both that Sydney's behavior related to the adolescent emancipation process, and that she herself had not emancipated until her twenties from a mother who completely controlled the lives of her sister and herself, and then only with the aid of intensive psychotherapy. She realized she had internalized and honored her own mother's expectations, and did not want Sydney to have to do it that way. She just wanted Sydney to take responsibility for herself and her schoolwork. Her father wondered if they should let Sydney sink or swim. He was sure she would sink, but did not want to be haranguing her all the time.

I told them that their reactions to Sydney were normal, but recommended that they exhibit maximum forbearance and take the long view of her development. By the latter, I referred to thinking in terms of how we hoped she would be functioning a few years from now, not next month. I also observed that Sydney needed to see that they did not enjoy criticizing her. I suggested that they ask Sydney how she thought they might help her stay on track with schoolwork, other responsibilities, and her bulimic problem, and be guided by her response, even though her thoughts in the matter might be changeable. I outlined for them the progression of Sydney's approach to her symptoms that I had previously reviewed for Sydney herself. They could identify all of the factors I mentioned and felt relieved.

With respect to the transference, Sydney presented her backsliding to me as if it had been worse than it apparently was. I think she was testing to see if I wanted to criticize her for these setbacks, or (conversely) whether I had confidence in her ability to wrest control over her symptoms. As noted, my stance was to emphasize the latter, as much conveyed by my attitude as expressed in words. The latter were oriented toward pointing out how her own behaviors represented her self-righting efforts at mastery.

The alternating purging and not purging recurred with a vengeance in the context of talking about contention with her mother, whom she felt was always criticizing her. Thus, doing and undoing of her bulimic behavior reflected this interpersonal dilemma of whether or not to gratify her mother's perceived need to criticize. But, as Sydney began to take herself to the brink of purging (i.e., starting and then stopping), it seemed likely that she was basically struggling internally to consolidate a confident sense of self-control over her urges. The latter is a central feature of normal adolescent development.

Following my meeting with her parents, Sydney reported that things were better with her mother who had apologized for becoming so angry with her. For her part, Sydney would try to be more forthcoming with her mother about her circumstances at school. Urges to vomit had been fewer that week, and she was able to say "no" to herself. So, if she had been complying with her mother's tendency to criticize, she was trying to reverse it.

Sydney requested that we not meet for the two weeks of their upcoming Christmas vacation. She considered this an ultimate test because of the amount of eating in which her family engages at that time of year. She felt she could do it. The technical question for me was whether she was trying to determine if I had confidence in her (if she were ready for this), or whether I wanted her to fail by being willing to leave her on her own prematurely in a particularly challenging setting (if she were not ready for this challenge). She went on to talk about having felt anxious during the past few weeks but could not identify its source. She added that her friends were feeling the same way.[11] Given her follow-up association about being anxious, I could not tell which response she wanted from me regarding the proposed two-week hiatus. So I suggested we not decide immediately.

In sessions that followed, Sydney described the vicissitudes of her continuing efforts to come to grips with purging. She now felt the urge both before and after meals. In the past she would think, "I'll eat this and then purge". Something similar had happened that day when she chose to eat a sweet, but decided to just enjoy the calories and not induce vomiting. It was getting easier to not purge. She was coaching herself to maintain the idea that she could find other ways to deal with tension.

At the same time, her social life was progressing in a natural manner—from apprehension about going to dances or accepting dates (presented to me as not wanting to go), to attending them and finding them "not that much fun", to deciding that the personality of boys who were interested in her was more important than their looks (even if her friends felt otherwise). And she began to experiment with different styles of dress—from "glam" (glamorous) to "grunge" to "preppie" garb on consecutive days. This imparted a charming, albeit mildly caricaturish quality to the typical trying-on-different-identities-for-fit behavior of adolescents. Sydney was also using the Internet to inform herself about bulimia, and brought her findings to our sessions.

She was apprehensive about the Christmas holidays because all members of her extended family were big eaters. We did not meet during those two weeks. She reported that her mother had "by chance" come upon her on the one occasion she purged during that period. Her mother had been contentious with her father and brother as well as herself during the holiday season.

Her mother called to say that Sydney's behavior deteriorates when she is doing poorly regarding her eating problem, and she had been horrible the previous week. Then, after sharing that observation with Sydney, who acknowledged it, her mother reported that Sydney's problematic behavior had ceased. I think that was because her mother approached Sydney on that occasion in a more conciliatory manner, which enabled Sydney to feel her mother did not want to criticize her. When Sydney arrived later that day she described having felt tense all week, "PMS-ing (pre-menstrual syndrome) all over the place". She had then become very upset, even though she knew she should not, after her brother said her thighs were out of proportion to the rest of her body. She was unable to prevent herself from vomiting, even with the technique that usually worked, which as looking at herself in the mirror and saying aloud that she looks good. She then commenced exercising compulsively. She felt better after the talk with her mother, and had not purged for two days. Interestingly, over the course of this session, she reported feeling increasingly better and more self-confident. That suggested again that her bulimic symptoms reflected, at least in part, compliance with what she felt someone else wanted her to feel—be it her brother teasing, or her mother or father criticizing her.

Her mother was upset by Sydney's failure to complete homework and to perform academically. Although the latter had always been the case, Sydney claimed that she and her mother had never had such fallings-out in the past. She thought that all members of her family had difficulty doing and learning things that did not interest them. And, conversely, when she was interested in learning something, she could devote her attention to it completely and productively. In fact, the latter was occurring at this time. Tension, which in the past would have been responded to by purging, was now being alleviated by learning something that appealed to her. She also observed that, similar to her father, she was disinclined to do things when she felt forced to by someone else, and vice versa. Her parents were presently embroiled in some low-grade contention with each other, interspersed with moments of forced pleasantry.

Sydney was challenging herself with increasingly problematic (greasy) foods, and finding it increasingly easier to withstand urges to purge. She wondered about stopping in a few weeks since she was running out of things about which to talk. I replied that was fine, but suggested re-evaluating at that time to decide whether to stop or reduce to meeting once a week. I added that we should stop when she felt confident of her ability to not purge. In this way I tried to keep the ball in her court and termination an issue within herself rather than between us.

Soon thereafter her mother called to reduce Sydney's appointments to weekly for financial reasons (though I offered to defer part of the payment), and to let her miss a session to participate in a school activity. Sydney subsequently said it was she rather than her mother who initiated the change, having told her mother that she no longer needed therapy. Her semester grades had been disappointing and a source of conflict with her mother. Sydney still felt under her mother's thumb; everything was all right if she gets good grades and stays on her mother's good side. She felt that her mother misinterpreted her moods as problematic and not normal. Sydney resolved to improve her academic performance. She had no urge to purge, was eating normally, and would like to stop meeting, though felt her mother would only approve of reducing to weekly meetings. She had invited a boy to the upcoming turnaround dance, suggesting further reduction of her normative developmental hesitation in the arena of boy–girl relationships. This was about six weeks before we terminated.

In the weeks that followed, there were some canceled appointments for extracurricular activities at school, a couple of episodes of purging in contexts that she felt were not typically bulimic (e.g., after eating food she later learned had not been refrigerated overnight). She expressed confidence that this pattern would smooth out. She was changing her group of friends to one that shared more artistic interests and were less "wild". And she let me know that she wanted to join Weight Watchers for help with self-regulation of her eating. So, she seemed to want a follow-on program in place before terminating therapy.

She felt ready to stop. She neither thought about nor had any urges to vomit, and could only recall what it was like in the past when she purged all the time. The dietary guidance she was receiving from Weight Watchers was reassuring. A similar program had been instrumental in her mother's weight loss and control. Also, the family's concern had now shifted to her brother, who was having behavioral and academic difficulties.

I asked when she wanted to say good-bye. She decided the following week. I wondered if there were anything else she wanted to be sure to bring up before we drew our work to a close. She hesitated and then told me about finding marijuana in her father's pocket, which was surprising, and made her think he was a hypocrite. She then rationalized her reaction away by observing that he is an adult and it was his business. She disclaimed disappointment, though noted that she had wanted to get it off her chest. She did not think this discovery would alter her own resolve to neither use marijuana nor drink, since she dislikes the effects of both.

Her mother called to report that Sydney seemed much more stable. She was acting normally, talking more to her parents, being more conscientious about her schoolwork, and exhibiting no evidence of purging. She felt Sydney was ready to stop.

At our last appointment, Sydney talked convivially about her daily activities, her friends, how much better were her parents than those of many of her friends, her spotty but improving academic performance, her mood, which was good except when she is tired, how she no longer thought about purging and was quite certain that she would tell her parents should those symptoms recur. She hoped she would never have to see me again, but wanted me to know that "I liked working with you". I returned that sentiment as we shook hands and said good-bye for the last time.

Discussion

Most points of discussion were elaborated upon in the case presentation. I will précis them in the terms of my paradigm for understanding adolescent development, discuss what this approach contributes to understanding and treating bulimia in adolescents, and finally reflect on how these ideas fit into the context of recent research.

In discussing Will's case, I emphasized working with clinical manifestations relating to two of the three precepts of adolescent development I have advanced to understand and treat adolescents. These are their wish to retain a positive relationship with their parents, and their need to experience parental sponsorship of their wishes/efforts to move forward. Similar issues were evident in Sydney's case, and, like Will, she, too, exhibited compliance and defensive identifications in response to such phenomena as her mother's tendency to criticize, her father's use of marijuana, and her brother's academic failure. But she did not work with my interpretations of these dynamics in the productive way that she responded when I identified and encouraged her behavioral and attitudinal manifestations of the third precept of adolescent development, which is their strivings to complete their development. Manifestations of these urges that Sydney exhibited included:

1. Efforts to take initiative in effecting her own cure: This feature had complicated Will's treatment, since his wish to do it alone had to be overcome to allow him to accept a therapist's help. By contrast, from our first meeting when she reported efforts to overcome her post-prandial feeling of fullness by eating less for breakfast, fostering Sydney's self-curative tendencies became the

major technical approach. A later example occurred after she recognized that bulimia served to reduce anxieties from various sources. Sydney then began to distract herself from purging by engaging in other activities (exercise, artwork, bathing, napping). Identifying self-righting tendencies and clarifying both what I thought she was trying to accomplish and how she was attempting to do so reinforced and supported her adaptive efforts at mastery.

2.   Adolescents' normative tendencies to practice perfecting skills are related to the first feature; this same penchant can be enlisted to overcome impediments to their forward movement. So, when Sydney presented what she had been doing to understand and modulate her symptoms, I encouraged that approach. Similarly, when it appeared that her symptoms were relatively ego dystonic, I encouraged her to actively resist the urge to purge. This is facilitated by another penchant of adolescents:

3.   That is an inclination to use abstract thinking to refine their self-reflective abilities. This is manifested particularly in adolescents' ability to split off observing ego from what had previously been primarily experiencing ego. (By contrast, preadolescents are more prone to reject the idea of thinking about things which trouble them, fearing that doing so will increase rather than reduce their tendency to act.) Sydney's early reflection about how "lame" it was to have these symptoms when she lived in such a beautiful area and had so much going for her, suggested that her symptoms were, or could readily be rendered, ego dystonic. So, I emphasized the wisdom of her own, early observation that she had started to think about her symptoms rather than just enacting them (i.e., using her mind to control her feelings and behavior).

(a)   A corollary feature deriving from adolescents' tendency to practice thinking abstractly is the manner in which they develop, accept, and utilize insight. An example is Sydney's observation of her use of displacement.[12] That insight did not answer the question of whether displacement from other anxieties gave rise to bulimic symptoms, or whether her bulimia became a convenient means of quelling anxieties from sources other than those associated with her weight, figure, and eating. But she was aware that displacement figured in both her underlying anxieties, and the behaviors adopted to reduce them. That insight allowed me to help her perceive that and how she was demystifying and detoxifying symptoms and anxiety associated with typical adolescent developmental conflicts. The latter included relationships with male and female peers, the intensity that develops in family interactions, apprehension about school performance, and the issue of feeling alone during the emancipation process. Displacement involved in reverting from bulimia to fingernail biting allowed me to invoke the historical context to utilize insight. That is, having developed self-control over a decade-long habit of fingernail biting, she could obviously do so with respect to vomiting.

4. Turning to peers, which is utilized to reduce loneliness in the process of emancipating and to de-idealize one's view of parents: Sydney began to allow peers' appraisal of her appearance to moderate what she realized was the distorted view that she held of her face and figure. With respect to this feature, I needed to do no more than be aware of this healthy use of friends' support in assisting Sydney to override her symptoms.

5. Experimenting and risk-taking, which normally help adolescents determine the limits and extent of their abilities: Accepting and presenting themselves with challenges in an effort to consolidate a confident sense of self-control and competence was observed in several of Sydney's activities. She tasted and enjoyed forbidden sweets without purging. She went into the bathroom to vomit but left without doing so. Then, late in treatment she challenged herself by eating greasy food, which previously had been anathema. Also, as she was dealing with control of her eating and purging, she attempted to go through a school day without talking to anyone. In pointing out both the parallel between these and her other experiments at home, and underscoring the developmentally progressive aspect of these activities, I was identifying the proverbial "method to her madness", in contradistinction to emphasizing a putting-herself-at-unnecessary-risk-of-failure type explanation. This latter technique helped Sydney organize her thinking when she felt it was scattered. It also underscored concretely my wish that she progress. Thus, it represented a sponsoring function for her development.

The bases of bulimia and treatment approach

Three factors stand out when trying to formulate the genesis of Sydney's bulimia: The maternal history suggested a familial dimension to bulimia and conflicts involving autonomy. Enjoying rich meals was an ego-syntonic activity in this family, and both her parents had struggled with self-control regarding weight regulation. Whether her parents' difficulties in the area of eating reflected simple gratification of an inborn predisposition/vulnerability or a learned common pathway for dealing with anxieties from various sources might be relevant in deciding whether serotonin-mediating medications might be helpful. However, that is beyond the scope of present knowledge in the field. Moreover, from a developmental standpoint, consolidating a sense of self-control over urges, including urges to eat, is such an important task for adolescents, that one would hesitate to focus the therapeutic approach on medication. This is especially so for an adolescent in whom the strength of her drive to master was so readily capitalized upon. Conveying to such an individual that self-control is gained through something put in one's mouth seems confusing at the least and inconsistent at worst. At best, it may be another of those situations where one wins the battle, in this case of purging, but loses the war involving the developmental issue of self control.

Another developmental consideration is the importance of peer relationships in aiding and facilitating the emancipation process from the childhood ties to parents. In Sydney's particular subculture, being overweight presented a problem in terms of her wishes to be found appealing to, and accepted by, peers for that very purpose. A case in point: Sydney had observed early in treatment being preoccupied with bulimia when alone in her room, but did not think about it when with her friends. This raised the possibility that coping with feeling alone in the process of emancipating to greater psychological autonomy was one determinant of her symptoms that peer relationships are important in moderating.

Termination of adolescent treatment

Termination of most adolescents' treatment is (of the necessity occasioned by their desire) relatively short in duration. Having made up their mind to stop, they think it makes most sense to do so sooner rather than later. That is because letting go takes precedence developmentally over hanging on in the emancipation process. In fact, the issue has usually been raised by the adolescent considerably earlier than the formal agreement to do so. Thus, many, if not most, adolescents have been working toward this goal, even though it may not have been mutually acknowledged between you for some time. In Sydney's case, it was four to six weeks, because the trial termination during the Christmas holiday was a self-imposed challenge geared toward determining for herself whether she could proceed on her own without treatment.

One last comment deserves mention: Sydney's treatment progressed quite easily and progressively, the credit for which is due to her. But it is important to also realize that, despite her parents' interactions, which might at times not have been optimal, each of them had struggled successfully with eating-related problems, had been helped by therapy, and supported Sydney being in treatment. The importance to the therapeutic outcome of their underlying sponsorship of their adolescent implicit in these factors cannot be overestimated.

Contributions from the clinical and research literature toward understanding bulimia

As noted, like suicide and bipolar disease, bulimia in adolescents is very uncommon. That is why adolescent bulimics (and anorexics) are grouped with adults—to achieve sufficient numbers for epidemiological and clinical studies. This has been justified by phenomenological similarities and by reports of few psychological differences between hospitalized adolescent and adult cases (Heebink, Sunday, & Halmi, 1995). Combining adults and adolescents may also be justified on the basis that many chronologically adult individuals are still psychologically adolescent. Emancipation occurs later in current day western society, especially among college students, who have frequently been the subjects of epidemiological studies. Those factors notwithstanding, there may be distinctive features in bulimic adolescents that in turn allow the normal adolescent developmental process to be capitalized upon in treating this subgroup.

For example, the intensity of adolescents' strivings to complete development and the fluidity of their ego resources potentially afford greater assistance to the therapeutic process than during other phases of the life span (Settlage, 1974). Writing from a libido-theory perspec tive, Anna Freud (1936) described unique characteristics of the adolescent ego's defense mechanisms. Children and adults typically respond to inner conflict by invoking defenses that facilitate compromise formation between complete repression and full conscious awareness of instinctual wishes. The result is neurotic symptom formation. By contrast, adolescents' defense mechanisms are less fixed and they are more inclined to alternate between indulging and completely renouncing the impulse. In bulimia, the latter are exemplified by bingeing and purging. Parenthetically, that feature of adolescents' defense mechanisms fits well with the classical psychoanalytic hypothesis that regressive, unconscious oral impregnation fantasies underlie bulimia and anorexia nervosa. Why did I not try to explore that possible dynamic? There are several reasons: First, the evidence from her descriptions of Sydney's thoughts and interactions with peers indicated that she was negotiating the movement toward heterosexual involvements in a normally progressive manner. Second, although she mentioned in her diary wanting to try sexual intercourse, this was not an issue close to her sensibility. She would have been more confused than enlightened had I tried to find some way to broach this, especially since her treatment was essentially moving well. Third, as will be noted, no single psychodynamic constellation fits all cases. Lastly, with adolescents, it is often best to deal with the issue of the moment and leave the rest for later, if further work is necessary—the technical matter of professional tact and tactics.

Also, in this latter area of tactical approach, it is worth mentioning that self-induced vomiting is a voluntary rather than an automatic act. Thus, it is reasonable to presume that bulimic adolescents have more self-control over their behaviors than, for example, do depressives over their symptoms. So, when a bulimic in therapy reverts to vomiting in the course of trying to get better, the clinician might be inclined to consider that there is more willful perversity or hostility toward the therapeutic efforts in this act than is implicit in the symptoms of other illnesses. As such, it becomes relatively easy for therapist and patient to become locked into an interpersonal struggle that predisposes to accentuation of the symptoms. By pointing out to these patients how they are trying to get better, the approach I am advancing minimizes the likelihood of such a struggle developing. It demonstrates how they themselves are experiencing their symptomatic behaviors as ego alien, and this supports their efforts to regulate their own self-esteem. Regarding the technique of responding to Sydney's recurrent purging, her consistent associations at such times were about her parents criticizing or becoming very focused on this behavior. As noted, I thought these represented her effort, albeit unconsciously, to coach me to not replicate her parents' attitude. So, pointing out what she was doing right rather than what she was doing wrong seemed the more therapeutic tack.

What the research literature reveals about bulimia in adolescents

As of a review in 1998, only a couple of epidemiological and clinical studies and no treatment studies limited to adolescent bulimics had been reported (Steiner & Lock, 1998). In the intervening years a few more studies limited to adolescents have appeared (e.g., Lock, Garrett, Beenhakker, et al., 2011; Marsh, Horga, Wang, et al., 2011). But research interest–attention has shifted from a psychological–clinical focus on the development and psychotherapeutic treatment of bulimia (and the other eating disorders) toward neurobiology (brain pathology) "utilizing cognitive neuroscience paradigms" (Eddy & Rauch, 2011, p. 1139). Such studies correlate the symptoms–features of eating disorders, including response to test stimuli, with patterns of activation in areas of the brain utilizing an fMRI technology (Lock, Garrett, Beenhakker, et al., 2011; Marsh, Horga, Wang, et al., 2011; Oberndorfer, Frank, Simmons, et al., 2013), and with altered brain structure utilizing voxel-based morphometry, a technique for automatic computational neuro-anatomy (Frank, Shott, Hagman, et al., 2013). It is not clear yet whether the brain changes identified represent cause or effect of the eating disorders (Alonso-Alonso, 2013). Either way, the anticipated, ultimate outcome of this approach would seem to be the development of effective medicinal interventions. Yet, this path may be complicated, for a long-time researcher in the field recently observed that gaining FDA approval for new medications may be difficult because of the small sample sizes in clinical trials, as well as the findings that CBT has proven superior to medicinal treatments (Halmi, reported in Watts, 2014). Halmi also observed that treatments for eating disorders have lagged behind those for other psychiatric conditions (reported in Watts, 2014). This is interesting, given the findings of a longitudinal study encompassing 8–25 years that all cause mortality and suicide in bulimia and other eating disorders were elevated (Crow, Peterson, Swanson, at al., 2009).

*   *   *

Regarding a possible unifying basis for bulimia, it should be noted that no pathognomonic, causal risk factors or single mechanism/pathway have yet been identified (Striegel-Moore, 1992; Strober & Humphrey, 1987). Rather, the development of eating disorders in adolescence and young adulthood is associated with a broad range of adverse environmental circumstances during childhood (Johnson, Cohen, Kasen, et al., 2002). This has led to reconsideration of common clinical lore about the earlier life experiences of future bulimics. Thus, frequently quoted characterizations, (e.g., of sexual abuse and the family environment of bulimics), are at best regarded as general observations consistent with the diagnosis, rather than definitive indicators of the source of bulimia (Pope & Hudson, 1992; Strober & Humphrey, 1987). This degree of heterogeneity with respect to familial and individual factors has led researchers away from efforts to find a single common pathway and toward identifying and determining the pathogenesis of different subgroups of bulimics and bulimic anorexics.

And with respect to treatment, though a few studies have shown higher recovery rates, albeit with significant relapse rates (see Herzog, Dorer, Keel, et al., 1999; Keel, Mitchell, Miller, et al., 1999), improvement and cure rates are roughly no greater than 50% from psychotherapeutic, medicinal, and combined treatments of grouped adolescent and adult bulimics. Moreover, no pre-treatment, post-treatment, or dropping-out of treatment predictors or other factors have been consistently identified that influence prognosis and likelihood of relapse (Agras, Crow, Halmi, et al., 2000; Freeman, Beach, Davis, et al., 1985; Olmsted, Kaplan, & Rockert, 1994). The sum and substance of the last two paragraphs (etiological heterogeneity and modest success of treatment) bespeak the wisdom of considering each case on its own, unique merits (Weiss, 1993). And particularly when treating adolescents, determining whether and how normative features of development can assist one in understanding and intervening with the patient.

Epidemiology

Interview studies report lower incidence rates than do self-report surveys, and reveal prevalence of less than 2% among junior high and high school girls (Crowther, Wolf, & Sherwood, 1992). Onset of illness was reported most frequently at age 16–17 in a study of adolescent females, and the lifetime prevalence of bulimia was calculated at 3% (Lewinsohn, Striegel-Moore, & Seeley, 2000). This figure is at the high end of the 1–3% reported in community surveys of cohorts including adult females (Fairburn & Belgin, 1990; Garfinkel, Lin, Goering, et al., 1995), and female twins (Kendler, MacLean, Neale, et al., 1991). So, bulimic symptoms may be more common but less entrenched in the adolescent population, or else adolescents may tend to exaggerate. That said, a recent nationally representative study of Norwegian individuals from 14–34 years of age found that compensatory behaviors decreased between 14–16 years of age and age twenty-three and older. Females were at greater risk of purging and males of bingeing (Abebe, Lien, Torgersen, et al., 2012). A small proportion of cases arising in adolescence continue into adulthood or recur (Lewinsohn, Striegel-Moore, & Seeley, 2000). But most adult cases of bulimia nervosa arise during adulthood, typically in the early twenties (Garfinkel, Lin, Goering, et al., 1995; Kendler, MacLean, Neale, et al., 1991; Kotler, Cohen, Davies, et al., 2001). Epidemiological surveys of adults report lifetime prevalence several times higher when less stringent criteria are used (Fairburn & Belgin, 1990).

Similar to adults, adolescents suffering from the partial syndrome are reported to be more similar to those meeting the full syndrome American Psychiatric Association *Diagnostic and Statistical Manual* criteria with respect to co-morbid diagnoses (depressive, anxiety, and perhaps substance abuse disorders) than are control subjects (Kotler, Cohen, Davies, et al., 2001; Lewinsohn, Striegel-Moore, & Seeley, 2000).

Support for the spectrum concept

When grouped on the basis of symptom severity (non-dieters, casual dieters, intensive dieters, dieters at risk, bulimia nervosa), college freshman women (who would probably be considered adolescents) tended to move to adjacent categories of greater or lesser severity when followed for six months. Symptoms that persisted typically did so at a milder level, and only a small proportion (15%) of at-risk dieters became bulimic. Interestingly, the cohort contained more dieters than non-dieters, so dieting was the normative behavior in that sample (Drewnowski, Yee, Kurth, et al., 1994).

Relationship to disordered
eating during childhood

Children in the primary grades become aware of societal attitudes about preferred body form, and some children wish for a different body type and even diet well before puberty (Thelen, Lawrence, & Powell, 1992).

The continuity and stability of disordered eating and eating disorders have been studied from childhood to young adulthood. A few, very modest trends have been identified between childhood eating patterns and subsequent bulimia: Eating too little was protective against developing bulimia. Pica and being uninterested in food or struggling around meals during childhood favored developing bulimia in adolescence and adulthood, respectively (Kotler, Cohen, Davies, et al., 2001; Marchi & Cohen, 1990).

Bulimic symptoms in early adolescence carried a modestly greater risk for similar symptoms in late adolescence. And bulimia in late adolescence conveyed an even greater likelihood of carrying the disorder into adulthood. Generally, the more severe the symptoms at an earlier point in time, the more likely they are to persist. So, simi-lar to the situation with adolescent suicide, prior similar behavior conveys a risk for future similar behavior. But the degree of risk is low, difficult to quantify in practical clinical terms, and there is great individual variation among those who develop the disorder (Kotler, Cohen, Davies, et al., 2001) and in the clinical course of the disorder (Fairburn & Belgin, 1990; Heatherton, Mahamedi, Striepe, et al., 1997); and differing risk configurations have been identified at different points during adolescence (Attie & Brooks-Gunn, 1989, 1992).

Relationship to obesity and perceived
overweight—present and future

While obesity is not necessarily associated with bulimia, bulimics consider themselves overweight or in danger of becoming so. Overweight doubled among adolescents during a recent couple of decades (Centers for Disease Control and Prevention (1997) reported in Field, Camargo, Taylor, et al., 1999). In one questionnaire survey of sixth, seventh, and eighth graders, approximately half of the girls and a quarter of the boys considered themselves overweight and were trying to lose or maintain their weight (Krowchuck, Kreiter, Woods, et al., 1998). In a much larger questionnaire survey of nine- to fourteen-year-olds, the prevalence of binge eating and purging was low (approximately 1%) for both boys and girls until age 13–14. Thereafter, purging began to increase in girls in association with concern about and misperception of being overweight, and purging in both sexes as well as binge eating in girls progressed with pubertal stage (Field, Camargo, Taylor, et al., 1999).

A study published in 1980 determined that the average woman was becoming heavier while the ideal figure as portrayed in the media and other venues (beauty pageant contestants, Playboy centerfolds) was increasingly thinner (Garner, Garfinkel, Schwartz, et al., 1980). Thus, it is reasonable to presume that bulimic symptoms will, if anything, increase, unless the tactic of clothing manufacturers to label larger garments with smaller sizes suffices to reduce women's dissatisfaction about their size, or unless there is a sea change in the present cultural attitude regarding preferred body shape.

Studies of adults and cohorts including adolescents and adults

The problem of accumulating patient cohorts for study and in comparing different studies is matched by the legion of problems inherent in individual studies. Discussing these difficulties in a different condition, but which I believe is applicable here, Esman (1994) cogently characterized the acknowledged limitations of the latter as "overreporting, underreporting, retrospective distortion, tendentious recollection, responses to overt or implied suggestion" (p. 1102). These factors have led to reconsideration of previous findings that had been reported frequently enough to become common clinical lore about the earlier life experiences of future bulimics. A history of sexual abuse in childhood/early adolescence is prominent among these ideas (Garfinkel, Lin, Goering, et al., 1995). In fact, it was identified in a small controlled sample of 10–15-year-old adolescent girls (Wonderlich, Crosby, Mitchell, et al., 2000). However, review of studies has determined that sexual abuse is not a specific risk factor for bulimia (Pope & Hudson, 1992), and does not occur at higher incidence than in a non-eating disorder population of 18–30-year-old women (Kinzl, Traweger, Guenther, et al., 1994). Sexual abuse prior to late chronological adolescence only correlates with bulimia when it is part of a family context including other (physical and/or psychological) abuses (Rorty, Yager, & Rossotto, 1994).[13] So, rather than being specifically associated with sexual abuse (Kinzl, Traweger, Guenther, et al., 1994) or other specific pathogens such as distant, controlling, or abusive fathering (Wonderlich, Ukestad, & Perzacki, 1994) (both of which have been implicated in several disorders), bulimia and other eating disorders are best understood as one among other outcomes in those raised in more generally dysfunctional families. Other outcomes include depression and substance abuse for dealing with internal conflicts (Garfinkel, Lin, Goering, et al., 1995) and personality disorders (Wonderlich, Ukestad, & Perzacki, 1994).

Thus, frequently quoted characterizations of the family environment of bulimics are best regarded as credible, general observations consistent with the diagnosis, rather than as specific pathognomonic indicators of the source of bulimia in their offspring (Strober & Humphrey, 1987). These include reports that when compared to controls, bulimics' families are more openly conflictual, disorganized/ chaotic, undercontrolled, tough, problematic in communicating, blaming, belittling/critical, affectively labile, active with mothers perceived as less warm, nurturing, caring, and varying characterizations of fathers as close in childhood but distant during adolescence, or neglectful and/or controlling (Calam, Waller, Slade, et al., 1990; Kinzl, Traweger, Guenther, et al., 1994; Steiner & Lock, 1998; Strober & Humphrey, 1987; van Furth, van Strien, Martina, et al., 1996; Wonderlich, 1992).

So, the development of eating disorders and weight problems in adolescence and young adulthood is associated with a broad range of adverse environmental circumstances during childhood (Johnson,

Cohen, Kasen, et al., 2002). Given what has just been described, it has been recommended that attention be turned from concentrating on risk factors *per se* to study of the "risk process". This would involve dynamic internal, interpersonal, and environmental factors in a developmental context/perspective aimed at establishing how the eating disorder begins and is sustained (Attie & Brooks-Gunn, 1992).

Bulimia in males

Lifetime prevalence for adolescent and young adult males is estimated at 0.2%, or approximately a tenth of that in females, and onset is a little later (18–26 years of age) (Carlat & Camargo, 1991). Treatment-seeking male bulimics are similar to females in most respects, although there is a larger proportion of homosexuals and bisexuals among male bulimics, men are more likely to be, or have been, overweight and to be less concerned about binge eating (Carlat, Camargo, & Herzog, 1997). Whether bulimia is a response to conflicts over homosexuality in adolescents, or whether they are coincidental factors has not been established (Carlat & Camargo, 1991; Robinson & Holden, 1986).

Genetic and familial considerations

The full bulimic syndrome has been reported significantly more commonly in monozygotic than dizygotic adult female twins (Garfinkel, Lin, Goering, et al., 1995; Kendler, MacLean, Neale, et al., 1991). But problems inherent in sample size and establishing zygosity have led to caution in speculating on the magnitude of a genetic contribution to this condition. It is generally thought that genetic vulnerability is not sufficient to cause bulimia nervosa. Also, the genetic predisposition may comprise features that do not relate specifically to eating problems. For example, it may be expressed in relative emotional instability. This then compromises the self-control of an individual who is challenged by urges to binge, which typically occur in the aftermath of strict dieting to lose weight—a situation that often precedes the onset of bulimia (Hsu, Chesler, & Santhouse, 1990).

Risk factors

It may seem ironic that the greatest gain for clinicians from epidemiological studies, as was the case in studies of adolescent suicide, has been discovering the heterogeneity of bulimics. That is because it is easier for us to think in terms of aggregated knowledge and downplay the exception (which we hope to achieve from epidemiological study) than it is for us to remain ever vigilant regarding individual cases. Allowing oneself to be lulled into a false sense of complacency by relying on statistics when facing an individual patient is a luxury that clinicians can ill afford.

Co-morbid conditions

Bulimic symptoms are not infrequently co-morbid with anxiety and depressive disorders, alcohol and substance abuse, though apparently have no or little significance on the course of the illness. Also, kleptomania has been reported (Herzog, Keller, Sacks, et al., 1992), as have a wide range of personality disturbances (Wonderlich, 1992). Most attention has been paid to the co-occurrence of depression, which may involve a quarter of patients but does not have prognostic significance, and borderline personality disorder, in which the symptoms are not more severe but the prognosis poorer than for non-borderline bulimics (Crowther & Mizes, 1992). Also, it has been reported that duration and severity of symptoms at presentation, and history of substance abuse and co-morbid Axis I disorders were prognostically significant (Keel & Mitchell 1997; Keel, Mitchell, Miller, et al., 1999). However, more recent data have concluded that bulimia and other eating disorders exhibit relative independence/uniqueness from other psychiatric problems. That is, co-occurring personality or other psychiatric disorders, or even assessments of global functioning, do not significantly influence the course of bulimia nervosa (Grilo, Sanislow, Shea, et al., 2003). A cohort of 102 females recruited from the community between ages sixteen and thirty-five and assessed every fifteen months for five years to trace the natural history of bulimia nervosa reported relatively poor prognosis with about a third remitting and a third relapsing every year (Fairburn, Cooper, Doll, et al., 2000).

Medical and dental complications

Medical complications of bulimia include electrolyte imbalances, which can affect cardiac functioning (potassium depletion giving rise to fatal arrhythmias), urinary infections and renal failure, leg cramping (also associated with hypokalemia) and tetany, epileptic seizures, esophageal tears, gastric disturbance, dehydration, orthostatic hypotension, parotid/salivary gland swelling, and malnutrition. The dental complication is erosion of the enamel and dentin, leaving the tooth vulnerable to fracturing (Carlat, Camargo, & Herzog, 1997; Russell, 1979; Steiner & Lock, 1998).

Clinical models of the development of bulimia

As noted, heterogeneity with respect to familial and individual factors (occurring in a multiplicity of family and personality types), difficulty determining whether risk factors are the cause or the result of the bulimia, and why bulimic rather than other symptoms developed (Rosen, 1992; Striegel-Moore, 1992; Wonderlich, 1992) have led researchers from searching for a single pathway to identifying the pathogenesis in subgroups of bulimics. But the models that follow attempt to provide an overarching explanation for the development of bulimia.

In the overview, these models roughly approximate those I described for adolescent suicide, namely a cumulative stressors model, an idiosyncratic response of an uncommon host to common stressor(s) model, and a psychiatric trait vs. psychological state model, which overlaps the latter general theory. At least for girls, a cumulative trauma model traces the development of bulimia from stressful features of the adolescent developmental process at puberty. The stressors include normative weight gain in the face of societal preferences for slender body configurations (which can draw the pubertal girl's attention negatively to her figure), and changes in social relationships with peers and parents (Attie & Brooks-Gunn, 1992). Coping with these issues can incline some pubertal girls (e.g., the less socially competent/popular, less self-contained) toward more serious symptoms than dieting, and perhaps more so in families where parents (usually mothers) are preoccupied with their own weight/figure and those same features in their daughters (Thelen, Lawrence, & Powell, 1992).

The uncommon host dealing with common stressors models accept the importance of what has just been described and the relevance of dissatisfaction with one's body in the genesis of bulimia. But these theorists emphasize different (though not mutually exclusive) factors as the crux of future bulimics' vulnerability to this disorder. Examples of the idiosyncratic feature of these potential bulimics include failure to live up to conflicting and unrealistic personal expectations (Levine & Smolak, 1992), a profound disturbance in the individual's perception and evaluation of her physical appearance (Rosen, 1992), and failure of repeated efforts at conventional dieting, which compromises self-esteem regulation (Heatherton & Polivy, 1992). An example of the psychiatric trait *vs.* psychological state model cites co-morbidity, particularly personality disorders, as features differentiating bulimics from non-bulimics (Johnson & Wonderlich, 1992).

These models all are consonant with the idea that bulimia arises in some individuals who are dissatisfied with their weight or appearance, and who resort to bulimia when they find themselves unable to reconcile that conflict in more conventional ways (e.g., dieting or altering their attitude toward their appearance). Each theory attempts to address the question of who among this group of individuals will become bulimic.

Course of illness and factors predisposing to persistence of bulimic symptoms

It is difficult to determine the course of illness in adolescent cases because they have not been studied independently (DeAngelis, 2002; Steiner & Lock, 1998). As noted earlier, one community survey limited to adolescent girls found bulimia to be more self-limited, circumscribed, and non-recurring than is often reported in cohorts involving adults (Lewinsohn, Striegel-Moore, & Seeley, 2000). Differing conclusions have been reported regarding whether bulimia nervosa patients (older adolescents and young adults) have less or greater concerns about maturing than comparison groups (Heebink, Sunday, & Halmi, 1995; Joiner, Heatherton, & Keel, 1997).

At ten-year follow-up, 80% of a cohort of college women was no longer bulimic and more satisfied with their body morphology, while 20% remained dissatisfied with their body and dieted chronically. Men, having gained more weight than the women, were more concerned with dieting, but bulimic attitudes had declined in both sexes during the intervening decade (Heatherton, Mahamedi, Striepe, et al., 1997). A persisting drive for thinness and dissatisfaction with body image are associated with unremitting bulimia (Kendler, MacLean, Neale, et al., 1991; Rosen, 1992) and with relapse six months after treatment for a cohort in which 17½ years old was the mean age (Freeman, Beach, Davis, et al., 1985).

Treatment outcome studies

In pooled outcome studies of female bulimics, which typically include patients from late adolescence through late mid-life, 50% of bulimics are symptom-free five years after presentation, 20% continue to meet full diagnostic criteria, and 30% have experienced relapse (Keel & Mitchell, 1997). Those findings were similar to a more recent, very large review (in which the age range of patients was not specified) that reported a mean recovery rate of 47.5%, and 26% for improvement and for chronicity (Steinhausen & Weber, 2009). Relapse more often occurs within six months after treatment (Olmsted, Kaplan, & Rockert, 1994), and less frequently from four years after presentation (Keel & Mitchell, 1997). Bulimics in treatment cohorts recovered more quickly than those in community samples, but outcome for both groups was the same five and more years after presentation (Keel & Mitchell, 1997). This may be in part explained by the finding that treatment is utilized most by women with greatest psychopathology (e.g., personality disorder/poorest functioning) (Keel, Dorer, Eddy, et al., 2002).

Accepting those figures as only a general, ballpark statistic for pooled studies of patients, no pre-treatment, post-treatment, or dropping-out of treatment predictors or other factors have been consistently identified that influence prognosis and likelihood of relapse (Agras, Crow, Halmi, et al., 2000; Freeman, Beach, Davis, et al., 1985; Olmsted, Kaplan, & Rockert, 1994; Steinhausen & Weber, 2009).

Medication

Antidepressant medications of several varieties (tricyclics, MAOIs, bupropion, trazodone, SSRIs) have all been shown superior to placebo in short-term studies. Approximately 50% of patients experience a 50% reduction of binge eating and perhaps purging in acute treatment studies. Complete remission is observed in less than 20% of cases. Dropout rates are high, and no consistent predictors of who will drop out, who will respond, or who will remit have been identified. In one study, continuing fluoxetine after an acute treatment period of eight weeks lengthened the time before relapse. But there was a tendency in both treated and placebo cohorts to worsen over time (Romano, Halmi, Sarkar, et al., 2002). A review of a quarter century of research found that psychotherapeutic approaches were superior to medication and behavior therapy in treating bulimia nervosa, the significance of which was limited by lack of clarity regarding the different modalities employed (Steinhausen & Weber, 2009).

Cognitive–behavioral therapy

This has been found more effective than medication (Steiner & Lock, 1998), but the rates of improvement also hover around 50%. For example, a recent study (Hollon & Wilson, 2014) comparing an "enhanced" version of CBT for five months with psychoanalytic psychotherapeutic treatment for two years reported 44% improvement in the former and 15% in the latter (Poulsen, Lunn, Daniel, et al., 2014). However, questions were raised about the comparability of the two treatment protocols as specifically practiced (Poulsen & Lunn, 2014; Tasca, Hilsenroth, & Thompson-Brenner, 2014). There are indications that the combination of cognitive–behavioral therapy and medication is superior to either alone, and that continuing medication for a year after successful acute treatment is of value in preventing relapse. To refine the effectiveness of this manual-based cognitive–behavioral treatment, researchers are attempting to identify subgroups of the patient population for which to alter the protocol. Promising as such approaches may prove to be, authors of a multi-site study have concluded that presently research findings are sufficiently inconsistent (owing in part to difficulties in comparing studies) that pre- or post-treatment outcome predictors offer "only general guidance to the clinician as to which patient will not do well in therapy" (Agras, Crow, Halmi, et al., 2000, p. 1303).

Short-term focal psychotherapy

One study found this psychodynamically oriented, exploratory interpersonal therapy almost as effective as cognitive–behavioral therapy, though its full effect took longer to achieve (Fairburn, Kirk, O'Connor, et al., 1986).

Combination of medication and focused psychotherapy

A meta-analysis of treatment studies found that the combination was superior to either medication or psychotherapy (e.g., cognitive–behavioral therapy or interpersonal therapy) alone. However, the dropout rates were notably high amongst patients taking medication in addition to psychotherapy (Hay, 2002).

Family-based treatment compared to supportive psychotherapy

A randomized, controlled comparison of these modalities involving forty-one adolescents (aged 12–19 years) found that about 40% of the family-based group were not bingeing nor purging after twenty sessions and about half that percentage after supportive psychotherapy. At six-month follow-up, those figures had dropped to about 30% and 10%, respectively (leGrange, Crosby, Rathouz, et al., 2007).

Light therapy

This has proven helpful, more so in bulimics with a seasonal component to the disorder (Lam, Goldner, Solyom, et al., 1994).

Concluding remarks

This discussion of bulimia leads to the conclusion that the developmental context in which psychopathology develops is complicated and without identifiable predictors. This state of our scientific knowledge need not render us nihilistic about the possibility that research may eventuate in specific causal elements and better treatments. It does suggest that great opportunity exists for trying to understand bulimia clinically and developmentally. Medicinal management and manual-based cognitive behavioral and interpersonal therapies share one important feature in common—great efficiency in the sense of ease of administration. For even when different parts of protocols are emphasized to more closely address and individual's needs, all patients are still given the same protocol. But, given the limited success of those treatments, it is worth considering an alternative general approach. That is approaching each case on its own, unique merits. And particularly when treating adolescents, determine whether and how features of adolescent development can assist one in understanding the patient's symptoms, and then serve as a guide for approaching that individual's treatment.

This approach may seem incongruous or a luxury that can no longer be afforded in the current treatment atmosphere. Yet, the combined facts of the number of patients who are not adequately treated by the currently popular treatments, and the accepted degree of heterogeneity in the backgrounds and pathogenesis of bulimia would seem to render the approach that I am recommending necessary rather than optional or out-dated. In fact, addressing bulimia from a developmental perspective with multiple (rather than a single) pathways leading to the disorder (Attie & Brooks-Gunn, 1989, 1992), and tailoring treatment to developmental stage considerations have been recommended (Steiner & Lock, 1998).

One conclusion I draw from the existing literature on non-medicinal treatments (notwithstanding the caveat that psychotherapy can make patients worse) is the likelihood that bulimics are helped by therapy. The specific form that any responsible therapy takes may be less important than the use that the adolescent patient can make of the therapeutic relationship to reverse her or his symptoms.[14] This may be especially so if, as I have tried to illustrate, the therapist can identify the adolescent bulimic's efforts at self-cure, and then follow that lead. It is relevant in this regard that 28% of the potential subjects of a randomized, controlled study of adolescent bulimics that compared CBT-based guided self-care and family therapy refused to participate because of possible assignment to family therapy (Schmidt, Lee, Beecham, et al., 2007). While there could be many reasons for such refusal, it is consistent with the premise emphasized in Sydney's treatment about the importance of the adolescent developmental imperative toward independence and completing one's development.

PART II

VICISSITUDES IN DEVELOPMENT: UNDERSTANDING SOME OUTLIERS

CHAPTER THREE

Revisiting homosexuality:
one possible developmental pathway

(Dilemmas at the interface of psychiatry and politics)

T his chapter addresses two questions: (1) Can a child's wish to achieve one basic developmental goal subvert the accomplishment of another, equally important developmental goal? Specifically, can the need for a secure object relationship override normative developmental progression toward heterosexuality to the degree that a person can develop an exclusive (in contrast to a so-called optional/preferential) homosexual orientation in order to gratify the former need? (2) If so, is there a window of therapeutic opportunity between puberty and mid-adolescence that can be capitalized upon to wrest a more conventional resolution for individuals who are at risk of undergoing such a developmental trade-off?

Background

In 1973, in an effort to protect homosexuals from discrimination, the American Psychiatric Association utilized an amalgam of civil rights, sociological, and clinical rationales to justify eliminating homosexuality as a psychiatric diagnosis. That contamination of the clinical by the political created a veritable conundrum, which has thrown all subsequent psychiatric study of homosexuality into disarray. For, since that time, it seems to have become awkward to discuss homosexuality even from the developmental perspective, at least if there is any indication that it is aberrant sexuality deriving significantly from psychological/environmental factors. As one author observed, removing homosexuality from the psychiatric diagnostic nomenclature had the effect of moving it "from the realm of psychiatric pathology to the realm of normal variants of sexual behavior" (Burr, 1997, p. 6).

Whether that inference can legitimately be drawn from the APA's three-sentence position statement, which specifically addressed "Homosexuality and Civil Rights" is debatable.[15] For example, Hooker, whose Rorschach study (1957) remains the basic reference cited in support of the psychological normality of homosexuals, observed in a less frequently publicized conclusion: "(Thus) one could defend the hypothesis that homosexuality is symptomatic of pathology, but that the pathology is confined to one sector of behavior, namely, the sexual" (p. 30; see also Hooker, 1972).

In any event, whether homosexuality is normal or abnormal sexuality is basically irrelevant to this discussion, which is about how a homosexual orientation might develop in certain individuals. Since it is generally accepted that many, if not most, end-point behavioral styles develop through interaction of endowment and experience, common sense dictates that at least some vicissitudes of sexual behaviors would also. But it is not known whether sexual orientation arises or can arise through a process of development in which each individual has an equal chance of developing a homo- or heterosexual orientation. Or, whether a homosexual orientation develops as a deviation from a default, heterosexual, position. If the latter, then it simply becomes a matter of whether the particular society wants to consider this difference within the purview of normality. Research data that have been utilized to resolve the question of the normality or abnormality of homosexuality will be considered here primarily to illustrate the types of problems created for professionals when clinical issues become politicized. Last, defining to whom one is referring as homosexual becomes important, particularly the distinction between willingness to engage in homosexual behavior in contradistinction to an obligatory homosexual orientation. For it is not generally accepted that all homosexual behavior has a unitary, underlying basis and psychosexual meaning (Livingood, 1972).

In modern historical times, homosexuality probably fell more within the province of psychiatry than other medical specialties for at least two reasons: Freud's psychosexual paradigm was the most influential view of psychological development. And, as is suggested by the twenty-four separate diagnostic categories of sexual and gender dysfunction and paraphilias in the American Psychiatric Association's *Diagnostic and Statistical Manual-5*, sexual behavior, desires, and functioning are considered to be notoriously responsive to psychological factors.

Sexual development during adolescence (see Bloch, 1995)

The importance of this developmental period in consolidating one's sexual identification has long been accepted in psychoanalytic and intrapsychically oriented psychotherapeutic approaches (A. Freud, 1936, 1958; Freud, 1905d). The upsurge of sexual drive that accompanies biological maturation (puberty) creates tension, which strives for discharge as it mounts in boys and girls. Both the inherited intensity of the drives and the degree to which their expression is influenced (historically dampened or inhibited) by the influence of one's family varies among adolescents. Then, sooner or later, albeit with considerable individual variation, the curiosity and urge to share the sexual experience supersedes masturbatory satisfaction. I am unaware of studies that have demonstrated a qualitative difference between the aim of sexual drive among heterosexuals and homosexuals. That is, for example, I have not found substantiation for the libido theory model, which would associate pregenital drive with at least some forms of homosexuality and genital drive with heterosexuality. Thus, and notwithstanding the oft-cited, anecdotally derived proviso (at least in prior generations) that emotional closeness facilitates this movement toward coitus in girls but is not such a prerequisite in boys, we can surmise that the drive is to discharge erotically stimulated tension. The major difference is in the sex of the object/individual with whom to engage in this experience.

Early narcissistically oriented object-finding in this process (which operationally amounts to a homosexual position) has also long been described in the adolescent process of consolidating a heterosexual identification (Blos, 1962; A. Freud, 1965). Although those love relationships are often sublimated, overt homosexual experiences do occur in early and mid-adolescence. The latter clinical observation is supported by recent demographic studies, which identify that (depending on the survey) the incidence of reported homosexual experiences falls off dramatically after age fifteen (Fay, Turner, Klassen, et al., 1989) or nineteen (Seidman & Rieder, 1994). These findings indicate that the greatest majority of those involved in early/mid-adolescent homosexual experiences do not become homosexual.

So, especially if the biological urges prove to not be qualitatively different in heterosexuals and homosexuals, early and mid-adolescence would appear to be the optimal time for intervening therapeutically to help youth who question, or are in conflict about, their sexual orientation. However, as noted in Chapter One, that is the period in development when it is typically most difficult to engage individuals in treatment, for they are concurrently struggling with the other basic developmental issue I have emphasized. That is the normative imperative to emancipate from the childhood psychological attachment to parents, and therapists readily become the transference objects of this conflict that inclines adolescents to bolt from treatment (Bloch, 1995). This dilemma of adolescent treatment and that of consolidating sexual development are illustrated in the following example.

Rachel

An eleven-year-old fifth grader was referred because of a resurgence of earlier problems with separation anxiety. Her father's new role in the foundation for which both parents worked was now going to require the two of them to make fund-raising trips together for a couple of weeks at a time. And although her maternal grandmother, who knew the children well, would be taking care of them, Rachel became so anxious about losing contact with her mother that it did not seem possible to leave her. So her mother was staying home.

Regarding the basis of this symptom, her perspicacious and candid parents felt that despite having done a good job of hiding their ambivalence from her, this daughter somehow sensed that they did not care about her as they did for her older sister. Sensitive and intelligent people, they were not sure whether their antipathy related to an earlier tragedy in their lives or was in response to this child's particular appearance and/or behaviors. While working as medical missionaries, their first-born child, a son, had died in infancy from an overwhelming tropical sepsis. They had mourned his loss, and ultimately dealt with their guilt about having remained in such a remote area with an infant by accepting solace from their religious conviction that it was God's will. They had looked forward to having more children upon returning to the U.S., where her father became involved in the administration of the foundation for which they worked and her mother continued active involvement in other aspects of its charitable function. They were delighted with the arrival of their next child, Rachel's older sister. But upon Rachel's birth, they were aware of feeling a bit wistful that she had not been a (replacement) son, though neither parent felt that was sufficient to account for the degree of their distaste for her.

They sensed that an underlying awareness on Rachel's part of their ambivalence contributed to her insatiable competitive drive to be the best at everything, to be approved of, and favored by all adults. They were also readily able to understand that certain other of her behaviors were defensive identifications with each parent that Rachel had developed from her experiences with them. For example, during her early latency, within a year after her mother suffered a depression, gained weight, and developed a distracted stare, Rachel became overweight and, at times, exhibited a similar stare. At other times, she evinced a somewhat supercilious, sharp manner that resembled occasional similar behaviors of her father. He was temperamentally inclined to be more harsh and critical toward her than was her mother, who, out of her sense of guilt, tended to be overindulgent. And even though they had worked hard not to reveal their dislike, they wondered if it had somehow contributed to her extreme tomboyish behaviors that had long been of concern to them. Even though neither parent had encouraged it, from relatively early on Rachel had always preferred to play with boys and engage in boys' games/sports. In contrast to her ultra-feminine sister, Rachel balked at wearing skirts/dresses, and when younger had bespoken wishes to have been born a boy, because they were stronger and had other advantages.

She seemed more neuter than boy-like to her parents when she began therapy. And Rachel characterized herself to her therapist as a tomboy, by which she meant that she responded neither like a boy nor a girl, and preferred toys and activities that had no gender connection.

Yet, within months after beginning therapy, and without in-depth exploration of this issue, Rachel began to evince more traditionally feminine interests. It was not dramatic, but a notable difference in manner and attitude. She spent more time establishing and engaging in friendships with girls rather than playing with boys, and showed greater interest in girl's clothing and make-up, and, subsequently, in looking glamorous. Her parents also reported that she was happier, more self-confident and self-controlled. It was difficult to understand these shifts, other than to attribute them to the interested, non-critical, basically approving attitude of her therapist, who was male.

Her presentation was typical of pre-adolescents—filling sessions with reports of her daily activities, boasting about her successes at school, expressing her peeves. The ego defense mechanism of undoing after expressing critical or superior attitudes toward others was more in evidence than reaction formation in dealing with anger and competitive feelings. She exhibited a kind of cock-sure, self-assertive confidence with her therapist. But this alternated with expressions of feeling unsure of herself and an expressed need for her therapist to be authoritative and she dependent on him for answers. This pattern of alternating independence and dependence, while not untypical of pre-adolescents, was noteworthy in this girl for the intensity of each pole of that behavioral spectrum. With respect to the problem that had brought her to treatment, she identified loneliness and fear of something happening to her mother (i.e., a phobic dynamic) as the sources of her reluctance to let her mother leave.

For the duration of her therapy, Rachel maintained a competitive relationship and a subtly patronizing hauteur toward the therapist (while, at the same time, remaining sensitive to feeling hurt or misunderstood by him). The former manner was interspersed with expressions of friendliness. The contrast of those two attitudes suggested that she felt decidedly ambivalent toward him. Yet, within months after commencing therapy, and coinciding in time with her shift toward more typically feminine behavior, Rachel became driven, purportedly out of curiosity, to learn about her therapist's personal life. She was seeking commonalties between them regarding everything from birth month to vacation activities to favorite TV shows. That particular therapist's disinclination toward self-revelation had the effect of heightening her curiosity to a maddening degree. During this period, she was also contending furiously with him in board games.

But, while being a fierce competitor, she would touch her therapist's hand or arm during board game play, in such a way as to convey her wish for congeniality, closeness, and physical contact. This pattern suggested that Rachel wanted her therapist to be positively, if not affectionately, disposed toward her, in spite of her intense competitiveness toward him. For her father, who spent much time with Rachel and encouraged competitiveness and excellence, was never physically demonstrative.

After a year of therapy, her parents reported that Rachel felt increasingly "free" to criticize both of them, and she complained that they favored her sister. Yet, she was most reluctant to acknowledge those critical attitudes to her therapist. Rather, with him she was inclined to defend and protect her parents, and rationalize any harsh behavior on the part of her father as being for her own good. Concurrently, she became quickly and increasingly disenchanted with her therapist, soon allowing that she had never had the courage to tell him that she had always hated coming to therapy. Often such feelings were expressed after brief or longer vacations, though she could not acknowledge this relationship to separations. In her increasingly captious, complaining, intermittently tearful, righteous reproaches of the therapist, Rachel emphasized that he had never answered any of her questions about himself, even innocuous ones. He was a stranger to her, yet he knew everything about her, which was egregiously unfair, and having to meet with him was driving her crazy. She was now just going to fill the hours with talk, not let the therapist get a word in edgewise, or explore anything. And that's what she did.

She eventually insisted on a plan that her therapist was hard-pressed not to accept: Since she had come to treatment because of separation anxiety, she could stop her treatment when both parents could go on a fund-raising trip together for two weeks. She accomplished this, after two years of therapy, at age thirteen. She left treatment still feeling disparaging and resentful toward the therapist. Yet, as she was walking out after their last session, expressing great relief at being free with a supercilious air of triumph, he noticed that she stopped and looked back and around the room wistfully a couple of times, seemingly trying to retain its image in her mind. It was as if her therapist's disinclination to disclose anything about himself had reduced Rachel to the poignant circumstance of having to hold on to an image of his office, which then, rather than he, became what she might miss. At that point, while her sexual identification did not seem to be consolidated, it appeared to be moving in the conventional manner (e.g., crushes on cute guys). The therapist attributed this in part to having mobilized Rachel's ambivalence toward parental figures, particularly her father in the transference. But she defended against awareness of that by enacting rather than analyzing that relationship; according to psychoanalytic theory, this is often the case with pre- and early adolescents. Or, in terms of more ego-oriented, control mastery theory, she was turning passive into active (i.e., rejecting the therapist as she had felt rejected by her father), albeit an unconsciously motivated action, undertaken in an effort to cure herself by identifying with her therapist's ability to tolerate such rejections without feeling devastated.

Subsequent contacts with Rachel

Given those last several months of intensely negative reaction/transference, the therapist was surprised when he next heard from her, eight years later at age twenty-one, that she remembered the experience and himself very positively. In the interim, Rachel had developed into a lovely, slender, shapely young woman. She had initially lost weight in early adolescence to become attractive to boys at school dances. She had had an academically successful high school experience. And she had been happy and highly successful at a prestigious women's college—until that summer prior to her senior year when she became very anxious, unhappy, and everything seemed difficult. Although at the top of her class, she had developed reservations about completing her pre-medical studies. She was unsure whether it was a matter of not wanting to become a physician, or not wanting to follow her parents' path into medical missionary work as she had planned.

However, she was returning to see her therapist primarily because of a resurgence of separation anxiety as her best friends, who were a year older, graduated. All were women, several of whom were experimenting with lesbianism, though had boyfriends as well. Rachel feared being very lonely during the next school year, and bemoaned the fact that, unlike all her friends and her sister, she had never had an intimate relationship. Heterosexual involvements had been unsatisfying, because she found that guys who were interested in her were either unappealing or manifested exactly those traits of her father that she found difficult to tolerate. She wasn't sure, but thought that she herself was "probably gay", or at least had a "low level of lesbianism".

Her therapist observed to Rachel that although much of what she was telling him centered around her lesbian-tinged friendships, he thought the core issue of the moment was interpersonally rather than gender based. Specifically, the loss of her good, older friends through graduation had precipitated a recrudescence of her earlier childhood separation anxiety. This had originally developed in pre-verbal childhood, when she had not felt secure in the absence of her parents. She had adapted well by using her impressive cognitive abilities to become precociously intellectually independent, and by staying active all the time. But the potential for re-experiencing this had remained. And when such anxiety is re-activated in later life, the same feeling of helplessness accompanies it; but it no longer has the objective significance it did when she was a young child. Rachel immediately stopped crying and felt relieved. Her subsequent associations supported that idea that her anxiety was a response to feeling that her sense of security was threatened by the loss of those friends.

She went on to decry the fact that all her friends had guys they were probably going to marry, but she had no one. She hadn't even dated much, and all her attractions were to women. Emerging in this context, those associations raised the question of whether her attraction to women was for the security-engendering qualities she associated with her mother more than sexual interest. She agreed to keep an open mind about her basic sexual orientation.

Her therapist next saw her almost a decade later when she met with him to share some impressive insights accrued through a combination of self-analysis and therapy at her medical school. In fact though, at her insistence, her therapist there had consulted periodically with her original one. Her revelations included her conclusion that survivor guilt regarding her sister, who had been disappointed in love and struggled with anxiety, caused Rachel to act at times less confident than she felt. However, whether the determinants of her own homosexual orientation had included deference to her sister's hyper-femininity had not been explored. A second insight was that emancipatory guilt with respect to her father, who, as she experienced it, always insisted on the rectitude of his own views, inclined her to act less autonomous than she truly felt, in an effort to propitiate him. And, most important, she had faced her underlying sense of his antipathy (though not that of her mother), and had "cried her eyes out" in working through that deep unhappiness and her fury toward him. She had gained understanding of her life-long intolerance for being alone that drove her to always actively seek some interesting distraction, to avoid feeling "bored" (i.e., anxious). For even now as then, when she had nothing to do, thoughts of bad things which she had done or that had happened in her life intruded into her conscious- ness, and she felt bad, guilty, or ashamed. The latter suggested that at some level of her sensibility Rachel still struggled with the common idea of children that they are responsible for bad things that have befallen them, in this case her sense of her parents' ambivalence toward her.

During that period, in her early and mid-twenties, Rachel had tried dating male medical students, but they, as her earlier male dates, always seemed to exhibit those characteristics of her father that drove her to distraction: basically an intolerance for any but their own ideas. And men never held the appeal that women did. She wished it were otherwise, but felt in her bones she was homosexual. Yet, the only sexual activity that she enjoyed was vaginal entry with a dildo (i.e., the typical heterosexual source of gratification). Moreover, as soon as she had won over a desirable woman, she quickly lost interest in sex in favor of the kind of cuddling that she enjoyed with her mother; she would then become preoccupied with fear that she could not retain the interest of the other woman. Rachel felt this matter was deeper than the relationship with her father, and probably related to her mother. She had agonized about how to cure this vague but deep feeling that there was something wrong with her, that anyone who was attracted to her was a loser, and she would not be able to hold on to anyone she successfully pursued. (While some might attribute her reaction to the impact of a so-called "heterosexist society", it seems to have little to do with that, especially since she was unaware of guilt associated with her sexual orientation, and she claimed that her parents were very accepting of it.)

By the time she completed medical school in her mid-twenties, having decided upon specialty training rather than missionary work, the narcissistic aggrandizement she had experienced earlier from being seen with particularly desirable women had faded. She much preferred kissing and cuddling, and the warmth and sensitivity of women to sex, which she now found almost disgusting. She felt readily willing to sacrifice sex for the pleasure of a relationship with a woman. Then, in her late twenties she developed a love relationship with a woman mentor in her residency program, whose endearing qualities were reminiscent of her mother, and toward whom her sexual interest quickly waned. She feared that her own sometimes brusque, impatient manner (a defensive identification with her father) would be hurtful to her partner, whom she planned to join in medical practice after completing specialty training.

*   *   *

To recap, as a tomboy during her childhood Rachel had at times voiced a wish to have been born male because boys were advantaged. Yet, both then and when she was in treatment as a pre- and early adolescent, she did not seem to experience any doubt about her ultimate sexual orientation, and had talked a number of times about having a husband and two children. Moreover, during that treatment, her tomboyishness appeared to be giving way to age-appropriate heterosexual interests. Later, in high school, she sensed conflict in the area of her sexual interests and experienced to her dismay a foreboding that she might be homosexual and wished it were not so. Still later, in college and beyond, as she continued to question her sexual orientation, she was clear that the only sexual experience that appealed to her was the conventional heterosexual one of vaginal intercourse, albeit with a dildo. In her heterosexual dating experiences, she invariably chose men who exhibited those of her father's traits that she found most frustrating (presumably this pattern was an unconscious effort at repetition for mastery). Then, during and particularly following a period when she felt narcissistically aggrandized in escorting particularly desirable women, she experienced the rapid waning of any sexual interest after successful object finding. This was complicated by her fear of being unable to sustain the interest of the other, which related directly to her childhood fears with respect to her parents. And her interest with the love object was almost exclusively to partake in the kind of physical holding that she had enjoyed with her mother.

Discussion

Regarding the development of homosexuality

My question is: What happened here? From a clinical, developmental, and diagnostic perspective, is it possible that one bedrock developmental issue, namely Rachel's psychological yearning to feel securely loved and wanted, that is, successfully nurtured, overrode the normative progression of another bedrock issue, heterosexual development, to the degree that her sexual orientation became inverted in a permanent way?

Most people select partners who represent the familiar in important respects. Problems arise when one (often unconsciously) selects their mate for the problematic familiar traits of the parent, or where the preponderance of more or less traumatizing qualities outweighs the more desirable and security-engendering traits. In those situations, the individual finds him or herself repeating for mastery a relationship that had been unsettling, and often such unions have great difficulty lasting, or at least in bringing happiness and a sense of fulfillment to the individual.

The personality traits of this young woman's father inclined him at times to act verbally harsh, critical, and to seem aloof. That made him more difficult than her mother to relate to comfortably. The latter, while perhaps equally ambivalent, was better able to contain or hide it by virtue of her guilt and milder personality style. Thus, if this child's developmental need was to feel more secure in an object relationship, her mother seemed more benign and held out greater promise of offering this to her. So, this young woman chose women as the objects of her affection and desire—primarily to experience a greater felt sense of acceptance and security. Unconsciously, she had not felt this basic desire and need to have been sufficiently fulfilled during childhood and adolescence. If it had been, she would have been left freer to choose someone who did not remind her so specifically of those of her mother's behaviors/traits that made her feel accepted/safe.

The question is whether her choice of a woman rather than a man was significantly influenced by dynamic, psychological factors. Or, are these separate, parallel developmental tracks, evolving entirely independently of one another? The difficulty in being able to discern this with confidence turns on understanding the basis of Rachel's early, notably tomboyish behavior. The latter is a frequent trait in girls, though relatively more often recalled by future lesbians than heterosexual women (Bell, Weinberg, & Hammersmith, 1981, cited in Friedman & Downey, 1993, p. 1172; Saghir & Robins, 1973). Unfortunately, there is no way to determine whether it was biologically driven, or psychologically motivated by subliminal awareness of not being acceptable to her parents as she was.

With respect to object choice we do know that:

1. The opposite situation can occur. That is, in some individuals the choice of sexual object can be overruled psychologically by the wish to discharge sexual tension. The common example is that of incarcerated prisoners who do not have access to partners of the opposite sex.
2. As noted earlier, in the process of finding and consolidating one's heterosexual identification, adolescents can engage in homosexual experiences.
3. In recent years, female homosexuality has been, if not more prevalent, certainly more frequently studied, and often described as a matter of preference rather than obligation.
4. We also know from the pre-sexual liberation era, when female delinquency was almost exclusively sexual delinquency, that many of those adolescent girls resorted to early heterosexual experiences in misguided efforts to secure gratification of pre-genital nurturing needs that their mothers had failed to provide (Blos, 1957, 1976). Those adolescents used heterosexual experiences to ward off awareness of and/or to gratify essentially "homosexual" (in the sense of pre-genital) yearnings with male partners, but these girls retained their heterosexual orientation.

Rachel raised the possibility of a much more dramatic solution to a similar developmental yearning, which was reversal of the normative direction of the object of her sexual desire—the complete domination of the drive for sexual love by the drive for object love. Or, stated another way, the demands of the sexual instinct for discharge are subordinated to the search for a secure love object. That appeared to be becoming a lasting adaptation in this young woman. If so, is such an adaptation accomplished or maintained at the expense of the person's sexuality withering prematurely?

Forsaking an apparently established heterosexual identity in favor of a homosexual relationship motivated by a search for intimacy rooted in the maternal relationship has been described in middle-aged women (Kirkpatrick & Morgan, 1980). That condition might be related developmentally or psychodynamically to this young woman's state. One can but wonder whether those middle-aged women did not have the developmental option taken by this young woman because of the greater strength of societal reinforcements for heterosexual orientation when they were adolescents. These women presumably sought unfulfilled maternal nurturance. I think that Rachel was looking for more secure object love from either parent, so the issue was not sex-specific for her; rather, her solution was sex-specific.

Regarding the issue of treatment

With respect to the possibility of treating her then potential homosexuality, Rachel had begun to exhibit notably more conventionally feminine attitudes and behaviors during her therapy in pre-adolescence and early adolescence.[16] As this occurred, she was driven to develop a more three-dimensional relationship with her therapist. In retrospect, this may well have been her attempt to extract a corrective ego experience from a male. Or, at least, it might have been capitalized upon as such in that therapy. For you will recall that frustration and dismay over the therapist's failure to reveal anything of himself was ostensibly what motivated Rachel to leave treatment. Granted that was only part of her motive for rejecting him, given the developmental imperative to emancipate that figured in her effort to overcome separation anxiety. But it was, nevertheless, a conscious, serious consideration, which is where we begin psychotherapeutic explorations.

As a general rule, I have not found self-revelation on the part of the therapist to be useful in promoting therapeutic change. But there are almost certainly situations when it is helpful, in specific, circumscribed doses (for examples see Bloch, 1995, pp. 275–278). This might have been a case where Rachel's therapist could have responded more directly to her relatively innocuous requests without compromising the value he placed on relative anonymity. Sharing such things as his birth month, favorite activities, vacation destinations, etc., would not have required disclosing particularly personal facts about his life outside the office. Had he responded in that manner, his patient might have experienced him as less withholding and therefore less rejecting, and more interested in helping her feel that she could confidently consolidate a relationship with a man characterized by a sense of security derived from mutual sharing. That, in turn, would have given her a better purchase from which to grapple with both the developmental issues of consolidating heterosexual identification and psychological emancipation. As it was, she terminated that therapy having mastered her separation anxiety, but without having recognized or worked through its basis in her fear that she was unlovable, and thus could never enjoy a solid love relationship. The latter was an issue that resurfaced later in her life when attempting to establish a stable relationship with a woman.

Let me emphasize that the therapeutic relationship between this early adolescent and her first therapist turns out to not have been awry in important respects. For when she returned many years later, it was with a feeling of confidence in him and, thus, safety.[17] My point is that, in retrospect, this might have been utilized more effectively during her earlier therapy with the modification of technique suggested. My hypothesis is that had her therapist been able to maintain her treatment through puberty and into adolescence, when biology contributes to bringing sexuality into psychological development, then this young woman might have been able to continue to reduce her ambivalence about those of her father's behaviors that frightened her, identify her fear of being unlovable, and complete her development in the heterosexual direction that it was heading when she terminated that treatment.

Obviously, the circumstances I have described are not pathognomonic for creating a homosexual orientation. Hers is not the only type of adaptation developed by children and adolescents living with an accurate, subliminal, or unconscious sense of not being loved, or being unfavored compared to a sibling, or failing to be an adequate replacement child. In fact, what I am positing is probably rare compared to other types of resolution of such conflicts.[18] Rather, my point is that this may be one adaptation made by individuals who, for whatever reason, may be predisposed to conflicts over sexual identity. If so, then if a therapeutic relationship can be established in preadolescence that is secure enough to override the normative tendency to leave therapy, and thus allow the treatment to continue through the emergence and maturation of sexual drive in early and mid-adolescence, then one may have the optimal opportunity to resolve developmental conflicts in favor of a heterosexual alignment of sexual drive and object.

Difficulties encountered on the pathway
to understanding homosexuality

The earlier psychiatric/psychological literature, drawing on patient study and thus emphasizing psychopathology, seems to have been replaced by the appearance of a psychiatric, psychoanalytic, pediatric, and social science literature that is oriented toward persuading the mental health community of the normality of homosexuality and the relative magnitude of its incidence in the population.[19] Since, to a significant degree, cultures define the parameters of normal behavior, it is understandable that homosexuals would lobby in this direction. But it is my impression that in recent times mental health professionals have tended uncritically to accept these points of view and the data used to advance them, just as previously the opposite situation prevailed. Any position short of scrupulous neutrality and honesty adopted by a practitioner regarding an issue as important as sexuality would be detrimental to adolescent patients whom he or she serves. These tendentious arguments are well known and made in several areas. I will note a few examples to cite less frequently referenced counterbalancing data that support my impression that politics are currently significantly influencing clinical neutrality, and, in turn, clinical judgment:

References to history and cross cultural study

Societal reaction to homosexuality among females in primitive, peasant, or modern cultures has been much less studied or reported than in males. It is often reported that sexual behaviors among men have been "promoted" and "idealized" in some Classic and current civilizations (e.g., Remafedi, 1990, p. 1170). However, it is not at all clear that homosexuality amongst adults has ever been exalted or encouraged (Karlen, 1980). Moreover, "all known cultures are strongly biased in favor of copulation between males and females as contrasted with alternative avenues of sexual expression" (Ford & Beach, 1951, quoted in Carrier, 1980, p. 118). There is a certain logic, based on the assumption of species-preservative instincts or motives in living forms, be they genetically or environmentally determined, to the finding that heterosexuality, marriage, and procreation are primary objectives in all societies studied.

In those ancient and more modern cultures where sexual relationships between adult men and pubescent male youth have been accepted, these experiences are somewhat ritualized and apparently circumscribed. In antiquity, the adolescents were expected to cease that activity and to function heterosexually as soon as they exhibited the physical features of maturation. And the adult males lose interest in the adolescents when they are no longer pubescent (Karlen, 1980). In latter-day primitive cultures where anthropologists have described homosexual activity between male peers, it primarily occurs in circumstances where heterosexual partners are unavailable or between male adults and youth/children in ritualized practices related to cultural beliefs, for example, transferring masculinity (Carrier, 1980).

The anthropological literature has been inconsistent in equating transvestitism with homosexuality, an association that may have often been accurate in that the transvestite chose the sexual partner of the sex adopted. But, in those societies studied in which specific provision was made at least for cross-dressing individuals (e.g., berdache in some North American Indian societies), anthropological data suggest that their social role or function rather than their sexual behavior was emphasized (Kroeber, 1940, quoted in Carrier, 1980, p. 106). In peasant societies, it also seems to occur primarily where sufficient heterosexual outlets are not available. In general, as in prisons, the male assuming the masculine role of insertor suffers no opprobrium, but the insertee is devalued in the community. And as noted, in no cultures studied are exclusively homosexual relationships between adults embraced as a natural part of the social order (Carrier, 1980).

References to "ambisexual" behavior in
lower vertebrates and invertebrates

These have been advanced to establish the universality of homosexual behavior in the animal kingdom. Kinsey, Pomeroy, and Martin (1948) observed, "there is no scientific reason for considering particular types of sexual activity as intrinsically, in their biologic origins, normal or abnormal" (p. 202). One might infer from that observation that Kinsey and his colleagues are advocating that norms of sexuality in civilized societies be defined by biological phenomena. That is, sexual behavior that is observed to occur "naturally" in lower animals would be considered normal sexual behavior in higher mammals. But their primary point was that, at the time of their study, scientific classifications of "natural" sexual acts and those deemed "contrary to nature" were based on age-old theological classifications (upon which, in turn, legal determinations were founded) rather than on biological observations of what occurred in nature among lower mammals.

Even were one to accept the idea of classifying homosexual sexual behavior as normal because it is observed in all lower animal species studied, a couple of provisos stand out (Denniston, 1980). One involves accurate recognition that the behavior is homosexual. Some biologists have interpreted sexual behavior of male and female animals as homosexual when either is assuming the behavior or position usually ascribed to the other sex. (That would be akin to concluding that each partner of a heterosexual human couple is exhibiting homosexual behavior when the woman is on top of the man during intercourse.) Biologists call this inversion (Kinsey, Pomeroy, & Martin, 1948, p. 614–615); unfortunately, that term came to be used in the mental health field as synonymous with homosexuality.

Another consideration involves the significance of the homosexual behavior, and whether it occurs "naturally" or in response to unnatural circumstances. Investigators of lower animals conclude that issues of convenience for relieving sexual tension in the absence of heterosexual partners is one condition in which such behavior is exhibited, just as can occur in humans. But, more importantly, issues of domination/submission, which serve to maintain the hierarchy of the social order of that particular species rather than sexual object preference, are often, if not invariably, the operative motives for such behaviors (Denniston, 1980). If accurate, that would not seem to be a desirable rationale for considering homosexual behavior normal in a civilized society.

References to demographics and prevalence of homosexuality

(a) The Kinsey reports and more recent studies: Despite widespread awareness of significant sampling bias[20] (often acknowledged in

passing as "convenience samples") without discussion of it significance when extrapolating from their research samples, the Kinsey
reports (1948, 1953) continue to be quoted authoritatively regarding:

(i)   the incidence of homosexual behavior in the population, and
(ii) the concept that the sexuality of every individual falls on a 7-
      point spectrum between exclusive homosexuality and exclusive
      heterosexuality.

One's rating is based on psychic responses or/and overt contacts,
and does not, or not necessarily, remain static over time. Kinsey, a biol-
ogist, and colleagues observed:

> It is a fundamental of taxonomy that nature rarely deals with discrete
> categories. Only the human mind invents categories and tries to force
> facts into separated pigeonholes. The living world is a continuum in
> each and every one of its aspects. The sooner we learn this concerning
> human sexual behavior the sooner we shall reach a sound under-
> standing of the realities of sex. (Kinsey, Pomeroy, & Martin, 1948,
> p. 639)

Thus, from their perspective, one speaks more accurately of homosexual and heterosexual behavior rather than of a specific sexual
orientation.

It is not clear whether that approach illuminates or confuses the
concept of sexual orientation. The latter is basically a matter of self-
identification, a product of evolutionary advance. By virtue of de-
emphasizing the importance of human mental functioning with
respect to sexuality, Kinsey's observation could be seen as a kind of
primitivism. For, call it pigeonholing or not, self-definition regarding
sexuality (as well as other issues) is one unique, valuable way in
which humans capitalize on their cognitive superiority over lower
animals to create internal psychological order out of biological chaos,
relate to one another, and establish and participate in their social
order.

With regard to their original projections regarding males, the
distortion was greater regarding frequency of homosexual behavior
over time than in their estimates of exclusive homosexuality (which is
closer to the issue of sexual identification). Kinsey researchers revised
both those figures in subsequent re-analyses to account for the sample

bias. The latter figures for exclusive homosexuality, still presented as rough estimates, were 3–4% for college-educated, white males, and 1–2% for white females (Gagnon & Simon, 1973; Gebhard, 1972). Surveys published during the 1990s by other researchers estimated from <1%–4% for males and <1%–2% for females (Billy, Tanfer, Grady, et al., 1993; Harry, 1990; Janus & Janus, 1993; Laumann, Gagnon, Michael, et al., 1994; Sell, Wells, & Wypij, 1995; Smith, 1991: see Kinsey Institute, 1999 for summary). The Centers for Disease Control and Prevention National Survey of Family Growth's "key statistics" for 18–44-year-olds encompassing the period 2006–2010 reported 1.8% of males and 1.2% of females identifying themselves as homosexual (National Center for Health Statistics).

(b) Hooker's earlier-quoted Rorschach study (1957) also suffered from sampling problems. Not the least of these was the methodological difficulty presented by the fact that homosexual individuals sought this study to demonstrate they were psychologically indistinguishable from heterosexuals. The researcher's relative inexperience in administering the Rorschach test has also been cited as a factor in the outcome. The results of the two other projective tests she utilized, the Thematic Apperception Test (TAT) and the Make-A-Picture-Story Test (MAPS), were not included in the report because of the ease with which the homosexual cohort could be identified. Yet, interpretation of the latter tests in conjunction with the Rorschach might have shed light on psychological differences between the two cohorts. Among her conclusions was the observation: "It may be that the primary psychological defect, if there is one, in the homosexual lies in a weakness of ego-function and control and that this cannot be adequately diagnosed from projective test protocols" (pp. 29–30).

Homosexuality among adolescents

Regarding the incidence of homosexuality among adolescents (the subjects of this book), in a large, population-based survey, about 1% of junior and senior high school students reported homosexual experiences, and the same percentage identified themselves as predominantly homosexual or bisexual (Remafedi, Resnick, Blum, et al., 1992). These researchers' questionnaires adopted Kinsey's seven-point classification of sexual behavior in a general way rather than using an either/or hetero-, homo-, or bi-sexual orientation. Twenty-five percent of twelve-year-olds claimed uncertainty about their sexual orientation; this declined to 5% at age eighteen, with the greatest majority identifying themselves as heterosexual. (This is consistent with the Kinsey report (1948) that homosexual experiences (in males) are most abundant from pre-adolescence through the teens, and then drop off. Among females, while homosexual behavior was also found to be primarily the province of the younger and single, Kinsey and colleagues (1953) reported that the relative decline in its incidence followed marriage rather than the end of adolescence.)

The authors of the adolescent study (Remafedi, Resnick, Blum, et al., 1992) suggest that their incidence figures for homosexuality approximated those of Kinsey for adults. But, since the changes among the adolescents were largely in the direction of heterosexuality, their lower incidence figures may be more accurately extrapolated to adulthood than Kinsey's prevalence figures. This study supports common clinical experience in at least two respects: This developmental period more than any other is associated with expressed uncertainty about one's sexual orientation, and transient homosexual experiences are engaged in by some adolescents on their way to a final heterosexual orientation.

The latter data also support the long-recognized clinical observation that has been used historically as evidence that resolution of sexual orientation/identification occurs during adolescence (Freud, 1905d). More recently, such data have been attributed to the reluctance of homosexual youth, cowed by the "homophobia" of a "heterosexist" society, to so identify themselves during adolescence. Even granting, for that and/or other reasons, that adolescents are reluctant to acknowledge homosexuality in themselves and to others, the significant reduction of that 25% of twelve-year-olds who expressed uncertainty about their sexual orientation, the largest number of whom are or become heterosexual, does not lend much credence to the idea that expressed confusion about sexual identity among the vast majority of young adolescents is based upon reluctance to acknowledge themselves as homosexual.

That said, figures recently released by the National Center for Health Statistics from the 2002 National Survey of Family Growth suggest a landscape that in some ways resembles, and in other ways is different from, that presented above. The data are derived from interviews with 12,571 men and women between ages fifteen and forty-four. Four percent of men and women described themselves as homosexual or bisexual (note that the age span includes mid- and late adolescence). More females than males identified themselves as bisexual. And 14% of women aged 18–29 had had at least one sexual experience with a woman, twice the proportion of the equivalent experience among same-aged males. This suggests that more adolescent and young adult women are either experimenting with lesbianism than in the past, or are more willing to acknowledge it.

From psychological to biological causation

Psychiatric treatment, largely based on psychoanalytic developmental formulations (initially centered on oedipal, then on pre-oedipal conflict, and subsequently on separation–individuation difficulties) fell into disrepute on a couple of counts: Formulations developed from the study of patient populations were not thought to apply to those homosexuals whose sexual orientation is ego syntonic and, as such, perceive no need to seek psychiatric treatment for this, and who function without any distinctive character pathology, that is, psychopathology different from that found in heterosexuals.[21] Also, the clinical studies failed to demonstrate convincingly that a significant proportion of patients who were exclusively homosexual (as opposed to bisexual or sexually abstinent individuals) can be successfully treated to become heterosexual, at least when their erotic fantasies rather than only their manifest sexual behavior is considered. Yet, one authority estimated that 20–50% of highly motivated, exclusive male and female homosexuals could reach an enjoyable heterosexual adjustment from behavioral and psychodynamic treatment (Marmor, 1980). Also, 100% success was reported in one small sample of highly motivated men utilizing group behavioral therapy (Birk, 1980). To my mind, especially when compared, for example, with medication studies for depression and anxiety, these are not unrespectable outcome figures.

Whether because of disenchantment with psychological approaches to understanding the basis of homosexuality, or more for "political" reasons of the public being more positively disposed to homosexuals if they were "born that way" rather than having chosen/preferred homosexuality (Frnulf, Innala, & Whitam, 1989),[22] interest in biological (genetic, neuroanatomical, and neurophysiological) research gained popularity following the APA's 1974 position statement. The problems in these areas have been those of methodology and replicability of findings, interpretation of the data, and applicability of data from sub-human species to humans.

Familial aggregation studies

Frequently quoted family aggregation and genetic studies afford a good example of the first two of those noted problems—replicating findings and the same data being subject to opposite interpretations. Although apparently not replicated in more recent studies (Townsley, 2001), 52% of monozygotic and 22% of dizygotic male twins, and 48% and 16%, respectively, of female twins raised together were found concordant for homosexuality (Bailey & Pillard, 1991; Bailey, Pillard, Neale, et al., 1993). Some authors have emphasized that the differential between monozygotic and dizygotic twins suggests "a powerful genetic influence" (e.g., Stronski Huwiler & Remafedi, 1998). Other authors emphasize that the 50% concordance amongst monozygotic twins is surprisingly low (e.g., King & McDonald, 1992), and that shared developmental/environmental experiences could account for all the studies' statistics (Byne & Parsons, 1993).

Familial aggregation studies suggest that female homosexuality also runs in families. Homosexual men have more homo- and bi-sexual siblings than do heterosexual men (Pillard & Weinrich, 1986). But more siblings of homosexual women identify themselves as bisexual than do those of male homosexuals (Bailey & Benishay, 1993). Although twin studies support a genetic component, genetic loading is not strong for either sex (Bailey & Pillard, 1991). They conclude that a large environmental component can (though not necessarily does) contribute to the development of homosexuality in any given woman. Consistent with that, in female monozygotic twins the non-shared environmental factors are more important in developing homosexuality than are the shared (common) environmental factors (Bailey, Pillard, Neale, et al., 1993). Such data raise a question about the validity of assertions like "substantial evidence has emerged that biology plays a preeminent role in the development of a homosexual orientation" (Stronski Huwiler & Remafedi, 1998, p. 112).

Moreover, the genetic/family aggregation research, which would be most helpful in clarifying this nature *vs.* nurture question, is in short supply. Those would be studies of monozygotic twins reared apart, which thus control for the confounding variable of shared developmental experiences. I could find only one such study that comprised six twin pairs, five of which included a homosexual and the sixth a bisexual twin. None of the four female pairs and one of the two male pairs was concordant for homosexuality (Elke, Bouchard, Bohlen, et al., 1986). The small sample size precludes definitive conclusions, even regarding possible differences in the bases of homosexuality in females versus males that has been suggested (Downey & Friedman, 1998; Kirkpatrick & Morgan, 1980; Riess, 1980, p. 300).

Neuroanatomical and neurophysiological studies

These studies present the replicability and applicability problems. More of the biological research has focused on homosexuality in males. In brief, none of the neuroanatomic (e.g., different-sized hypothalamic nuclei or corpus callosa), or neurophysiological/endocrine research that suggested differences between homosexuals and heterosexuals has been compellingly replicated or thought to be more than correlational, or directly translatable/transposable from mice and fruit flies to men and women (Byne & Parsons, 1993; Townsley, 2001).

Neurophysiological studies of female homosexuality

The biological findings in males are consistent in many, but not all, respects with those comparable studies of female homosexuality that have been undertaken to date. Demographic, genetic studies conclude that female and male homosexuality may share some causes but are also somewhat independent etiologically.

Neuroendocrinological studies have examined the effects of prenatal exposure to masculinizing hormones, either occurring in genetic syndromes like congenital virilizing adrenal hyperplasia or via progesterone compounds medically administered to maintain pregnancies (which can have an androgenic effect on brain development). These have been correlated (in the former condition) with the preference for more traditionally masculine play in childhood, and perhaps (in both) with more homosexual-type fantasy, and (in the latter) with a tendency toward homosexuality in adulthood, compared to girls not so exposed (Ehrhardt, Meyer-Bahlburg, Rosen, et al., 1985; Friedman & Downey, 1993). Thus, it appears that these partial states of prenatal androgenization can, but do not necessarily, have a "homosexualizing" effect during adulthood on the previously exposed individuals. This underscores again the variability of responses of which the human organism is capable.

Even without stronger confirmation from research, and perhaps because the currently most popular developmental theory is the biopsychosocial model, the consensus among students of the field is that there is probably a biological contribution to the development of homosexuality. Yet, since the genetic or other constitutional component is not a sufficient condition on the basis of current evidence, it remains unclear whether it is a necessary condition to develop homosexually.

Is homosexuality an option or an obligation?

In this general state of discomfiture in the field, the prevailing psychiatric idea about the development of homosexuality has become, at least according to one social scientist, "a form of sexual preference that is influenced by both biological and environmental factors just like heterosexuality" (Steinberg, 2005). Such characterization of a "preference" suggests some aspect of choice in the matter—free or otherwise, and this blurs the previously noted distinction that can be made between engaging in homosexual behavior and an exclusively homosexual orientation. That quotation could also be interpreted to mean that homosexuality and heterosexuality are equivalent expressions of normality—one is no more natural than the other. That idea would seem difficult to reconcile from an evolutionary point of view. In fact, efforts have been made to establish an evolutionary rationale for homosexuality (Wilson, 1975, pp. 343–344, quoted in Isay, 1989), but these are not persuasive (Futuyma & Risch, 1983–1984).

Why even mention, much less belabour, all this, since the thrust of current mental health efforts is to "depathologize" homosexuality in favor of helping society become more accepting of, and helpful to, homosexual adolescents, both of which are desirable goals? It is because in the current Zeitgeist, this position has been adopted at the expense of considering potentially maladaptive and treatable outcomes for some of those adolescents who experience greater uncertainty about their sexual identity than current trends would lead us to believe is the case. And while one can empathize with the social and personal struggles those adolescents whose homosexual identification is ego syntonic have had to face and surmount, that hardly justifies mental health practitioners forsaking their professionalism.

It seems almost certain that even the most conscientious clinician is going to approach an adolescent who evinces uncertainty about his or her sexual orientation differently if (a) that professional is persuaded that "sexual orientation is immutable from birth" (Isay, 1989, p. 21), or that there is no scientific evidence that the development of a homosexual orientation is related to any adverse conditions in childhood or adolescence, such as abnormal parenting, sexual abuse, or other traumatic events (Remafedi, 1990), or that "parents probably have little or no influence on the child's core feelings that define him or her as gender typical or gender variant" (Menvielle, 2003, p. 274), as opposed to (b) a professional who is persuaded either that sexual orientation is consolidated in adolescence, not in early childhood, and/or that environmental factors can have a more profound influence on the genesis of sexual orientation than simply the way one's sexual orientation is expressed.

In fact, no one knows what causes homosexuality or when a homosexual orientation is consolidated. Given that, mental health practitioners who deal with adolescents will better serve their patients by keeping a very open mind in exploring this matter with any adolescent. Every case has to be considered and approached as unique. Promoting humane attitudes toward homosexuality on the basis of it being as natural an alternative as heterosexuality does not serve well those adolescents whose sexual orientation is in flux on the basis of developmental interactions between unique constitutional qualities, interpersonal interactions, and broader environmental factors, and who can identify that confusion (Stronski Huwiler & Remafedi, 1998).[23]

The current rationale adopted to encourage adolescents who are struggling with their sexual development to accept the homosexual orientation includes emphasizing that it is somehow given and immutable (usually presented or implied as having a biological basis). We seem collectively disposed to the idea that things which are genetic cannot be altered psychotherapeutically and things that are psychological can be changed. But neither of those ideas is accurate; the opposite obtains in some conditions. As noted in the Introduction to Chapter One, placebos and psychotherapy have been shown to alter brain functioning in the same manner as medications. So, at our current state of knowledge, to presume the immutability of the emerging sexual identity of an adolescent who seems confused or uncertain seems premature. Thus, the most professionally responsible position for any clinician to take would be to ascertain as thoroughly as can be that a heterosexual orientation is not possible in any individual adolescent before focusing one's clinical efforts on helping such youth and their families adjust to their progeny's homosexuality. It does no adolescent or his/her parents any harm to acknowledge that the basis as well as the timing of when sexual orientation becomes established is not known, that there may well be a number of different constellations of constitutional and environmental factors which contribute to the ultimate outcome of sexual orientation, and that is what needs to be explored. For example, a clinical report described an approach to gender dysphoric children, those who wish to be the opposite sex (not homosexual), which focuses on the children as they are without actively attempting to help them accept their biological gender. A number of them lost their desire to be of the opposite sex while retaining stereotypic interests of the opposite sex (Rosenberg, 2002). This bespeaks the existence of developmental or other internal conflicts in at least some gender dysphoric children.

Challenges to therapists

Adopting a stance of interested neutrality, which translates into helping the adolescent determine who he or she is and wants to be, and helps them achieve that goal, presents different challenges for homosexual and heterosexual therapists. The former must overcome the natural tendency of humans to normalize one's own behavior, especially when it differs from the usual or accepted. The latter (heterosexual therapists) must overcome the natural suggestibility of humans to trends and fashions—for the same reason of wanting to fit in. Dealing with this issue in the current mental health climate is more of a challenge than surmounting the "homophobic and heterosexist" prejudices that are now so often leveled at the field. For therapists, despite their self-proclaimed independence, do not tend to take stances far from where the swinging pendulum is positioned at that point in historical time when they are practicing. The problem is compounded by the fact that adolescents, too, are very suggestible, despite their reputation for being iconoclastic. That is why hetero-sexual and homosexual therapists alike should approach them with interested neutrality.

Another challenge for therapists stems from the dependence of conscientious practitioners on the published research. Ironically, this is particularly so in this era when "evidence-based" treatment is emphasized by editors of journals and other leaders of our professions in an effort to make the mental health field more "scientific" (March, Szatmari, Bukstein, et al., 2007). This has spawned slews of "experts" who are, if anything, accorded greater influence than in times past by virtue of clinicians feeling cowed by the idea of not practicing "evidence-based" medicine. Given that, it is well to keep in mind that "science is not science unless its conclusions are examined as critically when they conform to our personal beliefs as when they oppose them" (Futuyma & Risch, 1983–1984, p. 157). So, a significant issue of professional integrity is involved. This places the onus on journal reviewers to insure the accuracy of the data and conclusions pub-lished. For a significant problem is created for clinicians who depend on the professional literature when basically unsubstantiated con-clusions, cloaked in the guise of being "evidence based", find their way into the literature. Then, by virtue of being repeated, forcefully or otherwise, these conclusions begin to take hold as documented truths. A specific example is that homosexual youth account for 30% of adolescent suicides (e.g., Policy Statement of the American Academy of Pediatrics 1993). That conclusion (Gibson, 1989), based on flawed sampling and data collection, was discredited by other researchers as well as by the Surgeon General, in whose report it was published (see LaBarbera, 2002; Shaffer, Fisher, Hicks, et al., 1995, cited in Stronski Huwiler & Ramafedi, 1998; Tuller, 2002). Yet, it continues to be published and quoted.

The issue of social norms

In addition to the just-addressed, most important consideration of professional integrity, the further danger of adopting the currently popular attitude regarding the issue of homosexuality with respect to adolescents involves the social or sociological dimension of the biopsychosocial approach. Again, the issue is one of balance. Much has been said about the down side of societal influences that historically tolerated, if not supported, discrimination against homosexuals. But nothing of which I am aware is being said currently by mental health professionals about the developmental value of societal norms in helping adolescents consolidate identifications. These norms, when firmly in place, serve a reassuring/stabilizing function in helping those adolescents who are in conflict about developmental issues to move toward the socially sanctioned side, by fostering and therefore reinforcing identifications with one's community (Erikson, 1956). In their absence, it becomes more difficult for individuals who are confused about their sexual identification to capitalize on that social force to help themselves resolve questions related to all facets of their identity.

Interestingly, the "gay pride" movement has appropriately capitalized upon this very factor in strengthening one's sense of personal homosexual identification by association with similarly oriented individuals, that is, within a subculture of homosexuals, including adolescents who consider themselves homosexual. It is not clear whether this "homosocialization" (Isay, 1989) functions solely as a support for those in the process of acknowledging their homosexuality, or currently can serve a proselytizing function for adolescents who are confused about their sexual orientation (as homosexual advocates consider "heterosexist" society does to gays). My point is that there seems currently to be no comparable "social" force from the mental health field, which similarly affords those adolescents who are uncertain of their sexual identification the opportunity to reinforce a heterosexual identity. I suspect that the lack of this has a subtly coercive impulsion in the opposite direction. Examples of this phenomenon have been described currently in such institutions as all-women's colleges (e.g., Chiu, 1997).

Societal acknowledgment/acceptance of such norms may play a more important role during an era when parents are less involved in the hour-to-hour supervision of their children and adolescents than when households were more traditionally overseen by a parent. This circumstance, if anything, renders the assistance of societal forces more urgent. For the absorption of a sense of security occurs more solidly through positive identifications with available parents than via defensive identifications with less available parents (Bloch, 1995). Yet, in a curious way, support for a kind of norm-lessness seems to be developing among mental health professionals with respect to this matter of sexual orientation. This may be guided as much by well-intentioned wishes to be neutral and non-judgmental as by clinical experience.

An instructive, illustrative example appears in consecutive statements by two eminent, credible, clinical researchers writing about female homosexuality:

> ... some theoreticians have argued that sexual orientation is innocuous and never symptomatic. This perspective seems to us to do a disservice to many patients, and to be out of touch with clinical realities. Keeping in mind that sexual orientation, however defined, is not a unitary entity, we note that simply because the group defined as lesbian or gay is not inherently pathological does not mean that homosexual fantasies and/or activities are never symptomatic. They obviously can be and, in some patients, frequently are.

That extract implies that the authors have some norms for sexual orientation, attitudes, and behavior in mind. Yet, they continue:

> The same observation is applicable to heterosexual fantasies and behavior in other patients. The pervasive heterosexist bias of our culture sometimes makes it difficult for clinicians to detect that culturally approved behaviors, such as the wish to marry, become pregnant, raise children in the context of conventional family structures, become a homemaker, experience orgasms resulting from vaginal coitus, may all be manifestations of psychopathology. (Downey & Friedman, 1998, p. 493)

I presume that the latter counterpoint to their first statement was included in an effort to be scrupulously neutral, but it effectively seems "politically correct." For with the possible exception among their enumerated examples of some motives (though not the wish) to become pregnant, their writing off features of accepted, healthy, adaptive cultural standards as reflections of heterosexist bias does not make sense to me, and seems inconsistent with the implication of their own first observation. Essentially, established social norms exist and, by inference, play an appropriate role in assessing the normality of behavior.

Exploring any patient's associations in an interested, neutral manner is not the same thing as promoting or accepting norm-lessness in an effort to appear non-judgmental and sensitive to the feelings of homosexuals. Acknowledging and accepting societal standards, which not everybody meets but which contribute to consolidating and stabilizing the individual's personality and interpersonal relatedness, does not predispose to developing the societal equivalent of either insufferable, domineering character rigidity or bigotry. And at the same time, it helps avoid development of the societal equivalent of perverse, polymorphous character fluidity.

The dilution of this component in the societal crucible in which adolescents are developing promotes/predisposes to lack of certainty, lack of self-confidence (often masquerading as exaggerated self-confidence or self-absorption), greater tendency toward experimentation, and perhaps greater ambiguity in some individuals' sexual identification. It certainly is possible that greater societal tolerance of sexual variation/deviation has simply made it easier for such individuals to so identify themselves. But it is as likely that it predisposes to polymorphous sexuality and contributes to the more frequent reports in recent years of psychosexual hermaphrodism, so-called bisexuality. One needs ask whether during earlier generations when norms with respect to sexuality were more clearly defined and held, were adolescents in flux helped to consolidate and live comfortably with the conventional sexual orientation? Or, were those in flux left to lead adult lives of "quiet desperation" trying to fit into a sexual orientation with which they were truly not comfortable? I have found no data bearing on that question, but presume that both resolutions occurred. But in either event, any social reinforcement for a final bisexual orientation would hardly augur well for an individual's ability to accomplish what I believe remain basic tenets of completing sexual development and achieving psychological maturity with respect to object relatedness. That is the ability to form an exclusive partnership in which one shares both erotic fulfillment and ego interests in achieving the dual aims of lasting companionship and procreation. Interestingly enough, those who come to treatment because of bisexual orientation are reported to be more successful in achieving a heterosexual orientation than are the exclusively homosexual, suggesting the wish of the former group to be heterosexual.

Homosexuality in women

The latter observations about more polymorphous and shifting sexual identifications bring the discussion closer to current thinking about homosexuality in women. Bisexuality has been identified to be much more frequent in women (14%) than in men (7%) (Bailey, Pillard, Neale, et al., 1993). Different and more varied pathways to lesbianism than to male homosexuality, particularly with respect to the contribution of nurture relative to nature, have been reported (Downey & Friedman, 1998).[24] In emphasizing the diversity of paths to lesbianism, Downey and Friedman comment on three descriptive types and suggest that many more pathways may exist. They describe those who recall having felt different for as long as they could remember, those who develop lesbianism in mid-life after lengthy marriages[25], based on a greater need for intimacy than their husbands and children are providing (see Kirkpatrick, 1989; Kirkpatrick & Morgan, 1980), and "political lesbians" whose "sexual" orientation is motivated by shared beliefs about the domination and subjugation of women by men (De Fries, 1979). Socarides (1989) identifies nine different clinical groups of lesbians based on correlating their manifest attitudes and behavior with their underlying, intrapsychic conflicts.

* * *

If variations in the development, expression, and practice of homosexuality do exist, and homosexual behavior is not a unitary entity, then it is a phenomenon that develops uniquely in individuals. As such, it remains an appropriate subject for study from a developmental and psychodynamic perspective. If it can be demonstrated that in some individuals homosexuality develops as an adaptation to a painful psychological reality, then whether or not the homosexual functions well in other areas of his or her life, or whether this is within the purview of normality, becomes less important than comprehending how it develops as a profound adaptive resolution to developmental conflicts, and whether better resolutions could have been effected by psychotherapeutic intervention.

The tenor of our times with respect to the issue of homosexuality obliges one to ask or consider, why bother, if homosexuality is inherently no more pathological or maladaptive than heterosexuality, why not just see what happens, let "nature" take its course? The answer is several-fold: First, it should be clear that "nature" did not simply take its course in this young woman; she struggled with significant internal conflicts. Secondly, as she herself said, she would have preferred to be heterosexual, and she struggled with her sexual identity to a degree that most adolescents and young adults do not. And in the final analysis, if one can have the choice, heterosexuality is still the easier route in life which is complicated enough in the best of circumstances.[26,27]

Thus, it would seem that homosexuality, at least in females, is not necessarily or invariably as simple as a variant of normal sexuality. Given that, it becomes important for therapists of adolescents to determine those for whom it is a condition amenable to change and those for whom it is a condition more amenable to facilitating adaptation— those who can and those who cannot be helped psychotherapeutically to consolidate a heterosexual identification. It is not justified at the current state of our knowledge to paint either group with the brush of the other. And as I have indicated, in much of what appears today in the professional literature, the pendulum has swung too far in the direction of simply prescribing efforts to make the environment more accepting. The danger of predicting subsequent sexual orientation from earlier life behavior is borne out at least in the follow-up studies of boys who exhibited feminine behavior in childhood (Green, 1987, Zuger, 1984). These studies are usually cited to demonstrate the opposite phenomenon, that as many as two-thirds to three-fourths became homosexual. But even if one increases those percentages to account for study subjects lost to follow-up, that still leaves a significant minority of relatively extreme-type cases who ended up heterosexual.

My point is not to dispute the value of helping homosexual adolescents, their families, and society to adapt to each other. Rather, my point is that there are more early adolescents who are confused about their sexual orientation or sexuality than there are those who know they are, or will become, homosexual. To treat them all as if they are the latter is inappropriate given the present state of our knowledge.

But the current child and adolescent psychoanalytic/psychiatric/ psychological and pediatric literature convey the impression that this is becoming the standard approach. Every case should be considered unique, and evaluated on its own individual merits. Thus, I have tried to illustrate that for mental health professionals to adopt a stance that homosexuality *per se* is simply a normal variant of psychosexual functioning does as much, if not more, disservice to adolescents who are struggling with their sexual identity as it helps those whose sexual identity may be set.

CHAPTER FOUR

The relationship between suicide and homicide

(Dilemmas at the interface of psychiatry and the law)

T he previous chapter dealt with the objects of one's affection. This one focuses on the antithesis—vicissitudes of one's aggression. Specifically, it addresses how the most extreme and opposite actions that can be visited upon the objects of one's aggression, namely suicide and homicide, can develop and become so closely related psychodynamically. I will review the data from which I developed a formulation about how the latter phenomenon occurred in one youth.

Mark

In a curious counterpoint to the original People *vs*. O. J. Simpson, another trial, followed with only keen local, rather than international, interest, was unfolding during the same time period on the other side of the country. I was subpoenaed to participate in the penalty phase of that trial. The experience underscored a couple of facts, which are not only well known to trial attorneys and experienced forensic psychiatrists, but also sensed by the public at large. Yet, the magnitude of influence that psychosociological factors can have on trials had eluded me. Consideration of the latter is a secondary theme of this chapter.

The notoriety of the Simpson case requires little be said because it is still easy to recall: A black jury with a non-black judge acquitted a black man whose defense attorneys, in order to create reasonable doubt in the minds of that jury, had to beat back a prosecution case which identified motive from prior aggressive behavior toward one of the victims, no other reasonable suspects, impressive circumstantial and compelling DNA evidence. Also, the venue of the trial had been changed because the District Attorney of Los Angeles feared rioting if the outcome were different.

While that case was preoccupying the country, at a smaller city on the other coast, a trial was in preparation to be conducted within weeks of the Simpson verdict. It involved a homicide that had occurred close in time to the Simpson–Goldman murders. A twenty-two-year-old youth of mixed black and white parentage, who, like Simpson, had spent his childhood in San Francisco, walked out on to the beach at the resort where he worked, drunk, with some marijuana in his system, and with pistol in hand, intending to commit suicide. He encountered a couple of strangers and asked them to write him a suicide note. The male of that couple, a twenty-nine-year-old, popular, white bartender from the area, with an even higher level of alcohol in his blood and apparently cocaine in his system as well, evidently became confrontive with the suicider, and within a few minutes the latter shot the former. He then returned to his living quarters, shot up his room, called his mother saying he thought something bad had happened but he couldn't remember what, and held off police briefly before emerging in handcuffs they had tossed in to him. The next day he could not recall what had happened. Acquaintances and relatives reported that he had always suffered from amnesia after drinking, which he did occasionally.

The case languished for a while, until the local community became roused by concern that this event would harm the area's tourism, and the bereaved family of the victim began to agitate and press for a murder conviction with maximum penalty, which is certainly understandable. The case then became one of celebrity, owing to the interest of the local newspapers and television station. In this case, neither a change of venue nor dismissal of the jury panel, when it proved to be all white, were granted by the judge. So, the counterpoints were a black judge and white jury, in a white community that was perceived as screaming for conviction, in contrast to a black jury and a non-black judge in a black community being perceived as agitating for the opposite outcome for Simpson.

The jury took less than two hours to reach a verdict of murder in the first degree, which requires premeditation in that state. It also carries the death sentence, which is why the penalty phase ensued. At that phase, a few relatives, friends, teachers, and professionals who had known the defendant in California during his childhood were called to testify about his egregious upbringing, over which he had prevailed well enough to the point of this homicide. That particular upbringing involved being raised alone by a mother who was alter-nately devoted and concerned, psychotic, and exploitative. As a child, he had always turned to those who held out hope of offering him the stability and security he knew he needed. But invariably his efforts were thwarted by a congeries of circumstances over which he had absolutely no control. These repeated experiences of being let down left him to grow up feeling unable to assert himself in any effective way in the world around him. He was helpless not only in the face of his mother's illnesses, but also of modest social service resources and a legal system which at that time was committed to reuniting children with parents who had previously failed them.

For all we know, the jury may well have recommended the alter-native life sentence to the judge without the ghosts from the closet of Mark's childhood having been pulled out and paraded in front of them during the penalty phase. The judge accepted that recommen-dation from the jury and imposed the sentence of life without the possibility of parole.

My point is not the one repeatedly raised after the Simpson verdict that the rich and famous are much more likely to get off. This young man shot the other in the presence of a witness. He was guilty. Rather, two questions interest me: From the court's side, why was this adjudged to be premeditated? And from the perpetrator's side, why did he commit murder when all indications were that he was contem-plating suicide? The answer to the first question is deceptively simple. There is a difference between the legal definition of premeditation and what the world of psychology might consider reasonable conditions for establishing premeditation. As I understand it, from a legal stand-point, premeditation can occur within seconds; it is not necessarily a longer-time, contemplated intention. (D. Bloch 2006, personal communication.) But the comparison of the two cases may suggest that the answer to my first question is not so cut and dried.

My first point is about the psychosociology of the case. It stems from the counterpoints of a black jury with a non-black judge exonerating Simpson in a community which supported the latter, and a white jury with a black judge convicting a mulatto youth of the most severe degree of homicide, in a venue where conviction seems to have been favored from the tenor of the local news media reports there. That jury and populace knew of the recent Simpson verdict. (Parenthetically, that outcome probably struck fear and pessimism in the hearts of defense attorneys throughout the country, who feared a backlash against the defense side.) In that case we saw that intense public sentiment can influence everything from venue to jury selection to outcomes of trials. Thus, we are thrown up against the fact that although ours remains the best of all legal and political systems, because people are suggestible and can collectively bring great subtle pressure to bear on others, the outcomes of cases may often rest less on the evidence and common sense, and more on what is going on inside people. For even if Justice is blindfolded, it seems clear that she is not deaf to public sentiment. Thus, is it likely or at least possible that the widely held view that justice miscarried in the Simpson case influenced the specific degree of homicide sought and the reaction of the jury at Mark's trial?

My other point was that this young man went out to commit suicide (most likely looking for someone to talk him out of it) and ended up killing someone else. The counterpoint here is that Simpson threatened suicide following the murders. My second question, more directly relevant to psychiatry, involves how it is that suicide and homicide can get so close together. Some psychoanalysts might well interpret that confrontation on the beach as the classical one of Oedipus at the crossroads in which the son, with jealousy and murder in his heart, kills his father—the mythic basis for the Oedipus complex, which, in classical Freudian theory, is thought to dominate psychological development. The victim had apparently become contentious with the murderer. Other psychiatrists or psychologists with knowledge of Mark's background might conclude that the homicide reflected the intensity of this youth's unrequited wishes for a protective father figure to help him at times of need—at base to offset those of his mother's less desirable influences. And the welling up of fear and anger for never having been able to count on a man to protect him from his mother's erratic behavior emerged violently when his inhibitions were loosened by alcohol, to which he was pathologically sensitive. Neither of these formulations seems adequate.

Asserting that psychologically traumatic experiences in his up-bringing help explain the horrendous outcome obliges me to address one obvious point at the outset: that unfortunate as such traumata may have been, there must be many children whose life circumstances bear similarity to those of Mark, but who do not commit murder or suicide. So, what sets Mark's situation apart from those others? I will focus on what I consider the more psychologically unique experiences in his upbringing compared to some others who have faced similar problems. That will provide the basis of my formulation regarding how suicide and homicide can come so close together:

I became acquainted with Mark while serving as psychiatric con-sultant to a small therapeutic–educational program for children who are deemed learning disabled and also significantly emotionally dis-turbed. Basically, these were elementary school-aged children whose problems were sufficiently severe that they could not be managed and taught in the public schools, but they were not so severely disturbed that they had to be placed in residential facilities. It was a very labor-intensive program, with very small class sizes, very high staff:student ratios boosted by classroom volunteers and student teachers, and therapist specialists from several disciplines.

As part of the evaluation process, I met with children being considered for enrollment and sometimes their parent(s) or foster parent as well. Each child was seen in a single, screening interview for my estimation of his or her suitability for the program. Once children were enrolled, I would occasionally observe them in their classrooms. However, most of my information about individual chil-dren then came from the staff. I met with the staff twice weekly to discuss the behaviors and circumstances of individual youngsters in their charge in an effort to find more effective strategies for working with them in the classrooms. I would then dictate reports based on those meetings. During the two years Mark attended that program, I recorded nine such notes, ranging in length from one-half to two typewritten pages. That is the database from which I developed my conclusions.

Mark was enrolled there between ages seven years ten months and nine years ten months. He was referred for typical reasons: not learning during his second time through first grade, and unmanageable behavior. The latter included uncontrollable restlessness, impulsiveness, distractibility and inability to maintain his focus and concentration on learning tasks, unacceptable language, and some aggressive outbursts. This was not a unique presentation. Neither was it unique that he had been raised from birth solely by his mother, and had never seen his father, who was in a federal penitentiary. A little more unique and influential in his life was the fact that in his own, predominantly black, neighborhood, his peers did not readily accept him because his mother was white. Being a child of an interracial marriage living in a black neighborhood is also not unique. But in Mark's case, this was one of a pattern of experiences I will describe that never allowed him to feel secure and comfortable in any environment—in this example, with peers during childhood. Also, more unique was the fact that his mother worked on a night shift, and she and Mark seemed to be alone in the world without extended family nearby. So, Mark may have been home alone through the night from an early age, unless her boyfriend, who did not get along with Mark, was at their apartment. Thus, Mark had to develop early a kind of superficial, precocious ability to fend for himself. And, for example, the second time this seven-year-old boy visited the Center for his evaluation, he came by himself, halfway across San Francisco alone on the public bus system from a rough part of town.

More unique still were the circumstances surrounding his entry into the program. His mother worked quickly and in a very determined manner to get him enrolled. But then, within a couple of weeks after accomplishing this, she underwent a severe, psychiatric decompensation to an overtly psychotic, paranoid, and depressed state. It was as if she had sensed her own imminent regression and worked to get Mark to a place where he would be taken care of before she became very ill. That is, she was looking out for his welfare. But then, in a remarkably paradoxical way, as soon as she became paranoid and depressed, she resisted cooperating in any way with the program. She refused to come in to sign papers for his enrollment, was unable to be contacted, and thwarted almost all efforts of the program's staff to get help for her. She did let the staff know that she had lost her job and didn't have money to provide lunches for Mark, but she refused the staff's help to get her aid and avoided them and the Center. Mark began arriving at school dirty and disheveled, without lunches, reporting having spent the night in a newsstand, not knowing where his mother was, not able to get into his apartment, and not having eaten dinner or breakfast. His mother told him she was dying of cancer and was going to have him adopted by friends. She finally accepted a medical referral from the school staff at which she told the doctor that even if she did not have cancer she was going to die of a seizure disorder—neither of which she had. This period of his mother's deterioration culminated in a suicide attempt, followed by absconding from the hospital where she was being held for treatment of self-administered cuts.

At that point, the school was able to have Mark removed temporarily from his mother's care. Again, he was not the first boy who has had such a frightening experience with a psychotic mother, or the first who has had to look after a parent as much as being parented by that parent. Neither was he the first child who was not even able to trust that his parent would help him understand reality—he had to reality test for his parent. At a meeting with his teachers, Mark's mother accused five people of staring at her, and it was (then) eight-year-old Mark who told his mother that five people were not staring at her; no one was staring. But from this pattern of her behavior, one can perceive how Mark could not develop any sense of confidence that his parent would consistently care for and protect him, and if his parent could not, who could, much less who would?

During my single interview with him, this small, seven-year-old represented himself to me as something of a fighter, though he seemed much more scared of fighting and being fought with. For example, he told me that a "crazy" kid in his neighborhood had threatened to kill his baby-sitter if she did not give him some food. Mark claimed to have hit that kid in the face once and subsequently feared him returning with a pipe or knife, but luckily that boy had moved away. Through this and other examples, Mark revealed himself to be primarily a frightened child whose efforts to hide this by portraying himself as tough and aggressive were not sufficient to bind his anxiety. And Mark's anxiety about the dangers of the world around him and his helplessness to feel protected from them seeped out in restless, distractible, impulsive behavior.

During that interview, Mark also revealed efforts to help himself bind anxiety in more appropriate, normal ways for a seven-year-old.

Most notably, he exhibited efforts to utilize obsessional mechanisms. For example, he lined up things in an orderly fashion, as a way to feel less anxious, and thus in greater control of himself by organizing his environment. And perhaps most importantly, in spite of his distrust, Mark exhibited a strong desire to be helped. He reached out to form relationships that held out the possibility of helping him feel sufficiently safe and secure that he could focus his attention on adaptive developmental tasks such as learning. Given the degree to which his experiences to that point might make it difficult to turn to others, I understand his tendency to do so as a reflection of inherent strivings to complete development.

The major point I will make in the data that follow about his life is that for the duration of the two years we knew him, efforts were made to provide Mark with the stable, safe environment he needed. Each time Mark tried to grab on to the opportunity. He was not a disaffected child, alienated from human relationships. Neither was he a predatory child who already, at the tender age of eight, was looking to take advantage of, or hurt, others. However, each time he started to profit from those opportunities, the rug was pulled out from under him, without him being able to do anything about it. He was never able to feel secure or protected for any significant length of time. He was helpless to have any influence over what happened to him. And he could not count on others to meet his appropriate needs. This rendered him not only chronically fearful and vulnerable, but also resentful and readily frustrated, as he struggled valiantly against his understandable feelings of distrust while continuing to try to extract from his environment what he needed to move his development forward. I am also quite certain, based on clinical experience, that these conditions also bred into Mark another underlying feeling that confounds the life of such individuals immeasurably. I shall mention it shortly.

Mark was placed in a group living setting where he was certainly exposed to bigger, tougher boys. His fright about that living arrangement, as well as his mother's situation, were evident. "I must be crazy," he told a staff member, "Otherwise why would I be hanging from the window there." He was expressing his fear and need for protection, and looking for the staff to help him. But at the same time, he was trying to protect his mother by saying that he himself was crazy, that is, that he was just like her, not better or better off than her.

Then, within six months, he was placed with a therapeutic foster parent—a single man. In this man's care Mark's behavior began to stabilize significantly and his learning at school flourished dramatically. Yet, even this situation was fraught with anxiety for Mark. For this gentleman was evidently overtly homosexual. And while he took care of Mark in an exemplary manner, you can imagine Mark's dilemma and fear, at least initially, when he was placed alone in the home of a strange man whom he identified as homosexual. Then later, after feeling more certain that he had nothing to fear from this man, when this child (who desperately wanted to form a solid attachment to a protective parenting figure) began to like and perhaps trust his foster father, Mark had to wonder if that meant he himself were gay. This was conveyed, for example, when Mark came to the Center and accused his male teacher of being gay and having a gay mother. The dramatic improvement in both his deportment and academics wrought through the joint and collaborative efforts of his foster father and Center staff to sustain a stable, constant, and consistent environment proved short-lived.

For within months of this occurring, Mark's mother, now feeling better able to take care of him, petitioned to regain custody. Mark had to be apprised of this possibility, and that there would be a court proceeding. Thus, he was again placed in the uncertain position of not knowing what would happen to him and having absolutely no control over his life. His behavior and scholastic progress deteriorated as dramatically as they had improved. At school, when he felt on the verge of losing control, he would provoke another child until that one lost control. Such turning passive into active, albeit a common way of alleviating inner turmoil by causing another to feel that way, and then by comparison to feel in better control of oneself, is relatively maladaptive.

Despite his love for his mother, he feared visitations with her, and was very aggressive toward the female staff members after those visits. His mother was not yet as stable as she thought, for she did not show up for some visitations. Also, on occasion, she evidently took him to bars. Mark reported to his teacher that he was holding a gun belonging to a friend of his mother, and asked of his head teacher, didn't she think it was important to learn how to handle guns? Thus, his mother revealed sufficient evidence of persisting instability and lack of judgment that Mark was ultimately left with his foster father.

But this was not effected before weeks had passed when Mark did not know what would happen. Also, he could anticipate being reunited with his mother within less than a year. So, although Mark began to settle down again and learn, he was still never able to live with any sense of confidence that he would be held in a protective and support-ive environment as long as he needed, to be able to count on the constancy of a protective adult, and to not have to worry about what would happen to him.

And, in fact, that is what happened. Within a year, he was returned to his mother's custody. She was moving to a suburban area but refused to let the Center find a suitable school for Mark, to pave his way and reduce the uncertainty of what he could expect, or to have any further connection with the staff. She wanted to, and did, sever all contact with the school. That was the last I saw or heard of Mark until receiving the subpoena.

A relationship between homicide and suicide

Although his mother has figured importantly in what I have related, my point is not to criticize or blame her for his problems any more than to criticize the social services department and legal system in San Francisco for not wresting a more permanent, stable solution for Mark. The latter were well intentioned and overworked, and I think his mother always had his best interests at heart. But she was strug-gling with serious psychiatric illness that impaired her judgment at times and rendered her unable to provide appropriately for Mark's developmental needs. Rather, I want to emphasize what may be rela-tively unique in his case compared to some other children who have endured similar experiences:

Mark presented as a child whose actions conveyed a desperate wish and need to live in a stable, secure environment that would foster his healthy psychological development. He was strongly oriented toward forming relationships, which could provide that. He had the ability to learn and significant intellectual potential as best we could determine. The way he responded during those times of relative stability in his life supported this contention. But he never experi-enced any sustained period during which he could feel confident that he would be protected from danger emanating from without or from within himself. Nor did he ever have the opportunity to feel that he could exert any effective influence over others to get his needs met. Instead, he always had to live helplessly with dramatic uncertainty. It was this repeated holding out of hope that he could have the stability he needed, only to have it almost immediately taken away or threatened, that makes his situation more unique than that of other cases with which I am familiar. As I noted, this pattern, augmented by identification with his mother, contributed to the development of significant distrust of others. Being caught between awareness of wishes to have secure, helpful relationships while at the same time distrusting others is a dreadful bind that he always had to struggle against as he tried to complete his psychological development normally.

Frustration is basically the emotional response to feeling helpless. Whenever Mark felt frustrated in his wishes to get what he needed from others he felt vulnerable and scared, and typically was inclined to re-experience long-standing rage and hurt. I noted earlier that such individuals develop one more ingredient, which is crucial in the welter of feelings that are always close to the surface and ready to erupt at moments of frustration: Children who have come to believe that adults (and particularly parents) will not respond to their appropriate developmental needs almost invariably develop the idea that they must not deserve what they want and need. At some level of their sensibility, they live with a chronic sense that they are either responsible for their parent's neglect and deserve to be punished, or that punishment will somehow then relieve their guilt. And they engage in self-punishing, self-destructive actions. To walk around feeling at one and the same time both legitimately needful of something from others but undeserving and without understanding why you feel this way can be as confusing as it is frustrating to someone who always risks feeling this dilemma when thwarted. In such situations, Mark risked turning his anguish and confusion into aggression directed toward himself out of guilt or on to those who have frustrated him out of blame. That is how I think suicidal and homicidal urges can develop so closely together. And that is what I surmise happened on that fateful spring evening. It is more complicated than simply a vicissitude of the instincts, that is, dealing with aggressive drive by turning it on to others or on to oneself. And I am positing that this type of psychodynamic figures in the cases of some other youth who commit murder or suicide.

In sum, if this formulation is relevant to other individuals, it might offer additional insight into what we already realize. That is, many of the aggressive crimes committed today by young people do not simply reflect the accentuation of behaviors learned in their day care centers or on the streets. Rather, they stem from these youths' responses of abject disappointment and disillusionment with parents who afforded them neither their birthright of protection from harm's way nor a sense of confidence that their developmental needs would be met. Subliminally despairing in their awareness that they cannot count on parents to afford them a sense of safety, they conclude that they are at the mercy of a capricious environment over which they have no influence. Thus, they struggle against a sense of vulnerability about being able to control their own selves. This developmental experience, not surprisingly, breeds a personal sense of distrust.

Yet, in an effort to complete their development, they still always strive to wrest a sense of control both over these internal feelings of insecurity, anger, and guilt, as well as over the outside world (their environment). But in the face of that anxiety, they are prone to become angry, but often not even so much angry as simply reactively aggressive—this being the only way they feel that they can protect themselves from their fear and ambivalence toward others. The coexistence of anger and guilt, the latter invariably associated with feeling that they must be bad to have been dealt their particular hand in life, may help us understand how homicide and suicide can get so close together, and why we may await more rather than less of this as the current generation spawns the next.

Postscript

Subsequent appeals to secure a new trial (automatically set in motion in that state) were not successful. That left an appeal for clemency for relief from life-long incarceration, but that, too, was denied (though can be made again each five years). We might presume that clemency proceedings are potentially every bit as subject to the kinds of influences I described with respect to trials. Mark has continued to seek any remaining alternatives, such as new evidence appeals, without success to date. When I wrote to confirm that the book will be published, Mark was forty-one years old and beginning his twentieth year of imprisonment. His reply included a reflection on the difficulty at times of remaining positive and focused without support from inside or outside the penitentiary, while at the same time always realising that "I did it to myself." Yet, he has not given up hope and continues to make every effort and take advantage of any educational and other opportunities he can find or create for his personal growth, and he has assumed a leadership role in helping others there. He has been a model prisoner.

Clearly, this is both a tragedy for all involved and a conundrum. Mark took the life of another. So should he ever be freed? The only true solution is to prevent this kind of vulnerability and its aftermath from occurring. That can only be accomplished in the home and the responsibility falls squarely on parents and parental surrogates. The next chapter focuses on less dramatic, but much more common, current practices of parents that are contributing to children feeling insufficiently protected and deprived of a psychologically secure upbringing. These increasingly frequent and accepted parental behaviors, too, carry significant implications for each succeeding generation.

PART III

DILEMMAS AT THE INTERFACE OF INDIVIDUAL PSYCHOLOGY AND SOCIOLOGY

The impact on civilization of its malcontents, or normalizing psychopathology and pathologizing normalcy in present-day America: an unfortunate natural outcome of developmental needs

Societal attitudes or practices which change dramatically within a short period of time may offer a better opportunity to identify any role that individual psychology plays in altering social institutions than do such changes that evolve slowly. I will discuss three institutions that currently present such opportunities. One involves changes in what is considered a normal developmental phenomenon of adolescence, namely risk-taking behavior. Here I believe we have witnessed a trend toward more dangerous behavior within the last generation or two. The other two phenomena are particularly interesting because they involve changes by adults in the direction of embracing practices that heretofore had been considered undesirable and hurtful to children and adolescents. I am referring to the increased frequency of divorce and prevalence of sending one's children to day care. My interest is particularly in those who experienced divorce and/or day care in their own childhoods, for they can serve as the points of reference for their own later behavior. In other words, they serve as their own control subjects. I was unable to find statistics on these particular groups. But currently the incidence of both divorce and day care utilization are so relatively high that significant numbers from those sub-groups must be encompassed in their midst. My point is that most adults consider their parents' divorce and/or their own experiences in day care (if they recall them) to have been undesirable, unhealthy, sources of significant unhappiness, and damaging to their own development. Yet, many then go on during adulthood to divorce and/or to send their own children to day care. Why do they not instead strive mightily to spare their own children from what they had painfully or traumatically endured?

Traditionally such matters, at least with regard to divorce and day care, have been the province of sociologists, social psychologists, and perhaps the common wisdom of the populace, explanations from which might seem sufficient at first blush. By the latter I refer, for example, to economic necessity, economic superfluity (the old "Pa's rich and Ma don't care" attitude), increasing secularization of society, and the suggestibility of individuals to strident voices of determined interest groups (e.g., the "equality movements" gone awry). But do such changes of societal norms primarily reflect relative enlightenment in successive generations? Or, do these changed attitudes and behaviors develop as accommodations to economic circumstances? Or, are they the effect of psychological browbeating by, or moral shaming of, the majority with the agenda of determined minorities? Or, do they at base result from the tendency of individuals to resolve in similar ways psychological conflicts or traumas that many of them shared in common during their upbringing? These four alternatives do not exhaust the possible sources for such change. Yet, they do represent a reasonably encompassing spectrum of explanations—to wit, accumulating wisdom, groups' struggles to survive in famine or liberty to feel indifferent in feast, tyranny, and the collective impact of individuals' efforts to adapt. While posited as an either/or question, it may be that no single factor offers sufficient explanation.

I will propose that a universal developmental response, involving vicissitudes of identification with one's parents, is a necessary factor for such sea changes in societal attitudes to take hold and be perpetuated in the next generation. The bedrock motive for children and adolescents to identify with their parents was articulated by Freud in *Civilization and Its Discontents* (1930a) (acknowledgment of which is reflected in the title of this chapter). Freud observed that children's most basic psychological need is to feel assured that they are safe and secure in their parents' care. Thus, gratifying one's parents becomes the child's highest priority. Weiss further elaborated that the child, in his or her efforts to retain the parent's love, "develops a powerful wish to obey his parents, be loyal to them, and be like them", and "condemns in himself whatever, in his opinion, threatens his ties to his parents"; the latter include attitudes or behaviors which seem to upset, or are disapproved of by, their parents (Weiss, Sampson, and the Mount Zion Psychotherapy Research Group, 1986, pp. 46–47). That premise enables us to comprehend how children can relatively readily come to accept and endorse as legitimate, justified, and correct even those parental attitudes and behaviors that they (the children) feel do not make sense or realize are just wrong. Identification becomes a basic means of so honoring parents.

Adolescents, too, are strongly motivated to retain an underlying sense of their parents' approval. This contention that adolescents wish to retain a positive relationship with parents seems at odds with their reputation for hostility toward, and withdrawal from, parents. Yet, it holds true even as they negotiate the developmental imperative to emancipate to greater psychological autonomy from the influence of their parents' wishes, proscriptions, and judgments. Perhaps the most compelling evidence for this is the common observation that after having resolved the developmental imperative to emancipate, these now young adults and their parents find they are much more alike than either thought possible during the adolescence of the former (Anthony, 1970). This underscores that the so-called adolescent rebellion is more about psychological independence than about necessarily changing underlying and persisting attitudes and values. This need to sustain a sense of parental approval, in conjunction with their need for active parental sponsorship of their efforts to become more psychologically independent, wreaks havoc on the progressive development of those adolescents who must bear witness to inappropriate, unbecoming, illegal, or otherwise self-denigrating or self-defeating parental behavior.

Certainly, rebellious and oppositional behavior can represent adolescents' efforts to bolster feelings of independence from parental hegemony. But such attitudes and behavior are often accompanied by conscious or unconscious guilt, which is warded off either by acting blameless or by blaming their parents.[28] And particularly when such behavior inhibits or hampers the adolescent's progressive development, I have found that it more often reflects either: (1) unconsciously motivated compliance on the part of the adolescents with what they have concluded (objectively accurately or not) is needed by or is most gratifying to one's parent(s). Their motive is to secure their parents' approval (love). Or else, (2) an identification with their parents, or adopting an equivalent of those maladaptive/unbecoming parental behaviors which distress or disgust the adolescent. Identification is basically imitative behavior, adopted and integrated into the developing personality. It is probably the most important way that children and adolescents learn behavior (Bloch, 1995).

While their basic motive is to preserve the relationship with their parents, adolescents can have opposite psychodynamic motives for imitating (identifying with) parental behaviors. One is love and admiration. Adolescents tend to imitate activities their parents enjoy or endorse, both because such must be desirable if their parents derive pleasure from them, and because they feel that imitating them will make them more acceptable to parents. The paradigms for this can be thought of as, "I want to be like my parents who make me feel good and secure", and "If I do things my parents like, they will like me more" (Bloch, 1995).

But adolescents also identify to avoid feeling dissatisfied with, superior to, or contemptuous of their parents for weakness they perceive in them. The paradigm in these circumstances can be thought of as "I'm not better than or disdainful of my parent, I'm just like my parent." So, even as adolescents become progressively more competent, their needs for approval and to feel parental sponsorship are so important to successful psychological development that there is a strong, natural, survival-based tilt within the individual's psyche toward supporting the parents' views and behaviors as the right and proper ones. Thus, adolescents are often unconsciously motivated to adopt disquieting parental behaviors in an effort to preserve a positive image of, and relationship with, their parents. I call these defensive identifications (Bloch, 1995).

The following brief examples illustrate vicissitudes of these phenomena of defensive identification and compliance based on what they perceive gratifies or fulfills parental needs.

Example 1: A man calls a psychiatrist about his ten-year-old daughter, who has just been suspended from school for four days because of rudeness to her teachers. She has been destructive at home, tearing things up, slamming things that get in her way. She has assaulted her father a few times, seemingly totally out of control, so that he has had to call the police, fearing that she is a danger to herself and him. He is at a loss to know what to do.

In response to a question from the psychiatrist, the father reported that, prior to five months ago, her behavior had been fine, except for a few problems at school, though "nothing out of the ordinary." When asked what had happened five months ago, he replied in an ashamed or embarrassed tone that her mother was incarcerated in a women's state prison—for violent felonies, assault, burglary, and assault with a deadly weapon. He then immediately diverted from that to noting that his daughter has friends who treat their parents as she is treating him—cursing them and getting their way—controlling them. So his daughter has witnessed that in others. The psychiatrist said he guessed that the daughter's behavior had a lot to do with her mother's incarceration, and asked how she had reacted to it. Her father did not recall her having shown much reaction. However, he added that she did evince considerable anxiety when he divorced her mother subsequent to the incarceration. He went on to say that she had been arrested for burglary a week ago and spent the night in Juvenile Hall, about which her attitude had been, "So what!"

He said that he himself was disabled, and their health care was provided by "MediCal insurance" (Medicaid). He had physical therapy later that week, so wanted to schedule an appointment the following week. The morning of that scheduled appointment he left the psychiatrist a message canceling it, saying only that he would call again to reschedule, which he never did.

This ten-year-old daughter was dealing with the loss of her mother by identifying with (imitating) her mother's behaviors. Her distress, which emerged after her father divorced her mother, was evidence that she worried about her mother. And compunction about her mother's behavior was communicated in her own equivalent behaviors, which demonstrated that she was no better than, and in fact was just like, her mother (a defensive identification).

Her father may well have followed through with another professional. But his preoccupation with his own physical therapy, difficulty scheduling more than one appointment in a week, and his tendency to identify the root of her problem in the influence of her friends to the exclusion of acknowledging its relationship to the incarceration of her mother and the divorce bespoke a readiness to disclaim or at least de-emphasize the role of parental behaviors and attitudes in the genesis of his daughter's difficulties.

Example 2: A fifteen-year-old whose academic performance had always been mediocre despite high intelligence came into the office one day wondering about the meaning of the word "hypocrisy." He wondered if the following observation was an example of hypocrisy: His mother always gives him a lecture for an hour about poor grades. Yet, on those occasions when he brings home excellent grades, she invariably passes them off unenthusiastically and non-encouragingly with "Oh, that's nice."[29] This youth had long since concluded (albeit unconsciously prior to this insight) that what gratified his mother more than good grades was to be able to indulge her wish or need to carp and condemn him for mediocre performance.

Children exposed to such contradictions between what parents preach and practice typically conclude that the behavioral message emanating from their parent's unconscious wishes is the more important one to gratify. Thus, in an effort to gain the acceptance of a parent he perceived as critical, this youth compromised his own development (academic progress in this case).

Example 3: An eighteen-year-old reflected on why he never plays chess. As a child he had played with his father and older brother hundreds of times—and had never won a single match. He had concluded that his father did not want him to be a winner, and so, rather than complying with that unstated/surmised parental dictate, he just lost interest in playing.

Many parents, under the seemingly appropriate guise of not wanting to patronize a child by "giving" him or her the game, and further justifying this stance by considering it the best way to learn, have the effect of inhibiting their children's competitive activity. That places such adolescents at a disadvantage in American culture. For these children have concluded, accurately or not, that the parent, and by extension others, cannot tolerate losing. So, they either lose to bolster their parents, or they drop out of competing. This particular example was paradigmatic of that youth's experience growing up the youngest in a large family and the lowest in a pecking order. Although highly intelligent, he was performing marginally in high school, from which he was ultimately expelled for desultory performance.

Example 4: Twenty-year-old Will (Chapter One) illustrated how someone at the threshold of adulthood sacrificed his forward movement so
as not to seem superior to his competitive father, who was no longer
able even to walk, and from whom Will yearned for sponsorship.

These examples encompass the developmental time span from
preadolescence to young adulthood. In each—by getting into trouble,
by failing to perform academically, by withdrawing from competition,
and by dropping out of school respectively—the child compromises
his or her own developmental progress in response to parental behaviors. Again, the common mechanisms vary between:

- identifying with (imitating) maladaptive parental behaviors,
- complying with perceived parental wishes even if these differ
  from what parents say they want,
- failing as a way of either protecting a parent from feeling worse
  about him or herself, or keeping the adolescent from feeling
  superior to, or contemptuous of, the parent.

I will now consider the role that these psychodynamics involving
identification may play in the recent changes observed in adolescent
risk-taking behavior, and then in divorce and day care.

Risk-taking behavior during adolescence

Historically, before researchers tended to isolate specific symptoms for
closer study, risk taking was subsumed under the rubric of adolescent
turmoil (Bloch, 1995). It is still probably generally accepted that
adolescents take risks to test the limits of their own endurance and
their society's tolerance; in so doing, they temper remnants of infan-
tile omnipotence fantasies and enhance their sense of reality. That
explanation identifies risk taking as a normal feature of adolescent
development. It addresses both intrapsychic (the adolescent's endurance) and interpersonal (society's tolerance) dimensions of the
phenomenon. But this explanation does not adequately account for
risk-taking behavior that becomes particularly dangerous. Many
adolescents probably rarely, if ever, put themselves at serious risk.
And there have always been those relatively few who put themselves
at extreme risk. But it is my impression that more current adolescents

do so than did their counterparts two generations (i.e., 60–70 years) ago.

The developmental tasks have not changed over the millennia, and the avenues for risk taking are largely the same. Given that, can today's more frequently serious risk taking be adequately explained by environmental factors? Those factors are society's greater tolerance for behavior that can be risky, plus the availability of risk-taking opportunities that have narrower margins of safety than were common in the past. By the latter, I refer to such facts as crack cocaine being more readily addicting than beer, AIDS more dangerous than syphilis in the penicillin era, and today's economy cars less safe than the larger, heavier, slower, better-encased-in-steel autos of the 1940s and 1950s. It does seem likely that the greater dangers inherent in our more user-friendly environment for taking risks contribute to more worse outcomes. Yet, these factors do not seem sufficient to explain the failure in judgment that accompanies egregious risk taking among adolescents. This seems especially so when considering a paradoxical aspect to what was just described. That is, more dangerous risk taking is occurring in an era when more, rather than fewer, preventive factors are readily available. Perhaps the best example is the dramatically greater incidence of teenage pregnancies currently when many more contraceptive alternatives not only exist, but also are more widely accessible than was the case two generations ago.

Recent imaging studies suggest that adolescents' failure in judgment reflects neurological immaturity (*Time*, 2004), and this certainly can be a factor. Yet, not all adolescents take undue risks and the same adolescent can exhibit impressive judgment in some areas or at some times and take significant risks at others. Moreover, as the example of teen pregnancies suggests, unless the brains of adolescents two generations ago matured earlier, other factors must be involved. So, it is difficult to ascribe risk taking solely or largely to differences in timing of maturation within the pre-frontal cortex.

Few behaviors exhibited by anyone under the sun are new. So, when encountering a frightening or worrisome behavior in clinical practice, my first reaction is to wonder whether this behavior has been adopted from interaction with someone else, essentially by identification. My clinical impression is that more parents of the last couple of generations of adolescents have engaged in, and continue to engage in, risky behaviors than did parents previously. Furthermore, the

parents' "delinquencies" are often not kept hidden from their progeny. Illicit drug use is perhaps the best example. My supposition is
consistent with the National Survey on Drug Use and Health report
that illicit drug use among young teens dropped a little each year
between 2002–2005, but increased each year in the 50–59-year-old
group and in the 18–25 year age group (Freking, 2006). Thus, it follows
that more adolescents will engage in the same behavior than did their
counterparts sixty years ago—as noted above, either out of a wish to
be like their parents or defensively to retain the positive image of their
parents they want and need to maintain.

A second motive for risk taking that can become problematic
relates to efforts to secure sponsorship. It has been reported that when
parents exhibit either too little interest or too much control, or are
poor role models, their adolescents will turn to a peer group (see
Bloch & Niederhoffer, 1958). The peer group now becomes their ersatz
family, which assumes the sponsoring function in their emancipation.
Being part of the peer group requires conforming to the conduct of its
members. This amounts to being like those peers in order to feel
securely part of that group. Adolescents are eager to arrogate adult
prerogatives. So, the behaviors of a peer group that is functioning
more autonomously from parental influences often tend toward the
leading edge of experimentation. In this context, some adolescents
will overcome their own reservations about the riskiest behavior of
the boldest among them, and will imitate these most foolhardy in their
group. Their motivation is the same as that of adolescents who imitate
stupid parental behaviors—to preserve a good image of that friend, by
proving that they are no better than him or her. These adolescents are
doing the wrong thing, but for the right developmental reason—
namely, to feel sponsored. This element is probably at play not only in
the behaviors of predatory adolescent gangs, but in cliques of adolescent girls as well.

A third motive for problematic risk taking involves efforts to
surmount impediments, which individual adolescents consciously or
unconsciously sense are hindering their strivings to complete development. This mechanism usually involves turning passive into active,
and often arises when adolescents attempt to master psychic trauma.
The ten-year-old girl described above whose behavior aped that of
her incarcerated mother is a good example of turning passive into
active. This common mechanism will not be further elaborated in

discussing risk taking because it involves more idiosyncratic, case-specific features than the broader, collective tendencies represented by the other two motives (efforts to retain a positive relationship with parents, and to feel sponsored by a peer group).[30] Also, it is a prominent feature in the psychodynamics of divorce and day care utilization, which are considered in the next section.

What I have described does not adequately explain all dangerous risk-taking behavior.[31] But it illustrates how individual psychology may play an essential role in rapid societal change. It also offers a framework for organizing one's clinical thinking when faced with this type of behavior based on the premises of adolescent psychological development that I have advanced. That is, determining whether the dangerous, risky behavior represents (albeit seemingly paradoxically) the adolescent's efforts to retain a relationship with his or her parents, or to feel sponsored, or to overcome impediments experienced in their strivings to complete development.

Faced with the same developmental tasks, in the context of these developmental needs, large numbers of adolescents will exhibit similar reactions and behaviors. I am suggesting that the collective impact of these common, individual reactions is a necessary ingredient for significant changes in the character of risk-taking behavior to have occurred and persisted in the last couple of generations of adolescents. What I am proposing does not explain one basic question: What was different about the upbringing of large numbers of the parents during whose watch these changes began? I passed that question off at the outset of this discussion to those who study larger group phenomena. Rather, I have addressed how and why changed parental behaviors become integrated into the development of their children and adolescents, which then allow for the perpetuation of patterns in our society that these very same individuals had considered unhealthy.

I will now illustrate the necessary role that these same psychodynamics play in the evolution of changes that have occurred in the last couple of generations regarding divorce and day care. The influence of these factors essentially results in normalizing pathological and maladaptive attitudes and behaviors experienced during one's own upbringing and perpetrating these on the next generation. The magnitude of the numbers of children and adolescents involved in these experiences suggests a potentially very significant impact of their collective responses on society. By 1990, almost one-half of children of married parents had lived through divorce by age sixteen. The majority of American children had spent at least part of their lives in a single-parent household. More than half of the mothers of preschool and school age children held jobs outside the home, and there was not much evidence that fathers were picking up that slack in child rearing. Furthermore, only 5% of children had regular contact with a grandparent (Hamburg, 1995).

Divorce and day care

Rarely does a clinician in practice hear adolescents or adults fondly recall their parents' divorce or day care (if they can remember it) as positive experiences in their development.[32] Neither do adults raised in intact but troubled families often suggest that divorce and day care would have been preferable. Even those who think in retrospect that divorce would have been a better alternative almost always emphasize that it would have made the lives of one or both parents better, and in turn that might have improved their own lot—albeit as a secondary or a side-effect benefit. And children in day care, even those who have known no different, almost universally either voice or convey (often in blatant behavior) their preference for staying at home with a parent.

To be sure, phenomena equivalent to divorce and day care have existed from the beginning of civilized time—mates living separately, and children raised by other than their parents. Yet, in recent generations (probably receiving at least partial impetus from enactment of the first "no-fault" divorce law in 1969), those adults who decried divorce or day care during their own upbringing have grown up to endorse, even if not embrace, what they had painfully and bitterly experienced or what they have observed in the families of their friends. An interview survey by University of Chicago researchers in 1998 reported that 67% of adults over eighteen years of age did not agree that parents ought to stay married for the sake of their children (San Francisco *Chronicle*, 1999). How do such dramatic shifts come about?

As noted earlier, because these are sociological phenomena, the explanations advanced usually range across larger scale issues than those more unique to individual psychology. Contributions from several areas are cited, applicable to different, partially overlapping sub-groups of those adults who divorce and those who send their children to day care. These include:

- economic necessity: In an inflationary world it is necessary for both parents to work, predisposing to both day care and divorce;
- liberation/equality movements: Women should be able to fulfill all their personal ambitions without having to choose between options; parenthood should not really have to involve personal sacrifices which require either parent to select among options;
- the wonder of technology: The explosion of technological advances can somehow pick up the slack created by parental unavailability;
- learned behavior paradigms: Divorce and day care are natural outcomes in the lives of adults who experienced these phenomena as children and thus have never known otherwise. These are the norms for those groups.

Even adding to these factors the suggestibility of the American public to accepting "politically correct" but unrealistic interpretations of the concept of equality of opportunity, we are still left to wonder how so many people become willing to expose their own children to what they themselves either observed in peers or personally recognized (even if not in so many words) to be these avoidable impediments to child and adolescent development.

At the outset, we should ask whether I am constructing two straw men. That is, have the recollections of those who experienced divorce and/or day care as psychologically damaging exaggerated the detriment to their later lives, even if not the emotional pain at the time? The long-term follow-up research on effects of divorce remains controversial. Some researchers emphasize the resilience of these children while others document lasting detrimental effects (Duenwald, 2002; Hetherington & Kelly, 2002; Wallerstein, 1991; Wallerstein, Lewis, & Blakeslee, 2000). With respect to the outcome of day care, differentiating the relative adverse impact of day care attendance from other features within the home/family environment is difficult at best and impossible at worst (Frankel, 1990). Also, the research on day care has been almost exclusively short-term (to age 5–6 years) (Frankel, 1990). One study, which did carry the assessment through adolescence, illustrates the complexity of differentiating the effects of the variables from the side of day care (how much, how long, what type) from those of the parent's personality and attitudes (Moore, 1975). Although more recent studies have assessed attachment issues, earlier research focused on cognitive development and subsequent educational achievement. While the latter is important, it is not more relevant than the emotional and subsequent personality development of day care attendees and the potential impact of these effects on their own adult lives. For, except in cases of egregious child rearing practices, clinical experience suggests that the effects of suboptimal child rearing often insinuate themselves more silently and insidiously, and their influence does not show up until adulthood when they ominously adopt or accept maladaptive parental stances as normal and acceptable. So, those researchers who support such changing child-rearing practices as day care by showing that such children learn as well as home-reared children may have focused on issues which are less crucial for subsequent generations, and perhaps especially with respect to personality development and the capacity for mutuality in relationships.

Even with respect to the latter issues, however, studies of the relationship between maternal employment and cognitive development and behavioral problems in young children (i.e., 3–6 years of age) are mixed—some positive, others negative. Some of those disparities are accounted for by study design. At least one study in which efforts were made to control for the kind of confounding factors noted above identified reductions in cognitive test scores and increases in body weight toward obesity among ten- and eleven-year-olds from socio-economically "advantaged" households, even when the mother worked only moderate amounts of time. The same detriments were not observed in "disadvantaged" children of the same ages who were found to experience some benefits from their mothers being employed (Ruhm, 2006). In this context, it is also worth recalling that the kibbutz experiment in group child rearing failed to be sufficiently gratifying for parents and their children to endure.

Surveys of both the adult public and of adolescents/young adults suggest a continuing and, if anything, increasing preference for traditional family life. The American public considers it best that young children be raised at home by their mothers (Sylvester, 2001). A review of surveys of adolescents and young adults covering the period 1975–1995 that drew upon several polling resources found the importance of lifelong marriages and family life strongly and increasingly endorsed (Whitehead & Popenoe, 1999). Serial surveys of high school seniors (*Monitoring The Future* project at the University of Michigan) reported that in 1995, 80% felt they would marry and 78% considered a good marriage and family life "extremely important "and another 14% considered it "quite important" (Johnston, Bachman, & O'Malley, 1997). In 2005, a good marriage and family life were "extremely important" to 76% and "quite important" to 14.5%. Moreover, 87% would "definitely" or "probably" prefer to have a mate, 82% would probably marry, 83% felt it was very or fairly likely that they would stay in that marriage, and 86% felt they would be a good spouse. Also, 83% were "very" or "fairly" likely to want children, and over 83% would be a "very good" or "good" parent (Johnston, Bachman, & O'Malley, 2006). A Gallup poll of 13–17-year-olds in 1992 found that 88% thought they would marry, a figure that had remained relatively constant since 1977 (Bezilla, 1993). At the same time they evinced pessimism about achieving it. So, it is not the attitude and hopes, but, rather, the expectations that have changed. It is particularly noteworthy that late adolescents reported increasingly over that twenty-year time span that divorcing couples do not try hard enough to salvage their marriages, and that divorce laws are too lax.

My question is, what keeps these young people from living out their hopes and convictions? Is it simply that they do not comprehend the difficulties of reality? Clinical experience has long considered that late adolescents have acquired all the cognitive capacities of, and perceive the same options, as adults. But being unfettered by adult responsibilities, they can reach different conclusions from those of their parents' generation—typically more idealistic ones when discussed in this context. So this is possible. But I am not convinced that the realities of living and surviving which come with adulthood are sufficient to explain why people who, as adolescents, obviously held strong convictions about these phenomena—or at least about divorce from this data—then forsake them in their own adulthood. Something more must be at play for such changes to occur between adolescence and adulthood. I will suggest that is a commonly shared developmental response to these experiences by a significant number of adolescents. The psychodynamics of this phenomenon that allow successive generations to accept and promulgate divorce and day care are the focus of this discussion.

At issue is the tendency of adolescents, beneath their overt expressions to the contrary, to unconsciously perpetuate the need from their childhoods to make their parents' attitudes and behaviors right. Their basic motives are to maintain their own inner sense of security, which requires thinking that their parents are acting in their (children's) best interests and not antithetical to them. This sense of security, when accompanied by parental sponsorship of their growing competence, is what ultimately enables them to move forward and engage the outside world independently and complete their development.

When later, during adulthood, they repeat their parents' maladaptive behaviors with their own spouses and children, their common motive is an effort, at one and the same time, to maintain that view of their own parents, and to resolve their own traumata through passive into active repetition for mastery. The earlier, classical psychoanalytic interpretation of passive into active behavior maintained that it is motivated by a desire to re-experience neurotic gratification. But since it is difficult to uncover any gratification in such repetition, it is better understood as the individual's effort to master trauma through repeating/perpetrating actively on someone else what he or she had previously experienced passively and traumatically.[33] I believe that this commonly experienced psychodynamic is at play in adults who compromise their own children's psychological development by repeating their own parents' inappropriate choices, rather than exercising their prerogative to improve upon the latters' parenting practices. It is a necessary and perhaps sufficient condition for the perpetuation of divorce and day care as well as a myriad of maladaptive behaviors in adults.

Data from the 2005 *Monitoring The Future* report (Johnston, Bachman, & O'Malley, 2006) is consistent with that thesis for explaining this paradox, though certainly other interpretations are possible for the inconsistencies in the following examples: Seventy-six percent and 74% of females and males, respectively, agreed or mostly agreed that being a mother/father and raising children was one of the most fulfilling experiences a woman/man can have. Almost 90% considered it "extremely" or "quite" important to give their children better opportunities than they had. Seventy percent and 77% felt that mothers and fathers, respectively, should spend more time with their children than they do now. Yet, only 30% "agreed" or "mostly agreed" that it is usually better for everyone involved if the man is the achiever outside the home and the woman takes care of the home and family. In the background of these attitudes, 64% of 14,584 responding high school seniors had a mother who worked half-time or more from "most" to "all or nearly all of the time" when they were growing up, and the mothers of another 20% worked "some of the time". Only 27% "agreed" or "mostly agreed" that a preschooler is likely to suffer if the mother works; and 67% "agreed" or "mostly agreed" that a working mother can establish just as warm and secure a relationship with her children as a mother who does not work outside the home. When the father works full time and mother is at home, 58% considered it "acceptable" or "desirable" that the wife do most of the childcare for pre-school children (and 82% endorsed both doing it equally). How can we reconcile widespread beliefs that parents should spend more time with their children, but absence from the home does not compromise the maternal relationship?

How do such paradoxes escape the perpetrator's awareness and become ego syntonic? Again, it is in part the same issue of protecting one's parents. For it is my clinical impression that many of these children and adolescents of divorce and/or day care struggle against their inevitable, often unconscious, conclusion that parental self-interest has taken precedence over interest in them. Being left relatively alone, that is, in day care and after-school care when younger, and to their peers or own devices when older, children of day care and divorce begin to identify with what they experience as their own parents' self-absorption. At the same time, they feel that they must look after their own interests because they can count on no one else to do so. So, their need to make their parents' way the right way now becomes augmented by feelings of necessity. It is a short step from there to adopting/integrating an attitude that nothing or no one should get in the way of fulfilling one's own wishes and needs; this is how they concluded that their parent(s) functioned. This type of dynamic may help explain why, in 2005, only 20% of high school seniors thought most people could be trusted, 40% considered that people are just looking out for themselves, 42% thought most people try to take advantage of you, and only 20% thought people would try to be fair (Johnston, Bachman, & O'Malley, 2006). Trust begins at home. Public opinion surveys noted in the earlier-referenced Carnegie Corporation reports support this conclusion. While parents of all socioeconomic classes were found to be "troubled" about raising their children, two-thirds of them reported being less willing than their own parents to make sacrifices for their children (Hamburg, 1995).

The salient factors that now come into play involve the effects of their adaptive efforts to substitute narcissism, by which I refer to self-centeredness or self-absorption, for true reciprocity and mutuality in adult relationships. The underlying motive is to quell anxiety associated with premature separation from parents, and the lack of confidence they develop in what they can expect of others in relationships. This ultimately culminates in the nature of these children's capacities as adults to relate truly interdependently with others. Such factors, relating to the dynamic nature of personality, cannot help but influence what each generation of non-parent raised children and those whose parents cannot live together bring to their own parenting. And normalizing the pathological aspects of their own upbringing has become a powerful, societally-supported outcome of this process—that is, not expecting that compromises are possible or advisable in marriage, and that having one's children raised in day care is adequate and justifiable.

Yet, ironically, even as these shifts are occurring in our society, the importance of the integrity of the parent–adolescent relationship as guarantor of healthy adjustment in the latter has been underscored by recent research. The largest-ever survey/interview study of American adolescents (Resnick, Bearman, Blum, et al., 1997) reported that the risk of drug and alcohol use, suicide attempts, early violent behaviour, and sexual activity is significantly reduced when a strong emotional connection exists between adolescents and their parents (and teachers). This data, which bears directly on the earlier-discussed issue of risk taking in adolescence, certainly has similar ramifications for the adults these adolescents grow up to become. Notwithstanding individual variation, the average-expectable children of day care and/or divorce probably have a more conflicted emotional connection with their parents than do those raised at home in intact families.

In their efforts to adapt and feel more stable and secure, people exhibit a strong tendency to convince themselves that the manner in which they were uniquely raised is normal, even if not optimal. This is an inherent tendency, an organizing principle, associated with the need to fit into the going order as well as into one's family of origin— to be considered normal, to consider one's thoughts, feelings, and behaviors congruent with those on whom their sense of security depends.[34] I realize this sounds paradoxical because most adolescents can articulate the deficiencies of their parents and some are particularly interested in doing so. But they then repeat them, and that is what I am trying to understand. My point is that deep down where they live, they unconsciously have to make their parents' way the right way. This phenomenon is observed across the spectrum of what most would consider normal and abnormal environments. This intergenerational transmission of maladaptive behaviors is most clearly observed and thrown into sharpest relief among those raised in the most egregious circumstances. It has been epitomized in the adage that "today's abused become tomorrow's abusers". It is easy to think that this occurs simply as a learned experience: that is, the individual knows no other way of dealing with children. But abused children universally realize that it is not helpful behavior. So, it is not sufficient to attribute the perpetration of such behavior on the next generation solely to learning. I am suggesting that those identifications with the aggressor parent have the psychodynamic bases that I have elaborated.

The regressive evolution of this phenomenon shows itself in increasingly more bizarre ways in each successive generation. In this process, the first generation of modern-day children to become products of divorce viewed the experience with shame and embarrassment, guilt, and disillusionment. Some also silently railed against their parents for betraying their birthright while remaining at a loss to apprehend it other than to struggle with guilt that they were somehow to blame. As more and more divorced children see their numbers swell, while universally retaining their wish to live harmoniously in a stable family with both parents, they begin to lose not the hope for this which, as noted, truly springs eternal, but the expectation that it will occur. Their embarrassment and guilt are not less, but their anticipation of what they can expect from family life fades. Experiences in day care do nothing to offset the latter, and by the second generation or so, we find adults who have the earlier-noted strong concept of self-centeredness bred of necessity from their interpretation of their parents' behavior and attitudes toward them. They evince an internal stridency about their views which brooks little self-examination because their self-esteem is not so much low as hard but friable. And they harbor little confidence in interdependency. As a result, they have few if any qualms about the reasonableness of subordinating children's development to parental careers or jobs and other interests.

In an effort to maintain their psychological sense of well-being, to deal with the hurt and feelings of having been betrayed by their parents, they basically identify with those self-absorbed attitudes of the latter, lest they have to consider themselves expendable by their own parents. In this way, they ultimately normalize the institutions of divorce and day care. Some even trivialize family life by effectively making children of their own "afterthoughts"—the last thing they do to give themselves the illusion or form of completing their development. Their ultimate indifference, and proof positive that their future children mean little more than the acquisition of something that others have, is seen in the movement toward designer fetuses (e.g., see Withrow, 2007), by those parents who, having tarried too long at their other pursuits to be able to conceive, still want this one last evidence of their perfectibility.

My intention is not to criticize individuals caught in this spiral. Rather, it is to offer at least partial explanation for why the acknowledged importance of lasting marriages and child-rearing by parents have become shibboleths that are increasingly honored in the breach rather than in the observance. My point is that it is a natural outcome of relative economic affluence, fueled by suggestibility of people to downsides of the women's movement, which somehow convinced people that there is world enough and time, and technology guarantees that hard choices never have to be made—it is possible to do everything. Neither of which are even half-truths. As designer fetuses suggest, the outcome is taking us surprisingly close to Huxley's fantasy. So, we should not be surprised if mothers and fathers are spending more time at the gym working on their "hardbodies" than on their children's sense of emotional security and well-being. As I said, this outcome is a natural, common sense progression of the effort to adapt to an unpalatable reality by normalizing it. It might seem that my brief is with women, since they are the traditional at-home child raisers, but this is neither so nor intended. For one sees many mothers who would prefer to raise their children and who perceive the children's anxieties in their day care experiences with anguish and dismay. But they are, in fact, bullied into working outside the home by the combination of their husband's insistence, which gets a strong boost from feminine rhetoric, and by an unwillingness to live within the means of a single income.

Those reports touting the lack of negative effects of day care on children and those supporting the same conclusion about divorce are reassuring only to those who subscribe to these practices. But they must have to turn a blind eye (or deaf ear) to the facts that children and adolescents do not seem to be faring well. For rates remain significant for such widely diverse phenomena as obesity, median school performance, drug and alcohol use, incidence of psychiatric diagnoses (unless the latter are an artifact of current diagnosing trends, as discussed below), teenage pregnancy, and delinquency. In order to live with these and other realities, such as adolescent suicide (p. 43) and the astonishing rates of sexually transmitted diseases (U.S. Food and Drug Administration, 2014), and higher homicide rates among 10–24 year-olds than among all other ages combined (Centers for Disease Control & Prevention, 2013), the parental generation has to discount common sense. The latter refers to the fact that children and adolescents go through a process of development in which their parents' judicious, active participation is indispensable for healthy development in the average expectable case. The earlier-quoted study (p. 195) confirmed that the relationship between adolescents and their parents serves a primary preventive function against engaging in self-destructive and risky behaviors—behaviors that hardly augur well for their adult selves.

Ironically, recent demographic data, that are probably the result of the conditions I have been describing, may be harbingers of what strike me as very reasonable solutions to the dilemma. For, according to a *New York Times* analysis of census results in 2005, just over half of American women were living without a spouse, and for the first time households of married couples became a minority (Roberts, 2007). Many of these people living singly are parents. But such shifts will, one hopes, be accompanied by greater acceptance of the alternative of not having children unless one truly wants to raise them and has not only the motivation, but also the means to do so.[35] That is, as noted above, no sense of shame, personal inadequacy, or loss of one's sense of perfectibility will be associated with being childfree. Women will not be thrown into the type of dilemmas reported by those who try to balance careers and child-rearing, such as expressed in the following quotations: "As a working mom, you always feel like you aren't doing either job well enough—a mother or a worker. There is not enough time in the day—not enough time to spend with my kids" Yet, this forty-one-year-old mother of three would not choose to stay at home, especially at "this point in my life". "I think the later you have kids, the harder it is to not go back to work. I'm too old to deal with a two year old 24/7" (Parent, 2007). Such sentiments are not untypical. To my mind, they reflect underlying ambivalence about the role of mother compared to that of out-of-home wage earner. So, if the old adage about not being able to serve more than one master is accurate, then what would be so bad about making a choice, and not having children if a couple's heart is primarily elsewhere?

Other recent trends may reflect awareness in the populace of the undesirability of the current situation with respect to child rearing. It is not clear whether these shifts reflect parental acceptance that working mothers cannot do justice to both roles, or increasing preference of mothers to be homemakers, or exhaustion and limits to the degree that one parent can alter her or his schedule to accommodate work outside and inside the home. Significantly more working mothers now prefer part-time employment (Noveck, 2007). The four-decade acceleration in the number of women participating in the workplace began falling off in the mid-1990s. Since 2000, that trend has affected most categories of women—the most notable, unfortunate exception being single mothers whose rates have increased (Porter, 2006).

*Postscript: Pathologizing normalcy: a counterpoint to
normalizing pathology from within the field
of child and adolescent psychiatry*

I have asserted that those adults discussed must effectively disregard the importance of development as a process in their children/adolescents, and it is this discounting of developmental process that predisposes them to normalize psychopathological circumstances. At the same time, in a remarkable parallel with an opposite outcome, a significant movement within the field of child and adolescent psychiatry endorses an approach that increasingly honors the developmental perspective more in theory than practice. This, in turn, predisposes to an outcome opposite from normalizing pathology: pathologizing normalcy.

With the advent of the so-called scientific revolution in psychiatry, the developmental model has increasingly been paid lip service in favor of symptom-based criteria for making diagnoses. Under the laudable guise of dedication to this purportedly more medical/scientific/evidence-based model, any number of mental health professionals, researchers, journal editors, and practitioners alike are pathologizing many adolescents whose problems are those associated with development rather than psychiatric illness. Again, the commonalty is a basic disregard for the concept of development.

The result has been that any child or adolescent whose symptoms fulfill the American Psychiatric Association *Diagnostic and Statistical Manual* diagnostic criteria, which are based on epidemiological studies, immediately becomes a candidate for medicinal treatment. This practice completely side-steps the significance of developmental psychology and psychopathology, by virtue of taking a "one size fits all" approach to psychological development. To be sure, and to their credit, epidemiological and clinical researchers and psychopharmacologists have continued their efforts to refine diagnostic specificity and determine who will be helped by which medication. But in order for that whole approach to fly, it has been necessary to eviscerate the developmental model. This can most readily be seen in the concept of "adolescent turmoil" discussed earlier. This was long accepted as a normal, anticipated condition in which many symptomatic behaviors were understood to often reflect internal conflicts associated with trying to feel more autonomous in the process of integrating adult sexuality, aggression, enhanced cognitive functions, and one's own moral code into his or her developing personality structure.

To be sure, adolescent turmoil is not inevitable and psychopathology can be misdiagnosed as adolescent turmoil (Masterson, 1967; Offer 1969; Offer & Offer, 1975). But that concept has been supplanted by the assertion that the majority of adolescents experience mild and temporary periods of perturbation, and only psychosocially disadvantaged youth experience morbidity (Steinberg, 1990). Yet, symptoms in adolescents often can be best understood in the context of what they are trying to accomplish developmentally at the time of their appearance, and if the clinician is not thinking about a relationship between symptomatology and development, then this will not be considered, to the detriment of adolescent patient and practitioner alike.[36] The following brief example illustrates this distinction.

The mother of a sixteen-year-old high school junior called a child psychiatrist about their daughter's "violence". She was hitting both parents and occasionally her next younger sibling hard on their arms and sometimes in the face—unwilling or unable to stop when they asked, implored, or demanded that she desist. Neither could she put off discussing the matters about which she was so exercised until she had calmed down.

She had recently been evaluated by a well-trained, experienced, competent, respected child psychiatrist in the community whose orientation was toward the current symptom-based approach. At their second appointment, he diagnosed bipolar disorder and strongly recommended medication. She refused and did not want to return to see him. However, shortly thereafter, an even more aggressive outburst occurred at home. The police were called and took her to a hospital psychiatric unit. She was observed there for several hours and then sent home, despite telephone consultation with the psychiatrist who strongly urged the hospital staff to medicate her. Her parents were now seeking a second opinion.

She was an appealing adolescent who presented herself to the second child psychiatrist as an open, insightful, articulate, and self-composed individual. Her mild initial reserve seemed to respond to the psychiatrist wondering what she thought this interview would be like, his sharing what he had been told about her, and asking what she would like to talk about. She observed that the first psychiatrist seemed to have a check-list of symptoms in mind. That left her with the impression that he was trying to fit her into a diagnostic category. While not saying so in as many words, the sense she conveyed was of not having felt listened to, much less understood.

The second psychiatrist, working from a developmental model, ascertained that these behaviors were of recent onset (three months). They occurred only at home and in response to what she experienced as intolerable, helpless frustration over her parents' punishments (e.g., lengthy "groundings" that she felt were out of proportion to her infractions). She had concluded that her father was intent upon keeping her under his thumb. This was squelching her efforts to feel more independent. Equally as dismaying, she experienced the manner in which they sometimes punished her as involving baiting and switching tactics, which made them seem sadistic. Whether objectively accurate or not, this was her perception, which is where we start our assessment.

With respect to diagnostic considerations, he learned that while she had not been an angelic child, there were no significant problematic behaviors in her background or in her current life, and, as noted, all her "violence" was confined to home. She was not chronically irritable, had no current or past behaviors suggestive of problems with focusing her attention, hyperactivity, or hypomania, and never experienced racing thoughts. She was taking honors courses at school. She had a couple of long-time friends and some of more recent acquaintance. She was involved with her first boyfriend, about whom her feelings were mixed. She had insisted that he use a condom on the rare occasions when they had intercourse. She acknowledged drinking and using marijuana occasionally with friends. She was very involved in a form of dance, which required much practice, many performances, and competitions.

In reflecting on her family she shared her own ideas about why her parents acted as they did toward her. These included her perspective on her parents' internal conflicts and contention between them. The psychiatrist used her data to raise some possible explanations for her behaviors that went beyond her response to frustration. She was able to perceive the possibilities that she might be protecting her parents' relationship by drawing the fire on to herself and away from their conflicts, and thus, in a curious way, protecting them. She also could see that she might experience survivor guilt toward that one of her siblings with whom she was most contentious—musing that she had never thought of that before. That sibling had struggled with some developmental problems that this girl had never had to face.

The psychiatrist explained to her that the first psychiatrist might have had good reason for considering the diagnosis and recommendations he made. However, he himself thought her symptoms were better understood in terms of what she seemed to be trying to accomplish developmentally, and that trajectory was being compromised by the kinds of inner conflicts they had just considered. His initial impression was that she was not bipolar and not in need of medication. But he recommended that they meet weekly to be sure his clinical impression was accurate and to see if they could work to reduce her outbursts. She agreed.

He subsequently met with her parents to gather background data and share his initial impression. They emphasized, and not without some justification, the rationale of their own approach in the face of their difficulty trusting her, the degree of her outrageously obdurate and uncompromising attitudes, and out-of-control behavior. They did not observe symptoms suggesting that she was psychotic. The family histories included some depression, but only one distant relative who had been diagnosed bipolar. In other respects, they confirmed their daughter's description of the stability of her earlier and current life. They agreed to the diagnostic/therapeutic trial of weekly psychotherapy.

She did not subsequently exhibit violent outbursts toward anyone, and became more tractable with her parents. She may have bipolar disorder, but there was no compelling evidence, especially when her behaviors were considered from the developmental perspective of what she needed to and was trying to accomplish at that time. The second psychiatrist was able to help her see the sense in her misguided efforts to feel more independent, that is, doing the wrong thing for the right reason.[37]

It is likely that a serious misdiagnosis was avoided. But what is a clinician to do? How can one know which is the right way to approach diagnosis and treatment? While not infallible, there still is rarely, if ever, any substitute for careful, considered clinical judgment. I am suggesting that this should always be dominated by the developmental perspective. There are several, additional, unexpected benefits from weighing data in terms of the adolescent's psychological development: It helps off-set any tendency to get swept along with the tide of trends and fashions. The latter include not only phenomena like the "biological revolution" in the field, which can incline one toward rigidly adhering to statistical norms. It can also off-set the tendency to lose perspective in the face of movements for social equality toward which psychiatrists, as humanitarians, are sympathetic, and which can go awry. Here, the dangers include well-intentioned mental health professionals finding themselves drawn into political struggles by "embracing diversity" in such indiscriminate ways that they end up developing compulsive empathy, which amounts to pity. Such conditions more readily allow the strident to overtake the reasoned, and the unprincipled to prevail in the guise of righteousness. At that juncture, we are at increasing risk of the lunatics taking over the asylum. Clinical judgment and the developmental model help us, to paraphrase Kipling, "keep our heads when all about us are losing theirs and blaming it on us". Yet, as the last case suggests, ironically, the field that should lead the way in emphasizing the developmental approach has effectively fallen into line with, and under the sway of, adult psychiatry.

EPILOGUE

Twenty-plus years ago, it was recommended that I devote a final chapter of my earlier book to the issue of medicating adolescents. The enthusiasm engendered in those years about biological treatments has now been tempered by the relatively sobering outcomes of "evidence-based" studies, which have shown that they are not panaceas. This, in turn, has become the impetus for renewed interest in psychotherapeutic approaches (which also do not cure all). This irony merely highlights the likelihood that focus and productivity in our fields tend to swing in a pendulum-like fashion—typically a bit too far in each direction. This book might be viewed as an effort to edge the pendulum back toward the center. In fact, this is already occurring. For, currently, a more collaborative integration of biological and psychological treatments is being sought and achieved (see, for example, American Academy of Child & Adolescent Psychiatry, 2007b).

The benefits to adolescent patients of such a rapprochement go beyond treating those who do not respond to medications and enhancing domains of functioning that medicines do not affect. Perhaps the most obvious is the possibility of reducing known and as yet unidentified, long-term adverse effects of medicines on healthy development (see Leckman & King, 2007). These are often related to dose and duration of medicating. So, especially for recurrent or chronic conditions, treatments that reduce medicinal utilization are worth pursuing. This becomes particularly relevant as markedly greater numbers of children and adolescents are given serious diagnoses and placed on all types of psychiatric medicines and often on several concurrently. With respect to the former consideration, a *New York Times* series on these subjects in 2006 quoted government survey findings that six million American children have been diagnosed with serious mental disorders—a figure that has tripled since the early 1990s (Carey, 2006). The number of American children prescribed antipsychotic medications, almost half of which were for non-psychotic conditions, increased from an estimated 8.6 per 1,000 children in the mid-1990s to nearly forty in 2002, with little research evidence to support this use (Cooper, Arbogast, Ding, et al., 2006). An analysis of polypharmacy reported that in 2005, 1.6 million children and teens (mostly the latter) were prescribed two psychiatric medications concomitantly, a half million were receiving three, and 160,000 were given four together (Harris, 2006). Yet, evidence to support this practice (polypharmacy) is in short supply.

It has been suggested that the news media tends to report published studies of medication utilization in children with a negative bias (Grinfeld, 2006). Yet, in the face of such figures, it is not difficult to see why alarm is being registered in public and professional forums about these potential dangers to the future physical and mental health of children and adolescents (see Carlat, 2006). So, it is difficult to simply dismiss such concerns of the public as inadequately informed opinions. This is the more so because our mission is better served if the public perceives professionals' efforts as helping rather than harming the nation's youth. The current specter of conflicts of interest between pharmaceutical companies and psychiatrists who either receive grants to research their medications or to serve as experts/speakers in presenting these drugs to rank and file practitioners does little to allay that skepticism (e.g., Harris, Carey, & Roberts, 2007).

It is not clear, though, whether more current-day adolescents are developing psychiatric conditions, or whether clinicians have become more astute diagnosticians, or whether these increases are artifacts of modified diagnostic criteria. The latter has perhaps occurred with respect to attention-deficit/hyperactivity disorder (Carey, 2006;

Polanczyk, Silva de Lima, Horta, et al., 2007). And it certainly has with respect to bipolar disorder (American Academy of Child & Adolescent Psychiatry, 2007a; Ghaemi & Martin, 2007). For example, a Yale University study based on insurance claim data found that the rates of the latter diagnosis doubled among 7–12-year-old boys between 1995 and 2000 (cited in Carey, 2006). Yet, this dramatically greater incidence of pediatric bipolar disorder appears to be relatively unique to the United States, suggesting that the issue involves changes in the diagnostic criteria rather than in the prevalence of the condition (McClellan, 2005). The second possibility (improved diagnostic acuity) is probably always debatable. But, if the first (more prevalent psychiatric disturbance) is operative, then data presented here favor reconsidering solutions that many parents and mental health practitioners alike may be reluctant to hear, much less to heed. For with many demands being placed on busy practitioners and harried parents alike, the possibility that a pill or pills will reduce problematic behaviors becomes appealing. Hence, it is not surprising that people on both sides of that professional divide endorse, even if not embrace, such solutions.

Using serious diagnoses so that insurers will pay for medication and services follows and complicates matters.[38] For, by contributing to the current problem of too many children diagnosed with too many significant mental disorders and treated with too many medications, "evidence-based" psychiatry may be unwittingly colluding with the abandonment of parenting. For any increase in the prevalence of behavioral problems exhibited by American youth today may be more accurately laid at the doorstep of environmental neglect than attributable to changes in genes during our lifetimes. In a cell phone poll of 600 16–22-year-old California residents, conducted during the autumn of 2006, family breakdown topped the list (24%) as the most pressing issue facing their generation from among several choices offered of social, environmental, global, and other issues (New America Media, 2007). This suggests that today's adolescents are aware that something significant is missing from current family life, the crucible of every individual's development.

The solution is deceptively simple. It is supported by the survey data reported in Chapter Five (p. 195). It is basically akin to the old adage that there are no shortcuts to learning. Essentially, no feasible substitutes have yet been found for dedicated, full-time, appropriate parenting as the best antidote to developmentally crippling behaviors in adolescents. With the possible exception of certain aspects of cognition, in the average expectable child all aspects of psychological development—certainly object relatedness, modulation of impulse and expression of emotion, and self-esteem regulation—are significantly influenced by the relationship between parents or their surrogates and children/adolescents.

The rediscovery of the importance of parenting was epitomized in one article of that *New York Times* series on psychiatric disturbance in the current generation of children, entitled "Parenting as treatment for mental illness" (Carey, 2006). It described programs successfully helping parents in their interactions with their offspring. Other programs, in addition to those noted earlier, have proven effective as preventive interventions with parents whose pre-school children were determined to be at risk of developing conduct disorder (e.g., Hutchings, Bywater, Daley, et al., 2007).

The irony in this rediscovery resides in the fact that the field of child psychiatry began and grew up as the child guidance movement—outpatient treatment of children and adolescents, which included regular parental guidance.[39] The earliest of these clinics were developed to serve the delinquent, behaviorally disordered spectrum of which we now also see large numbers. (The further ironies include the fact that many parents are receptive to such help, but as noted, less attention is paid to this compared to medicinal intervention. Organized child and adolescent psychiatry in this country ceded that half of its birthright to psychology during the recent "scientific revolution".)

The equivalent lesson for mental health professionals is that no viable substitutes have yet been found for labor-intensive evaluations and long-term therapy for some adolescents (Fonagy & Target, 1994; Target & Fonagy, 1994a,b). But since time and intensity of involvement are not sufficient of themselves in many cases, we might briefly revisit the two complementary elements of psychodynamic therapy with adolescents. One encompasses long-recognized features of the therapeutic relationship about which our understanding continues to evolve. The other involves identifying and helping the adolescent to face and understand the emergence of their symptoms in a way that facilitates both their reversal and resumption of normal maturation. The developmental perspective forms the basis for this approach. Central to this model are ideas that psychological development evolves through the interaction of internal and external factors, and that earlier life experiences profoundly affect later adaptation. A corollary of the latter is that psychic trauma can wreck havoc on the process and outcome of psychological development. Individual practitioners and schools of thought may emphasize different specifics, such as how symptoms become manifest (e.g., faulty learning *vs.* resolution of conflict). But these underlying precepts are still subscribed to by most therapists who treat children and adolescents.

The two basic components of psychodynamic psychotherapy

The therapeutic relationship

The protective effects of congenial relationships in maintaining psychological as well as physical health are by now so well-known as to be taken for granted, from studies ranging from physical ailments through depression and suicide to longevity and even cognitive decline associated with Alzheimer's disease (DeVogli, Chandola, & Marmot, 2007; Wilson, Krueger, Arnold, et al., 2007). Basic psychological aspects of relationships are thought to be shared by most successful psychotherapeutic approaches. As noted, these are also thought to account for the placebo effects observed in medication studies. At base, the interest communicated by the researchers' attention to the patients' symptoms is experienced as caring about their welfare. But what is "caring" and how does the therapist communicate this to adolescent patients?

I have belabored the unique difficulty encountered in establishing a therapeutic relationship with adolescents, owing to their developmental imperative to emancipate (Part I). The challenge is to convey what is basically an adult-type interest in their welfare without it becoming experienced as parental in most cases. This task is further complicated by my impression that feeling rejected (by reason of the parental practices discussed in Chapter Five) figures importantly in the symptomatology of many current-day adolescent patients. The therapist must somehow offset that expectation of rejection without being experienced as parental, controlling, or seductive. This is attempted by communicating respectful, non-proprietary interest in the adolescent's welfare. By non-proprietary interest, I refer to conveying a sense of wanting the adolescent to achieve his or her own reasonable goals. Additional aspects of the approach that I find facilitate a therapeutic relationship include identifying and communicating appreciation of the adolescent's personal assets in facing his or her struggles, and ego support in the form of a non-critical and generally optimistic though candid attitude conveyed in a friendly, encouraging, non-worrying manner. Avoiding being drawn into transference reenactments is also important in fostering a therapeutic relationship.

If all one does is communicate these attitudes to any adolescent who is not overwhelmingly opposed to meeting with the therapist, then the patient will have a corrective ego experience, even if all other hoped-for therapeutic goals are not achieved. By corrective ego experience, I mean that the therapist's approach will help offset aspects of the parental relationships that have contributed to the development of maladaptive behaviors. Not infrequently some or many symptoms will moderate, and that treatment will ultimately be recalled by the patient as positive.

Clinical paradigms for understanding specific symptomatic behaviors

The therapeutic relationship helps create optimal conditions in which the adolescent patient's ego can function in treatment. It is a necessary condition for effective therapy, but, as just noted, often not sufficient to reverse all symptoms and allow the resumption of progressive development. Depending on the individual case, the additional ingredient involves variously integrating insight (i.e., offering knowledge as the power to become more self-directed and to progress developmentally), reinforcing the patient's adaptive behaviors, and/or more experientially, passing the patient's "tests" in the often unacknowledged transference.

The insight-oriented dimension of the therapy often begins by identifying clinical paradigms relevant to the individual patient. I use "paradigm" as a catch phrase for working formulations that relate the adolescent's maladaptive attitudes, behaviors, interpersonal relationships, or symptoms to their earlier-life bases in internal conflicts. These conflicts arose from efforts to reconcile either prototypic or more unique developmental issues. (That distinction between prototypic and unique will be illustrated in the case example that follows.)

Referring to these as paradigms rather than simply insights that relate the psychogenetic to the psychodynamic metapsychological points of view (which they are) is intended to facilitate recognition of them as integrated patterns. Although thinking in terms of paradigms risks oversimplifying complex issues, I have found it a helpful approach for keeping the big picture in mind when sorting out complicated clinical material. Often paradigms are identified by thinking concretely or symbolically about the essence of the patient's behavior as it might relate to prototypic developmental issues in light of what the therapist knows about the parents' interactions with their adolescent. The following example is intended to clarify my use of the term "paradigm".

A highly intelligent college freshman was attending class sporadically and putting himself in academic jeopardy by not turning in (often completed) papers. He considered himself homosexual, having had a few one-night stands arranged in the most impersonal of ways, but he never had experienced an on-going relationship or even much in the way of friendships. In these and his other dealings he remained preoccupied with social status and its accoutrement, and ever fearful of being found lacking in social standing by men who appealed to him. Despite being physically and intellectually attractive to women and interested in them, he was reluctant to approach co-eds for fear of being ridiculed. Yet, he claimed to live in constant fear of loneliness.

He was the only child of a mother who was given to putting on airs and who felt she had married beneath her status. Yet, while maintaining a subtle hauteur toward her husband, she herself had never capitalized upon her own significant credentials to contribute to the betterment of herself, her family, or her community. Her subtly patronized husband, the boy's father, was a diligent professional whose academic background had held out the promise of greater things than his career as a small town newspaper editor. Whether of his own preference or out of deference to his wife's commandeering the relationship with their child, he had remained somewhat distant from their son, who tended to look down upon his father as weak while looking up to his mother as being of high class. His father had been disinclined to intervene either in his wife's monopolizing of their son, or her indulgence of the boy's excuses to avoid attending school because it was too easy (which it may have been). But the latter had contributed to this adolescent developing a persisting pattern of forsaking personal responsibility and, in the process, failing to demonstrate and reap the full benefits of his abilities (e.g., not being accepted at prestigious colleges). At the same time, he marginalized himself socially. He considered his parents very incompatible (Mann, 2005).

In trying to sort through such material, what paradigms might help us understand his academic difficulties, his apparent uncertainty about sexual orientation, and his interpersonal relations? Different paradigms are not necessarily mutually exclusive, and may complement each other. But those that strike a more respondent chord in the patient will be where our exploration begins. From even this briefest of case histories, you may be able to identify more paradigms than the following three, which illustrate the phenomenon. At this early point in his treatment, is the most relevant paradigm one stemming from:

1. The child's need to feel secure in his relationship with parents? He grew up persuaded that his parents could not live together congenially, or proudly share a relationship with him. So, did he sense that the only way to achieve the basic need to feel secure was to cleave to one parent at whatever personal cost this entailed? Then, did the price of securing that relationship with his mother include complying with her attitudes (including rejecting his father), and adopting her maladaptive practices (defensive identifications), such as rationalizing irresponsibility with a supercilious attitude of superiority?

2. The wish for a close relationship with his father that could help him deal with his mother's over-involved possessiveness? Feeling rejected by his father's lack of involvement, the patient responded by overtly rejecting him in turn (compensation), and succumbing to his mother's influence (compliance). Thus, in his homosexual behavior, is he seeking to resolve his developmental need for approval, admiration, love, and help from a man, while at the same time dealing with feelings of rejection?

3. The adolescent issue of needing to feel more psychologically autonomous? His fear of being ridiculed kept him from relating to young women. Did that expectation stem from efforts to deal with his (accurate or inaccurate) conclusion that his mother was possessive (i.e., did not want him involved with other women), or that ridicule could be expected if he did not comply with her

wishes, and thus, by extension, those of all women? That is, was submission the price of relationships with women, and autonomy was not possible? (Clearly, that expectation of ridicule could represent something different from what I have hypothesized.) Then, during adolescence, he was thrown into a conundrum with respect to object relationships with both men and women. Fearing rejection by males and ridicule by females, he dared not involve himself meaningfully with either sex. That relegated him to what he claimed to fear most, namely loneliness. Or, was that ostensible dread defensive (i.e., a reversal), adopted to avoid awareness that he sought greater psychological independence, but unconsciously he did not feel he had permission to pursue this. In each of these latter alternative scenarios, the paradigm involved vicissitudes of achieving psychological autonomy from the influence of parent(s). The connectors between the outward behaviors and underlying, unresolved issue were, variously, compliance/submission and sacrifice (if responding to his mother's possessiveness), and reversal (if fear of loneliness was defensive).

I have used this example to clarify "paradigms" as brief, case-specific psychodynamic formulations that link earlier-life conflicts with adolescents' symptoms. Many paradigms can be seen to develop when the child encounters difficulty negotiating those two prototypic developmental issues that have been emphasized in this book: The earlier life one is the child's highest priority being to gratify his or her parents in an effort to secure a sense of safety (Chapter Five). Whether this issue is drawn into conflict turns on the child's interpretation of parental behaviors and interactions in the face of his or her needs from the parents. The first paradigm in the above case reflects this matter. The other prototypic developmental issue is the adolescent iteration of that earlier one, in which the youth must achieve a greater felt sense of psychological autonomy from the influence of his or her parents while retaining a basically positive, underlying relationship. The third paradigm in the example illustrates this. While related to the first paradigm, the second one (need for the love and help of the father) is less generic than the other two, and an example of a more specifically case-unique paradigm.

Since there are a finite number of ways to react to a limited number of developmental issues, the responses of many adolescents will differ in the particulars but not in their essence. Depending upon the individual's unique experiences growing up in his or her family, different facets of the same issue may be more evident than others. For example, when the issue of emancipation becomes problematic, some adolescents may be more aware of a concern that their parents will be hurt by their independence. For others, the idea that their parents need to be taken care of is more apparent. Some are more plagued by the idea that personal achievement can only occur at the expense of other family members. Still others may be convinced that feeling emotionally stronger than a parent is not acceptable or is out of the natural order of things. Another response is the adolescent feeling that he or she owes their parent(s) his or her life. A common attitude is that self-assertion in one's own behalf constitutes defiance of parents (Bloch, 1995). The specific symptomatic manifestations in any individual adolescent will reflect which of these or other ideas he or she harbors. The connectors between the adolescent's symptoms and the underlying operative issue in conflict include, but are not limited to, such mechanisms as compliance, defensive identifications, self-sacrifice, reversals, elements of the omnipotence complex, and displacement.

The treatment is then accomplished in several ways. One is through insight—identifying paradigms, clarifying how and why they may have arisen, sharing and bearing together the emotional dysphoria associated with having lived with their irrational aspects, and working them through by discovering their pervasiveness in the adolescent's life. In others, responding appropriately to paradigms enacted by the adolescent patient (i.e., tests of the therapist) is more helpful. A third feature involves reinforcing adolescent patients' accurate perceptions and sound judgment, and helping them perceive their adaptive efforts to cure themselves, that is, the sense rather than the non-sense in their behaviors. The degree to which adolescents respond to one or the other approach varies among individual patients. This is particularly the case with respect to consolidating the experience in the transference. Since adolescents tend to avoid direct consideration of the transference, often the treatment is accomplished by analyzing their conflicts with respect to their important relationships, and more silently "passing" (i.e., responding therapeutically to) their direct and reverse (passive-into-active) transference tests (Weiss, 1993). Some of the latter is achieved by simply maintaining the posture described above in establishing a therapeutic relationship.

Psychodynamic psychotherapy in the present era of treatment

Advocating psychodynamic psychotherapy might strike some as anachronistic or atavistic at best, and cavalier at worst. For escalating demands for services call for developing ever-more time-efficient means of treating an ever-increasing number of patients. Psychodynamic psychotherapy is not invariably lengthy, but tends to be more labor intensive, and thus expensive, compared to medicating (unless one does not have health insurance, and even then it can be pricey). Still, for some adolescents feasible alternatives may not yet exist. The saving grace is that adolescents will not abuse that privilege; they will not remain in therapy longer than necessary.

The other reservations about psychodynamic psychotherapy run the full gamut from learning it, through the intellectual integrity of the discipline, to demonstrating its efficacy. Regarding the first, if my own experience is any indication, the learning curve to proficiency is slow, albeit interesting and gratifying. Moreover, the enduring influence of its progenitor, Freudian psychoanalysis, highlights the best (expertise of those master craftsmen/women who are good teachers) and the worst (rigidity, authoritarianism, dogmatism) aspects of a guild-like system. The latter (down side) is compounded by the fact that case supervision is still probably the best method for learning psychodynamic psychotherapy. So, during that most suggestive time of their professional development, when they have least understanding of the field and of themselves, students must maintain a high level of intellectual self-discipline and judgment. This is necessary to avoid falling prey to rigid dicta of mentors and psychoanalytic and psychotherapeutic training programs, while, conversely, avoiding the shoals of undisciplined polymorphism. In recent years, strides have been made within the field to moderate these influences.

The second reservation regarding the intellectual integrity of the field is related to the latter issue of teaching/learning the discipline. Some of the most widely known and sacrosanct shibboleths of classical psychoanalysis upon which therapy was based may well have been more relevant to patients at the time when they were developed. But they have not proven to be as clinically useful or accurate paradigms in our era. The best example is the paradigm of the primacy of the Oedipus complex in development and in neurotic symptom formation. Fortunately, sufficient conceptual modifications have been introduced by many psychodynamic therapists, so this problem no longer justifies dismissing psychodynamic therapy out of hand.[40]

Last, with respect to demonstrating its effectiveness, until recently the results of long treatments have been available primarily in anecdotal form, like the cases presented here. Moreover, the unique impact of the therapist's style and manner may always make comparisons of treatments and gathering statistical data on outcomes and technique difficult. Yet, as noted in the Prologue, significant advances are being made and efficacy has been demonstrated by current-day "evidence-based" standards. Thus, this approach now has a greater claim to legitimacy in the current era's standards for treatment. So, if there ever were, there now seems no rationale for throwing the baby of psychodynamic therapy out with the lack-of-evidence-based bath water.

Final words

In this book, I have tried to accomplish three things: The first was to illustrate the applicability and specifics of a psychodynamic approach to severe pathology when medication is not effective, when therapy is the only treatment option acceptable to the adolescent, or when resumption of progressive development does not accompany symptom reduction. The second was to re-emphasize the profundity of the environment's influence on the developing child and adolescent by describing two cases of outliers from more typical development. This is intended to counterbalance rather than discount the current emphasis in our fields on the role of genetic, biological influences; I think the latter have been disproportionately emphasized during psychiatry's scientific revolution. The third was to extend the relevance of individual development to sociological phenomena.

Taken together, and extrapolating from these conclusions about development to the treatment setting, a credible case can be made for the value of psychotherapeutic approaches to undo the effects of psychological, developmental traumata, to move development in the normal or conventional direction, and help the current generation to not visit the proverbial "sins of one's fathers (and mothers)" on their own issue. These are some things that medication alone may never be able to do.

The latter allows me to close with another point–counterpoint. This one relates to Freud's observation (1915 1916, p. 199) that ontogeny recapitulates phylogeny. He was suggesting that the history of the race can be traced in the development of the individual. If my conclusion is accurate, that children's and adolescents' need to legitimize their parents' maladaptive behaviors toward them leads to perpetuating these practices in the next generation, then phylogeny also recapitulates ontogeny—and not always in a developmentally positive manner. But if so, we are fortunate to have the power within ourselves to reverse such unintended consequences of our ways.

NOTES

1. For example, this and other factors conspired to move psychotherapy from the center to the periphery of psychiatric residency training. Other contributing factors included the addition of significantly more ACGME (Accreditation Council for Graduate Medical Education) required areas of instruction and competencies to the training curricula, which have severely curtailed supervised training in psychotherapy. Then, upon entering practice following completion of residency, the combined demands to see large numbers of child and adolescent patients, many of whom are seriously disturbed, and the economic incentives provided by the health care insurers' pattern of reimbursement rates are predisposed to the currently prevalent treatment model, which splits therapy and medication management (Kaye, 2007).

2. It has been suggested that this part of the title might equally well refer to that one-third or more of symptoms and domains of functioning (e.g., development of adaptive skills) that are not influenced long-term by medications, yet are important for achieving an optimal therapeutic outcome for child and adolescent patients (Kaye, 2007).

3. A report to Congress, issued by the Center for Mental Health Services of the Substance Abuse and Mental Health Services Administration (SAMHSA) on November 7, 2007, emphasized the preeminent importance of parental involvement in programs developed to prevent future psychiatric problems in at-risk children (Daly, 2007).

4. Parenthetically, recently similar conclusions have been reported about publication bias leading to overestimation of the efficacy of cognitive–behavioral therapy and other psychological treatments for adult depression (Cuijpers, Smit, Bohl-Meijer, et al., 2010).

5. Determining a specific percentage accurately might not be possible, even with the benefit of meta-analyses. This figure is an estimate (probably conservative) derived from reviewing representative pharmacological studies of adolescents and adults, some of which are listed in the Appendix to this chapter.

6. Separation guilt is that experienced by those who feel that their wishes to have more than their fair share (i.e., greed) will destroy others who are important to them. So, they do not deserve or cannot have an independent life (Modell, 1965). Survivor guilt, the other pole of the continuum, a term adopted from the experience of survivors of the Second World War concentration camps whose family members had perished, has been expanded. It includes those who have prevailed or surpassed or found themselves at some advantage over a close family member with respect to whom they harbored no wish to have gained such an advantage. Yet, they fear that that their success has occurred at the expense of the other (Modell, 1971). The guilt can be either conscious or unconscious.

7. Specifically, recent statistics indicate that one-third of teenage ideators attempt suicide, perhaps 40% of suiciders have made a prior attempt, and among attempters, one in 400 teenage boys and in 4,000 teenage girls complete suicide (Centers for Disease Control and Prevention, 2000; National Center for Health Statistics 2001, cited in Shaffer & Greenberg, 2002).

8. It is important to realise that the rate of false positives in studies of adults is extremely high for the marker of hopelessness (Beck, Steer, Kovacs, et al., 1985).

9. Parenthetically, the same holds true for all but the most basic published conclusions about adolescent suicide (e.g., age and sex differences).

10. The symptom-based diagnoses, beginning with *DSM-III*, provided an antidote to the difficulties in documenting the psychodynamic constellations, which formed the basis of earlier nomenclatures. But that Scylla of subjective judgments about underlying psychodynamics was ultimately replaced by the Charybdis of excessive symptom overlap among diagnoses. The latter, as exemplified by these varied symptom constellations for juvenile mania, presents a current challenge. It is not clear whether greatly widening the range of symptoms now grouped as bipolar disorder amounts to re-aligning ourselves with earlier views of the illness or whether bipolar disorder is becoming a wastebasket diagnosis to

accommodate a technological lag between our nomenclature and an evolution of symptomatic manifestations of psychological malfunctioning. To wit, we now rarely see hysterical symptoms (e.g., paralyses, astasia/abasia) common in the time of Charcot and Freud. Instead, we observe more behavioral symptoms of excess than those of inhibition. Perhaps this is at least in part a reflection of loosened societal strictures against expression of emotion and impulse. However, it remains to be seen whether this presages a revision in the way we understand psychopathology and, thus, a new nomenclature, or whether these changes in symptom patterns will be accommodated by this widening of the margins of this current diagnostic category.

Efforts to address this problem are beginning to take form in considering the relationship of symptom complexes to the three domains in which psychiatric symptoms are expressed—behavior, cognition, and emotions. An example is the relationship of bipolar symptomatology to impulse disorders (McElroy, 2000). Another example is the recently reintroduced thesis with respect to the adult disorder that it is not an entity distinct from Unipolar Depression/Major Depressive Disorder (as was considered in both the last American Psychiatric Association *Diagnostic and Statistical Manual IV-R* and the recently adopted *DSM-5*), but rather it exists on a continuum with dysthymia, unipolar depression, and schizoaffective disorder (Ghaemi, 2006; Ghaemi, Ko, & Goodwin, 2002). A third example involves singling out symptoms, like impulsive aggression, that cut across diagnostic categories for independent study and consideration of (at least medicinal) treatment (Jensen, Youngstrom, Steiner, et al., 2007).

11. This phenomenon of contagion of feelings among friends is common among people of all ages, but most notable among groups of adolescents. It is often a feature of their efforts to establish emotionally closer relationships with peers as part of the process of emancipating from the childhood psychological attachment to parents. Thus, it may embody developmental significance for this group in a way that such empathy does not for adults and children.

12. Similar defense mechanisms have been reported in older adolescent bulimics (Heatherton & Baumeister, 1991) and in dieters (Polivy & Herman, 1999).

13. The latter observations are consistent with studies that have determined that the response to sexual abuse varies greatly among children and adolescents, ranging from severe persistent symptoms to no identifiable maladaptive effects. No specific syndrome or single traumatizing process has been identified. Symptoms depend on such factors as age, severity, duration, and forced nature of the abuse, relationship to the perpetrator,

and maternal support of the abused child. The latter protective factor, which favors recovery from symptoms, has also been described with respect to bulimia (van Furth, van Strien, Martina, et al., 1996). Sexually abused youngsters are as likely to develop internalizing as externalizing reactions, with symptoms related to the former usually resolving more readily than those associated with the latter (Conte & Schuerman, 1987, Kendall-Tackett, Meyer Williams, & Finkelhof, 1993).

14. Interestingly, a review of studies suggests a similar conclusion might be drawn with respect to psychotherapy for depression in adolescents (Mufson & Velting 2002).

15. That statement deplored discrimination against homosexuals, stating that "homosexuality per se implies no impairment in judgment, stability, reliability, or general social or vocational capabilities . . ." (Position Statement, 1974).

16. In one study, approximately one-half of homosexual women recalled heterosexual attachments, usually in early adolescence, and one-third reported heterosexual fantasies. Both phenomena evaporated by the end of adolescence (again raising the possibility that this may be an optimal time for therapeutic intervention) (Saghir & Robins, 1980).

17. In truth, an alternative or additional possible explanation is that her positive recollection reflected the degree to which children wish to forgive and consider parents'/parental-type figures' actions right, for reasons discussed in Chapter Five.

18. For example, a thirty-seven-year-old heterosexual bachelor had grown up in somewhat similar circumstances that also led to an overriding need to find a secure love object. However, his sexuality was influenced in a different manner from that of Rachel: He had been displaced at age ten months from the center of his mother's attention by the birth of his sister (who became a lesbian from late adolescence). His recollections from childhood that continued in his adult life were that his mother did not have time for or interest in him, and that she reacted to his expressed needs either with anger and criticism of him or with behavior communicating that she felt overwhelmed. He lived with a chronic desire to return to a blissful state of maternal nurturance, which was more likely a wished-for fantasy than an earlier life reality. Also, he lived with the chronic expectation that he would always be shunted aside in favor of the needs of his sibling or their mother. His father had not been around since shortly after his sister's birth.

From mid-latency, he recalled a several-year period of secretly wearing different articles of his mother's or sister's clothing, that is, an identification with his sister or mother as a substitute for the needed object relationship. This faded away after puberty. As an adult he wanted to marry and procreate, but was plagued by fears that he could not feel accepted by his partner or assured that she would be as devoted to his needs as to her own (i.e., maternal transference). And he feared that, in spite of himself, he would become jealous of his wife's attention to children they might have.

Whenever he did feel accepted by a woman, and thus could consider a relationship that was more than sexually based, he became preoccupied with how to secure the closeness, warmth, and succor he sought. He would find himself fantasizing about changing sexes or becoming homosexual like his sister. He would also become preoccupied with sexually amalagamated cartoon characters or fantasies involving images of women with penises and men with breasts (i.e., figures representing the possibility of being or having both partners in one). His sexual orientation, interests, and practices were exclusively heterosexual, though incorporated anal as well as vaginal intercourse.

Unlike Rachel, whose overriding need to secure a love object also stemmed from having felt profoundly rejected by both parents and disfavored compared to a sibling, this man's response influenced his sexual fantasies, but not his sexual orientation/identification.

19. Or, as the reviewer of a volume on homosexuality and psychoanalysis framed it:

> Because psychoanalytic knowledge about the homosexualities has long been clouded by political forces and prejudice, open-minded psychoanalytic clinicians should be eager for new insights on this topic. Decades of psychoanalytic theorizing misappropriated moralistic anti-sexual attitudes, allowing prejudice and coercion. More recently, oppositional forces of political correctness and an exclusive focus on the pathogenicity of homophobic attitudes have contributed to a similar constriction of scientific investigation. (Schuker, 2001 p. 1462)

20. The sampling bias in their study of males that had the most distorting effect on their incidence figures was the overrepresentation of males who had been incarcerated, a group with a significantly higher incidence of homosexual activity (Gebhard, 1972). It was subsequently estimated that perhaps more than 60% of the male subjects were either sex offenders, incarcerated criminals, pimps or other criminals, male prostitutes, a few pederasts, and individuals recruited from homosexual activist groups (Reisman, 2000, see also Pomeroy, 1972, p. 208). That error was corrected for in their study of females (Kinsey, Pomeroy, Martin, et al., 1953) by

eliminating women with prison experience (Gebhard, 1972). The greater confounding factors in the sample of the latter study included being exclusively white (which was also true of the male study), the educational level being slanted significantly toward the more educated (in whom higher incidences of homosexual behavior are reported in women but not in men), underrepresented age groups (those under sixteen and over fifty), geographic distribution (concentration in northeast, north mid-central states, and California), and perhaps the religiously devout, which were also drawbacks in the study of males.

21. The latter criticism has persisted despite Freud's observation that psychoneuroses are the negative of perversions, that is, differentiated only by whether perverse sexual fantasies are acted upon or repressed and give rise to neurotic symptoms (Freud, 1905e, p. 50).

22. A Time.com survey in 2000, however, suggests this is not the case.

23. Isay (1989) maintains that homosexuality in males is constitutionally based, established in early childhood, and that efforts to work psychiatrically with that issue during adolescence are harmful. Over and above the fact that he is talking only about males and perhaps about a sub-set of male homosexuals at that, the question remains whether his model applies to all youth whose sexuality deviates from the norm or who express confusion about their sexual orientation. Representing an opposite view, Socarides (1989), in line with Freud's idea (1905d, footnote added in 1915, p. 146) that the final sexual orientation is not determined until after puberty, identifies this as the "pivotal time" to undertake treatment of homosexuality.

24. Again, it is important to distinguish between individuals who identify themselves as exclusively homosexual from those who experiment or dabble in homosexual involvements during late adolescence and young adulthood, but who, like Rachel's college friends, anticipated marrying men and living heterosexual lives (which they evidently did).

25. Interestingly, Kinsey and colleagues (1953, p. 457) had described this phenomenon.

26. Marmor (1980, p. 274) makes a similar point.

27. Considering the broader picture of the importance of the circumstances in which children and adolescents develop, a recent sociological study is instructive, even allowing for the individuality of every case. A large, randomly selected cohort (correcting for the small size and convenience sample problems of prior studies and current reports) compared young adults (ages 18–39) raised in several different family circumstances (lesbian and gay parent(s), biological (heterosexual) parents who remained married, those later divorced, step-families, adoptive parents, single

parents, others). Those who had been raised in most alternative circumstances, and particularly those raised by a lesbian parent, reported significantly greater incidences of difficulties in a number of the forty social, emotional, and relational outcome variables assessed, when compared to those raised by biological parents who remained married (Regnerus, 2012).

28. An intuitive awareness of this enables parents to continue to exhibit forbearance in the face of rude, insolent attitudes and disobedient, insubordinate behavior on the part of their adolescent sons and daughters.

29. You will recall that Sydney observed a variant of this dynamic with her mother (Chapter Two).

30. See Bloch 1995, pp. 182–183 for additional case-specific examples of this third motive.

31. For example, a recent study, albeit with certain methodological limitations, correlated severity of risk-taking behaviors among Israeli adolescents with levels of exposure to, and relatively continuous threats of, terrorist attacks and with the existence of PTSD symptoms (Pat-Horenczyk, Peled, Miron, et al., 2007). These findings probably reflect the adolescents' efforts to master trauma by turning passive into active, which may represent a different basic motive (curing pathology) than that of much normative adolescent risk-taking behavior (advancing development). Of the three mechanisms I posited, this would be closest to the third.

32. I am not referring to the relatively few children whose physical or psychological safety is enhanced by removal from brutalizing household environments. Rather, I am referring to the vast majority of divorced children who can voice their strong preference for being raised in an intact home with two parents sufficiently devoted to them and each other to provide a basically harmonious, secure family life.

33. This is a common transference paradigm in psychoanalysis and psychodynamic psychotherapy. The patient's underlying, unconscious hope is that the psychoanalyst or psychotherapist will not respond as he or she had when exposed to similar circumstances. For if they do not, the perpetrator can identify with the other's less traumatized reaction, and this contributes to reversing the effects of his or her own trauma (Weiss, 1993). If the same inference can be drawn about the perpetrator's motive in everyday life, then the spouse and/or child become unwitting therapists to the other spouse/parent. There are many examples in which the spouse or children react in more neutral, "therapeutic" ways, and the perpetrator is afforded a corrective ego experience and improves his or her behavior. The reasons why this does not occur more frequently include the readiness with which children accept their parents' views and

the fact that choices of mates are often made on the basis of familiarity. That is, by virtue of being a more known entity, people will select spouses with whom there is therefore a greater likelihood of repeating their childhood experiences than with others who, in fact, may hold out greater promise of not doing so.

34. A vicissitude of this phenomenon in a different context (i.e., sexual orientation) was discussed in Chapter Three.

35. That said, and although the trends in industrialized nations are toward lower rates of childbirth in general (Samuelson, 2006), that has not been so in the USA. Moreover, in 2005, according to the Centers for Disease Control, almost four in ten babies in this country were born out of wedlock. Although most were among low-income women in their twenties, the rates had increased among 30–44-year-olds as well as 25–29-year-olds (Rosenberg & Wingert, 2006). So, the hopeful trend I am suggesting has not yet materialized.

36. A more comprehensive discussion of adolescent turmoil can be found in Bloch (1995, p. 172).

37. Shane, Shane, and Gales (1997, p. 192ff) present an analogous situation involving a younger adolescent approached from a developmental, but self psychology-oriented perspective.

38. This idea is supported by the sharp decline in the number of major depression diagnoses made in children and adolescents that has been reported since the FDA warning in 2003 about heightened risk of suicidal signs and symptoms among those taking SSRIs (Libby, Brent, Morrato, et al., 2007; Pfeffer, 2007).

39. Parenthetically, this contrasts with adult psychiatry in this country, which developed around the care of hospitalized/institutionalized patients rather than outpatient (clinic) patients.

40. There are, and have for years been, a number of psychodynamic schools (e.g., Jung, Adler, the interpersonal school of Harry Stack Sullivan, self psychology, schools emphasizing object relations, and others), plus therapeutic approaches with bases in psychoanalysis (Kleinian; control mastery treatment of Weiss & Sampson; Langs; Masterson; and others emphasizing the relational aspects of the therapeutic process). However, in our lifetimes, psychodynamic has been most synonymous with the intrapsychic dynamics of Freudian psychoanalysis. Probably all schools of therapy, except those based on social learning theory, bear some relationship to psychoanalysis.

REFERENCES

Abebe, D., Lien, L., Torgersen, L., & von Soest, T. (2012). Binge eating, purging, and nonpurging compensatory behaviors decrease from adolescence to adulthood: a population-based, longitudinal study. *BMC Public Health*, 12: 32. Also at www.biomedcentral.com/1471–2458/12/32, and summarized by Sinclair, L., Journal Digest, in *Psychiatric News*, April 20, p. 20.

Adatto, C. (1958). Ego integration observed in analysis of late adolescents. *International Journal of Psycho-Analysis*, 39: 172–177.

Adatto, C. (1966). On the metamorphosis from adolescence into adulthood. *Journal of the American Psychoanalytic Association*, 14: 485–509.

Agras, W. S., Crow, S. F., Halmi, K. A., Mitchell, J. E., Wilson, G. W., & Kraemer, H. C. (2000). Outcome predictors for the cognitive behavior treatment of bulimia nervosa: data from a multisite study. *American Journal of Psychiatry*, 157: 1302–1308.

Al-Adawi, S., Dorvlo, A. S., Burke, D. T., Al-Bahlani, S., Martin, R. G., & Al-Ismaily, S. (2002). Presence and severity of anorexia and bulimia among male and female Omani and non-Omani adolescents. *Journal of the American Academy of Child and Adolescent Psychiatry*, 41: 1124–1130.

Allen, B. (1987). Youth suicide. *Adolescence*, 22: 271–290.

Alonso-Alonso, M. (2013). Brain, reward, and eating disorders: a matter of taste? [Editorial]. *American Journal of Psychiatry*, 170: 1082–1085.

Ambrosini, P., Bianchi, M., Rabinovich, H., & Elia, J. (1993). Antidepressant treatments in children and adolescents I. affective disorders. *Journal of the American Academy of Child and Adolescent Psychiatry, 32*: 1–6.

American Academy of Child & Adolescent Psychiatry (1997a). Practice parameter for the assessment and treatment of children and adolescents with anxiety disorders. *Journal of the American Academy of Child and Adolescent Psychiatry, 36*(10 Suppl.): 69S–84S.

American Academy of Child & Adolescent Psychiatry (1997b). Practice parameter for the assessment and treatment of children and adolescents with bipolar disorder. *Journal of the American Academy of Child and Adolescent Psychiatry, 36*(10 Suppl.): 157S–176S.

American Academy of Child & Adolescent Psychiatry (2001). Practice parameter for the assessment and treatment of children and adolescents with suicidal behavior. *Journal of the American Academy of Child and Adolescent Psychiatry, 40*(7 Suppl.): 24S–51S.

American Academy of Child and Adolescent Psychiatry (2007a). Practice parameter for the assessment and treatment of children and adolescents with bipolar disorder. *Journal of the American Academy of Child and Adolescent Psychiatry, 46*: 107–125.

American Academy of Child and Adolescent Psychiatry (2007b). Practice parameter for the assessment and treatment of children and adolescents with depressive disorders. *Journal of the American Academy of Child and Adolescent Psychiatry, 46*: 1503–1526.

American Academy of Child and Adolescent Psychiatry (2009). Practice parameter on the use of psychotropic medication in children and adolescents. *Journal of the American Academy of Child and Adolescent Psychiatry, 48*: 961–973.

American Psychiatric Association (2002). Practice guideline for the treatment of patients with bipolar disorder [Revision]. *American Journal of Psychiatry, 159*(4 Suppl.): 1–50.

American Psychiatric Association (2013). *Desk Reference to the Diagnostic Criteria from DSM-5*. Arlington, VA: American Psychiatric Association.

Andrews, J. A., & Lewinsohn, P. M. (1992). Suicidal attempts among older adolescents. *Journal of the American Academy of Child and Adolescent Psychiatry, 31*: 655–662.

Anthony, E. (1970). The reactions of parents to adolescents and to their behavior. In: E. Anthony & T. Benedek (Eds.), *Parenthood: Its Psychology and Psychopathology* (pp. 307–324). Boston, MA: Little, Brown.

Apter, A., Gothelf, D., Offer, R., Ratzoni, G., Orbach, I., Tyano, S., & Pfeffer, C. (1997). Suicidal adolescents and ego defense mechanisms.

Journal of the American Academy of Child and Adolescent Psychiatry, 36: 1520–1527.

Apter, A., Gothelf, D., Orbach, I., Weizman, R., Ratzoni, G., Har-Even, D., & Tyano, S. (1995). Correlation of suicidal and violent behavior in different diagnostic categories in hospitalized adolescent patients. *Journal of the American Academy of Child and Adolescent Psychiatry, 34*: 912–918.

Attie, I., & Brooks-Gunn, J. (1989). Development of eating problems in adolescent girls: a longitudinal study. *Developmental Psychology, 25*: 70–79.

Attie, I., & Brooks-Gunn, J. (1992). Developmental issues in the study of eating problems and disorders. In: J. H. Crowther, D. L. Tennenbaum, S. E. Hobfoll, & M. A. P. Stephens (Eds.), *The Etiology of Bulimia Nervosa: the Individual and Familial Context* (pp. 35–58). Washington: Hemisphere.

Bailey, J. M., & Benishay, D. S. (1993). Familial aggregation of female sexual orientation. *American Journal of Psychiatry, 150*: 272–277.

Bailey, J. M., & Pillard, R. C. (1991). A genetic study of male sexual orientation. *Archives of General Psychiatry, 48*: 1089–1096.

Bailey, J. M., Pillard, R. C., Neale, M. C., & Agyei, Y. (1993). Heritable factors influence sexual orientation in women. *Archives of General Psychiatry, 50*: 217–223.

Bateman, A., & Fonagy, P. (2009). Randomized controlled trial of outpatient mentalization-based treatment versus structured clinical management for borderline personality disorder. *American Journal of Psychiatry, 166*: 1355–1364.

Beautrais, A., Joyce, P., & Mulder, R. (1997). Precipitating factors and life events in serious suicide attempts among youths aged 13 through 24 years. *Journal of the American Academy of Child and Adolescent Psychiatry, 36*: 1543–1551.

Beck, A. T., Steer, R. A., Kovacs, M., & Garrison, B. (1985). Hopelessness and eventual suicide: a 10-year prospective study of patients hospitalized with suicidal ideation. *American Journal of Psychiatry, 142*: 559–563.

Bell, A., Weinberg, M., & Hammersmith, S. (1981). *Sexual Preference: Its Development in Men and Women*. Bloomington, IN: Indiana University Press.

Benyon, S., Soares-Weiser, K., Woolacott, N., Duffy, S., & Geddes, J. R. (2008). Psychosocial interventions for the prevention of relapse in bipolar disorder: systematic review of controlled trials. *British Journal of Psychiatry, 192*: 5–11.

Berman, A. L., & Jobes, D. A. (1991). *Adolescent Suicide: Assessment and Intervention*. Washington, DC: American Psychological Association.

Bernstein, G., Anderson, L., Hektner, J., & Realmuto, G. (2000). Imipramine compliance in adolescents. *Journal of the American Academy of Child and Adolescent Psychiatry, 39*: 284–291.

Bezilla, R. (Ed.) (1993). *America's Youth in the 1990s*. Princeton, NJ: The George H. Gallup International Institute.

Bibring, E. (1937). Symposium on the therapeutic results in psychoanalysis. *International Journal of Psycho-Analysis, 18*: 170–189.

Bibring, E. (1953). The mechanism of depression. In: P. Greenacre (Ed.), *Affective Disorders* (pp. 13–48). New York: International Universities Press.

Biederman, J. (1998). Resolved: mania is mistaken for ADHD in prepubertal children. Debate Forum, *Journal of the American Academy of Child and Adolescent Psychiatry, 37*: 1091–1099.

Billy, J., Tanfer, K., Grady, W., & Klepinger, D. (1993). The sexual behavior of men in the United States. *Family Planning Perspectives, 25*: 52–60.

Birk, L. (1980). The myth of classical homosexuality: views of a behavioral psychotherapist. In: J. Marmor (Ed.), *Homosexual Behavior: A Modern Reappraisal* (pp. 376–390). New York: Basic Books.

Birmaher, B., Axelson, D., Strober, M., Gill, M. K., Valeri, S., Chiappetta, L., Ryan, N., Leonard, H., Hunt, J., Iyengar, S., & Keller, M. (2006). Clinical course of children and adolescents with bipolar spectrum disorders. *Archives of General Psychiatry, 63*: 175–183.

Bloch, D. S. (1999). Adolescent suicide as a public health threat. *Journal of Child and Adolescent Psychiatric Nursing, 13*: 26–38.

Bloch, H. A., & Niederhoffer, A. (1958). *The Gang: A Study of Adolescent Behavior*. New York: Philosophical Library.

Bloch, H. S. (1981). The role of strivings to complete development in the therapeutic process of child analysis. *International Review of Psycho-Analysis, 8*: 203–218.

Bloch, H. S. (1995). *Adolescent Development, Psychopathology, and Treatment*. Madison, CT: International Universities Press, paperback edition, 2007.

Blos, P. (1957). Preoedipal factors in the etiology of female delinquency. *Psychoanalytic Study of the Child, 12*: 229–249.

Blos, P. (1962). *On Adolescence*. New York: Free Press of Glencoe.

Blos, P. (1976). Postscript. In: *The Adolescent Passage*. New York: International Universities Press, 1979.

Boergers, J., Spirito, A., & Donaldson, D. (1998). Reasons for adolescent suicide attempts: associations with psychological functioning. *Journal of the American Academy of Child and Adolescent Psychiatry, 37*: 1287–1293.

Borst, S., & Noam, G. (1993). Developmental psychopathology in suicidal and non-suicidal adolescent girls. *Journal of the American Academy of Child and Adolescent Psychiatry, 32*: 501–508.

Botteron, K. N., Vannier, M. W., Geller, B., Todd, R. D., & Lee, B. C. P. (1995). Preliminary study of magnetic resonance imaging characteristics in 8- to 16-year olds with mania. *Journal of the American Academy of Child and Adolescent Psychiatry, 34*: 742–749.

Bowes, M. (2002). New sustained-release formulations of antidepressant medications. *Advances in Psychiatric Medicine.* Supplement to *Psychiatric Times,* July.

Brent, D. (1987). Correlates of the medical lethality of suicide attempts in children and adolescents. *Journal of the American Academy of Child and Adolescent Psychiatry, 26*: 87–91.

Brent, D. (2000). Children of depressed mothers. [Letter to the editor]. *Journal of the American Academy of Child and Adolescent Psychiatry, 39*: 136–137.

Brent, D., Baugher, M., Bridge, J., Chen, T., & Chiappetta, L. (1999). Age- and sex-related risk factors for adolescent suicide. *Journal of the American Academy of Child and Adolescent Psychiatry, 38*: 1497–1505.

Brent, D., Holder, D., Kolko, D., Birmaher, B., Baugher, M., Roth, C., Iyengar, S., & Johnson, B. (1997). A clinical psychotherapy trial for adolescent depression comparing cognitive, family, and supportive therapy. *Archives of General Psychiatry, 54*: 877–885.

Brent, D., Moritz, G., Bridge, J., Perper, J., & Canobbio, R. (1996). Long-term impact of exposure to suicide: a three-year controlled follow-up. *Journal of the American Academy of Child and Adolescent Psychiatry, 35*: 646–653.

Brent, D., Perper, J., Moritz, G., Allman, C., Friend, A., Roth, C., Schweers, J., Balach, L., & Baugher, M. (1993a). Psychiatric risk factors for adolescent suicide: a case-control study. *Journal of the American Academy of Child and Adolescent Psychiatry, 32*: 521–529.

Brent, D., Perper, J., Moritz, G., Allman, C., Schweers, J., Roth, C., Balach, L., Canobbio, R., & Loitus, L. (1993b). Psychiatric sequelae to the loss of an adolescent peer to suicide. *Journal of the American Academy of Child and Adolescent Psychiatry, 32*: 509–517.

Brent, D., Perper, J., Moritz, G., Baugher, M., & Allman, C. (1993c). Suicide in adolescents with no apparent psychopathology. *Journal of the American Academy of Child and Adolescent Psychiatry, 32*: 494–500.

Brent, D. A., Kolko, D. J., Allan, M. J., & Brown, R. V. (1990). Suicidality in affectively disordered adolescent inpatients. *Journal of the American Academy of Child and Adolescent Psychiatry, 29*: 586–593.

Brody, A. L., Saxena, S., Stoessel, P., Gillies, L. A., Fairbanks, L. A., Alborzian, S., Phelps, M. E., Huang, S-C., Wu, H-M., Ho, M. L., Ho, M. K., Au, S. C., Maidment, K., & Baxter, L. E. Jr. (2001). Regional brain metabolism changes in patients with major depression treated with either paroxetine or interpersonal therapy. *Archives of General Psychiatry, 58*: 631–640.

Brooks, D. (2013). Heroes of uncertainty [Op-ed column]. *New York Times.* May 28, p. A19.

Brotman, M. A., Kassem, L., Reising, M. M., Guyer, A. E., Dickstein, D. P., Rich, B. A., Towbin, K. E., Pine, D. S., McMahon, F. J., & Leibenluft, E. (2007). Parental diagnoses in youth with narrow phenotype bipolar disorder or severe mood dysregulation. *American Journal of Psychiatry, 164*: 1238–1241.

Brown, J., Cohen, P., Johnson, J., & Smailes, E. (1999). Childhood abuse and neglect: specificity of effects on adolescent and young adult depression and suicidality. *Journal of the American Academy of Child and Adolescent Psychiatry, 38*: 1490–1496.

Brown, W. A. (2006). Understanding and using the placebo effect. *Psychiatric Times, XXIII*(11): 15–17, October 2006.

Brubaker, C. (2013). The evidence for "evidence-based" child and adolescent psychotherapy. *AACAP (American Academy of Child and Adolescent Psychiatry) News, 44*(5): 235–236, Sept/Oct. 2013.

Burr, C. (1997). Homosexuality and biology. *The Atlantic* online at: www.theatlantic.com/issues/97jun/burr2.htm

Bushnell, J. A., Wells, J. E., Hornblow, A. R., Oakley-Browne, M. A., & Joyce, P. (1990). Prevalence of three bulimia syndromes in the general population. *Psychological Medicine, 20*: 671–680.

Byne, W., & Parsons, B. (1993). Human sexual orientation: the biologic theories reappraised. *Archives of General Psychiatry, 50*: 228–239.

Calam, R., Waller, G., Slade, P., & Newton, T. (1990). Eating disorders and perceived relationships with parents. *International Journal of Eating Disorders, 9*: 479–485.

Carey, B. (2006). What's wrong with a child? Psychiatrists often disagree. *The New York Times*, Health/Psychology section, 11 November.

Carlat, D. J. (2006). Bipolar disorder in children: is the diagnosis valid? *The Carlat Psychiatry Report, 4*(8): 1–2.

Carlat, D. J., & Camargo, C. A. Jr. (1991). Review of bulimia nervosa in males. *American Journal of Psychiatry, 148*: 831–843.

Carlat, D. J., Camargo, C. A. Jr., & Herzog, D. B. (1997). Eating disorders in males: A report on 135 patients. *American Journal of Psychiatry, 154*: 1127–1132.

Carlson, G. (1995). Identifying prepubertal mania. *Journal of the American Academy of Child and Adolescent Psychiatry, 34*: 750–753.

Carlson, G. (2002). Bipolar disorder in children and adolescents: a critical review. In: D. Shaffer, & B. D. Waslick (Eds.), *The Many Faces of Depression in Children and Adolescents* (pp. 129–178). *Review of Psychiatry,* Vol. 21. Washington, DC: American Psychiatric Association.

Carlson, G. (2007). Who are the children with severe mood dysregulation, a.k.a. "rages"? *American Journal of Psychiatry, 164*: 1140–1142.

Carrier, J. M. (1980). Homosexual behavior in cross-cultural perspective. In: J. Marmor (Ed.), *Homosexual Behavior: A Modern Reappraisal* (pp. 100–122). New York: Basic Books.

Centers for Disease Control and Prevention (1997). Update: prevalence of overweight among children, adolescents, and adults—United States, 1988–1994. *Morbidity & Mortality Weekly Report, 46*: 198–202. Cited in: Field, A., Camargo, C. A. Jr., Taylor, C. B., Berkey, C., Frazier, A. L., Gillman, M., & Colditz, G. (1999). Overweight, weight concerns, and bulimic behaviors among girls and boys. *Journal of the American Academy of Child and Adolescent Psychiatry, 38*: 754–760.

Centers for Disease Control and Prevention (2000). Youth risk behavior surveillance—United States 1999. *Morbidity & Mortality Weekly Report, 49*: 1–95.

Centers for Disease Control and Prevention (2013). Youth violence: national statistics. Accessed at http://www.cdc.violenceprevention/youth violence/stats_at_a_glance/hr_trends.html (last visited October 2013).

Chang, K., Saxena, K., & Howe, M. (2006). An open-label study of lamotrigine adjunct or monotherapy for the treatment of adolescents with bipolar depression. *Journal of the American Academy of Child and Adolescent Psychiatry, 45*: 298–304.

Chiu, L. (1997). My roommate thinks she's a lesbian. In: C. Page (Ed.), *The Smart Girl's Guide to College* (pp. 57–62). New York: Noonday Press, a division of Farrar, Straus and Giroux.

Clarkin, J. F., Levy, K. N., Lenzenweger, M. F., & Kernberg, O. F. (2007). Evaluating three treatments for borderline personality disorder: a multiwave study. *American Journal of Psychiatry, 164*: 922–928.

Colom, F., Vieta, E., Martinez-Arán, A., Reinares, M., Benabarre, A., & Gastó, C. (2000). Clinical factors associated with treatment noncompliance in euthymic bipolar patients. *Journal of Clinical Psychiatry, 61*: 549–555.

Colom, F., Vieta, E., Martinez-Arán, A., Reinares, M., Goikolea, J. M., Benabarre, A., Torrent, C., Comes, M., Corbella, B., Parramon, G., & Corominas, J. (2003). A randomized trial on the efficacy of group psychoeducation in the prophylaxis of recurrences in bipolar patients whose disease is in remission. *Archives of General Psychiatry, 60*: 402–407.

Conte, J. R., & Schuerman, J. R. (1987). The effects of sexual abuse on children: a multidimensional view. *Journal of Interpersonal Violence, 2*: 380–390.

Cooper, W., Arbogast, P., Ding, H., Hickson, G., Fuchs, D., & Ray, W. (2006). Trends in prescribing antipsychotic medications for US children. *Ambulatory Pediatrics, 6*: 79–83.

Cooper, W., Callahan, S. T., Shintani, A., Fuchs, D. C., Shelton, R., Dudley, J., Graves, A., & Ray, W. (2014). Antidepressants and suicide attempts in children. *Pediatrics, 133*: 204.

Cosgrove, L., Bursztajn, H. J., Krimsky, S., Anaya, M., & Walker, J. (2009). Conflicts of interest and disclosure in the American Psychiatric Association's Clinical Practice Guidelines. *Psychotherapy and Psychosomatics, 78*(4): 228–232.

Croghan, T. W., Tomlin, M., Pescosolido, B. A., Schnittker, J., Martin, J., Lubell, K., & Swindle, R. (2003). American attitudes toward and willingness to use psychiatric medications. *Journal of Nervous and Mental Diseases, 191*: 166–174.

Crow, S., Peterson, C., Swanson, S., Raymond, N., Specker, S., Eckert, E., & Mitchell, J. (2009). Increased mortality in bulimia nervosa and other eating disorders. *American Journal of Psychiatry, 166*: 1342–1346.

Crowther, J. H., & Mizes, J. S. (1992). Etiology of bulimia nervosa: conceptual, research, and measurement issues. In: J. H. Crowther, D. L. Tennenbaum, S. E. Hobfoll, & M. A. P. Stephens (Eds.), *The Etiology of Bulimia Nervosa: the Individual and Familial Context* (pp. 225–244). Washington, DC: Hemisphere.

Crowther, J. H., Wolf, E. M., & Sherwood, N. E. (1992). Epidemiology of bulimia nervosa. In: J. H. Crowther, D. L. Tennenbaum, S. E. Hobfoll, & M. A. P. Stephens (Eds.), *The Etiology of Bulimia Nervosa: the Individual and Familial Context* (pp. 1–26). Washington, DC: Hemisphere.

Cuijpers, P., Smit, F., Bohlmeijer, E., Hollon, S. D., & Andersson, G. (2010). Efficacy of cognitive-behavioural therapy and other psychological treatments for adult depression: meta-analytic study of publication bias. *British Journal of Psychiatry, 196*: 173–178.

Daly, R. (2007). Report says family focus key to mental illness prevention. *Psychiatric News* [Newspaper of the American Psychiatric Association], 21 December, p. 19. See also: Promotion and prevention in mental health: strengthening parenting and enhancing child resilience. Posted at http://download.ncadi.samhsa.gov/ken/pdf/SVP-0186.pdf.

De Fries, Z. (1979). A comparison of political and apolitical lesbians. *Journal of the American Academy of Psychoanalysis, 7*: 57–66.

de la Fuente-Fernández, R., Ruth, T. J., Sossi, V., Schulzer, M., Calne, D. B., & Stoessl, A. J. (2001). Expectation and dopamine release: mechanism of the placebo effect in Parkinson's Disease. *Science, 293*: 1164–1166, 10 August.

DeAngelis, T. (2002). Promising treatments for anorexia and bulimia. *American Psychological Association Monitor on Psychology, 33*: 38–41.

DelBello, M. P., Hanseman, D., Adler, C. M., Fleck, D. E., & Strakowski, S. M. (2007). Twelve-month outcome of adolescents with bipolar disorder following first hospitalization for a manic or mixed episode. *American Journal of Psychiatry, 164*: 582–590.

DelBello, M. P., Kowatch, R. A., Adler, C. M., Stanford, K. E., Welge, J. A., Barzman, D. H., Nelson, E., & Strakowski, S. M. (2006). A double-blind randomized pilot study comparing quetiapine and divalproex for adolescent mania. *Journal of the American Academy of Child and Adolescent Psychiatry, 45*: 305–313.

Denniston, R. H. (1980). Ambisexuality in animals. In: J. Marmor (Ed.), *Homosexual Behavior: A Modern Reappraisal* (pp. 25–40). New York: Basic Books.

DeRubeis, R., Gelfand, L., Tang, T., & Simons, A. (1999). Medications versus cognitive behavior therapy for severely depressed outpatients: a mega-analysis of four randomized comparisons. *American Journal of Psychiatry, 156*: 1007–1013.

Deutsch, H. (1944). *The Psychology of Women (Volume I)*. New York: Grune & Stratton.

DeVogli, R., Chandola, T., & Marmot, M. G. (2007). Negative aspects of close relationships and heart disease. *Archives of Internal Medicine, 167*: 1951–1957.

Diener, M.J., Hilsenroth, M. J., & Weinberger, J. (2007). Therapist affect and patient outcomes in psychodynamic psychotherapy: a meta-analysis. *American Journal of Psychiatry, 164*: 936–941.

Donnelly, C. L., Wagner, K. D., Rynn, M., Ambrosini, P., Landau, P., Yang, R., & Wohlberg, C. J. (2006). Sertraline in children and adolescents with major depressive disorder. *Journal of the American Academy of Child and Adolescent Psychiatry, 45*: 1162–1170.

Downey, J. I., & Friedman, R. C. (1998). Female homosexuality: classical psychoanalytic theory reconsidered. *Journal of the American Psychoanalytic Association, 46*: 471–506.

Drewnowski, A., Yee, D. K., Kurth, C. L., & Krahn, D. D. (1994). Eating pathology and DSM-III-R bulimia nervosa: a continuum of behavior. *American Journal of Psychiatry*, 151: 1217–1219.

Driessen, E., Van, L., Don, F., Peen, J., Kool, S., Westra, D., Hendriksen, M., Schoevers, R., Cuijpers, P., Twisk, J., & Dekker, J. (2013). The efficacy of cognitive-behavioral therapy and psychodynamic therapy in the outpatient treatment of major depression: a randomized clinical trial. *American Journal of Psychiatry*, 170(9): 1041–1050.

Duenwald, M. (2002). 2 portraits of children of divorce: rosy and dark. *The New York Times* (Science section/Health & Fitness) (p. D1), 26 March.

Duman, R. S. (1998). Novel therapeutic approaches beyond the serotonin receptor. *Biological Psychiatry*, 44: 324–335.

Eddy, K., & Rauch, S. (2011). Neuroimaging in eating disorders: coming of age (Editorial). *American Journal of Psychiatry*, 168: 1139–1141.

Edlund, M. J., Wang, P. S., Berglund, P. A., Katz, S. J., Lin, E., & Kessler, R. C. (2002). Dropping out of mental health treatment: patterns and predictors among epidemiological survey respondents in the United States and Ontario. *American Journal of Psychiatry*, 159: 845–851.

Ehrhardt, A. A., Meyer-Bahlburg, H. F. L., Rosen, L. R., Feldman, J. F., Veridiano, N. P., Zimmerman, I., & McEwen, B. S. (1985). Sexual orientation after prenatal exposure to exogenous estrogens. *Archives of Sexual Behavior*, 14: 57–77.

Elke, D., Bouchard, T., Bohlen, J., & Heston, L. (1986). Homosexuality in monozygotic twins reared apart. *British Journal of Psychiatry*, 148: 421–425.

Emslie, G., Rush, A. J., Weinberg, W., Gullion, C., Rintelmann, J., & Hughes, C. (1997a). Recurrence of major depressive disorder in hospitalized children and adolescents. *Journal of the American Academy of Child and Adolescent Psychiatry*, 36: 785–792.

Emslie, G., Rush, A. J., Weinberg, W., Kowatch, R., Hughes, C., Carmody, T., & Rintelmann, J. (1997b). A double-blind, randomized, placebo-controlled trial of fluoxetine in children and adolescents with depression. *Archives of General Psychiatry*, 54: 1031–1037.

Erikson, E. (1956). The problem of ego identity. In: *Identity and the Life Cycle. Psychological Issues*, Monograph 1. New York: International Universities Press, 1959.

Ernulf, K. E., Innala, S. M., & Whitam, F. L. (1989). Biological explanation, psychological explanation, and tolerance of homosexuals: a cross-national analysis of beliefs and attitudes. *Psychological Reports*, 65: 1003–1010.

Esman, A. H. (1994). "Sexual abuse", pathogenesis, and enlightened skepticism (Editorial). *American Journal of Psychiatry, 151*: 1101–1103.

Eyman, J., & Smith, K. (1986). Lethality trends in multiple suicide attempts. In: R. Cohen-Sandler (Ed.), *Proceedings of the Ninteenth Annual Meeting of the American Association of Suicidology* (pp. 75–77). Denver, CO: American Association of Suicidology.

Fairburn, C., & Belgin, S. (1990). Studies of the epidemiology of bulimia nervosa. *American Journal of Psychiatry, 147*: 401–408.

Fairburn, C., Cooper, Z., Doll, H., Norman, P., & O'Connor, M. (2000). The natural course of bulimia nervosa and binge eating disorder in young women. *Archives of General Psychiatry, 57*: 659–665.

Fairburn, C., Kirk, J., O'Connor, M., & Cooper, P. J. (1986). A comparison of two psychological treatments for bulimia nervosa. *Behaviour Research and Therapy, 24*: 629–643.

Fay, R. E., Turner, C. F., Klassen, A. D., & Gagnon, J. H. (1989). Prevalence and patterns of same-gender sexual contact among men. *Science, 243*: 338–348.

Fergusson, D. M., & Lynskey, M. T. (1995). Suicide attempts and suicidal ideation in a birth cohort of 16-year-old New Zealanders. *Journal of the American Academy of Child and Adolescent Psychiatry, 34*: 1308–1317.

Field, A. E., Camargo, C. A. Jr., Taylor, C. B., Berkey, C. S., Frazier, A. L., Gillman, M. W., & Colditz, G. A. (1999). Overweight, weight concerns, and bulimic behaviors among girls and boys. *Journal of the American Academy of Child and Adolescent Psychiatry, 38*: 754–760.

Findling, R. (2010). Antipsychotics in young patients: results from the TEOSS Study. Medscape, 29 June.

Findling, R., Johnson, J., McClellan, J., Frazier, J., Vitiello, B., Hamer, R., Lieberman, J., Ritz, L., McNamara, N., Lingler, J., Hlastala, S., Pierson, L., Puglia, M., Maloney, A., Kaufman, M., Noyes, N., Sikich, L. (2010). Double-blind maintenance safety and effectiveness findings from the Treatment of Early-Onset Schizophrenia Spectrum (TEOSS) study. *Journal of the American Academy of Child and Adolescent Psychiatry, 49*: 583–594.

Fitzgerald, M. (1999). Impulsivity and suicide (Letter to the editor). *Journal of the American Academy of Child and Adolescent Psychiatry, 38*: 939.

Fonagy, P., & Target, M. (1994). The efficacy of psychoanalysis for children with disruptive disorders. *Journal of the American Academy of Child and Adolescent Psychiatry, 33*: 45–55.

Ford, C. S., & Beach, F. A. (1951). *Patterns of Sexual Behavior*. New York: Harper & Bros.

Frank, E., Kupfer, D. J., Thase, M. E., Mallinger, A. G., Swartz, H. A., Fagiolini, A. M., Grochocinski, V., Houck, P., Scott, J., Thompson, W., & Monk, T. (2005). Two-year outcomes for interpersonal and social rhythm therapy in individuals with bipolar I disorder. *Archives of General Psychiatry*, 62: 996–1004.

Frank, G., Shott, M., Hagman, J., & Mittal, V. (2013). Alterations in brain structures related to taste reward circuitry in ill and recovered anorexia nervosa and in bulimia nervosa. *American Journal of Psychiatry*, 170: 1152–1160.

Frankel, S. (1990). Effects of day care: implications of current knowledge. In: S. Chehrazi (Ed.), *Psychosocial Issues in Day Care* (pp. 83–99). Washington, DC: American Psychiatric Press.

Frazier, J. A., Biederman, J., Tohen, M., Feldman, P. D., Jacobs, T. G., Toma, V., Rater, M. A., Tarazi, R. A., Kim, G. S., Garfield, S. B., Sohma, M., Gonzalez Heydrich, J., Risser, R. C., & Nowlin, Z. M. (2001). A prospective open-label treatment trial of olanzapine monotherapy in children and adolescents with bipolar disorder. *Journal of Child and Adolescent Psychopharmacology*, 11: 239–250.

Freeman, R. J., Beach, B., Davis, R., & Solyom, L. (1985). The prediction of relapse in bulimia nervosa. *Journal of Psychiatric Research*, 19: 349–353.

Freking, K. (2006). Drug use up for boomers, down for teens. Associated Press, reported in *Marin Independent Journal*, Health and Science section, 8 September, p. A6.

Freud, A. (1936). The ego and the mechanisms of defense. In: *Writings (Volume 2)*. New York: International Universities Press, 1966.

Freud, A. (1958). Adolescence. *The Psychoanalytic Study of the Child*, 13: 255–278.

Freud, A. (1965). Normality and pathology in childhood: assessments of development. *Writings (Volume 6)* (pp. 184–197). New York: International Universities Press.

Freud, A. (1968). Difficulties in the path of psychoanalysis: a confrontation of past and present viewpoints. In: *Problems in Psychoanalytic Training, Diagnosis, and the Technique of Therapy. Writings (Volume 7)* (pp. 124–156). New York: International Universities Press, 1969.

Freud, S. (1905d). *Three Essays on the Theory of Sexuality*. S.E., 7: 125–243. London: Hogarth.

Freud, S. (1905e). *Fragment of an Analysis of a Case of Hysteria*. S.E., 7: 3–124. London: Hogarth.

Freud, S. (1915–1916). *Introductory Lectures on Psycho-analysis*. S.E., 15: 199–212. London: Hogarth.

Freud, S. (1926d). *Inhibitions, Symptoms, and Anxiety. S.E.,* 20: 87–174. London: Hogarth.

Freud, S. (1930a). *Civilization and Its Discontents. S.E.,* 21: 59–145. London: Hogarth.

Friedman, R. C., & Downey, J. I. (1993). Psychoanalysis, psychobiology and neurobiological perspectives. *Journal of the American Psychoanalytic Association,* 41: 1159–1198.

Futuyma, D., & Risch, S. (1983–1984). Sexual orientation, sociobiology and evolution. *Journal of Homosexuality,* 9(2/3): 157–168.

Gabbard, G. (1998). The impact of psychotherapy on the brain. *Psychiatric Times,* September, p. 1.

Gagnon, J., & Simon, W. (1973). *Sexual Conduct: The Social Sources of Human Sexuality.* Chicago, IL: Aldine.

Garfinkel, P. E., Lin, E., Goering, P., Spegg, C., Goldbloom, D. S., Kennedy, S., Kaplan, A. S., & Woodside, D. B. (1995). Bulimia nervosa in a Canadian community sample: prevalence and comparison of subgroups. *American Journal of Psychiatry,* 152: 1052–1058.

Garner, D. M., Garfinkel, P. E., Schwartz, D., & Thompson, M. (1980). Cultural expectations of thinness in women. *Psychological Reports,* 47: 483–491.

Garrison, C. Z., Addy, C. L., Jackson, K. L., McKeown, R. E., & Waller, J. L. (1991). A longitudinal study of suicidal ideation in young adolescents. *Journal of the American Academy of Child and Adolescent Psychiatry,* 30: 597–603.

Gebhard, P. H. (1972). Incidence of overt homosexuality in the United States and Western Europe. In: J. M. Livingood (Ed.), *National Institute of Mental Health Task Force on Homosexuality: Final Report and Background Papers.* DHEW Publication No. (ADM) 76–357, 1976.

Geller, B., & Luby, J. (1997). Child and adolescent bipolar disorder: a review of the past ten years. *Journal of the American Academy of Child and Adolescent Psychiatry,* 36: 1168–1176.

Geller, B., Todd, R., Luby, J., & Botteron, K. (1996). Treatment-resistant depression in children and adolescents. *Psychiatric Clinics of North America,* 19: 253–267.

Ghaemi, S. N. (2006). Antidepressants and the bipolar spectrum. The American Psychiatric Association 159th Annual Meeting APA Conference Chronicles, Conference Proceedings Highlights-APA 2006 (pp. 5–6). *intellyst*® Medical Communications, 2101S Blackhawk St Ste 240, Aurora CO 80014–1475.

Ghaemi, S. N., & Martin, A. (2007). Defining the boundaries of childhood bipolar disorder (Editorial). *American Journal of Psychiatry,* 164: 185–188.

Ghaemi, S. N., Ko, J. Y., & Goodwin, F. K. (2002). Cade's disease and beyond. *Canadian Journal of Psychiatry, 47*: 125–134.

Gibbons, R. D., Hur, K., Baumik, D. K., & Mann, J. J. (2006). The relationship between antidepressant prescription rates and rate of early adolescent suicide. *American Journal of Psychiatry, 163*: 1898–1904.

Gibson, P. (1989). Gay male and lesbian youth suicide. Supplementary data in *Report of the Secretary's Task Force on Youth Suicide (Volume 3). Preventions and Interventions in Youth Suicide*. Washington, DC: US Dept. of Health and Human Services.

Gitelson, M. (1948). Character synthesis: the psychotherapeutic problem of adolescence. *American Journal of Orthopsychiatry, 18*: 422–436.

Glass, R. M. (2009). Letters in reply: Psychodynamic psychotherapy and research evidence: Bambi survives Godzilla? *Journal of the American Medical Association, 301*: 1587–1589.

Godlee, F., & Loder, E. (2010). Missing clinical trial data: setting the record straight. *British Medical Journal, 341*: c5641. Published online 12 October.

Goldstein, T. R., Axelson, D. A., Birmaher, B., & Brent, D. A. (2007). Dialectical behavior therapy for adolescents with bipolar disorder: a 1-year open trial. *Journal of the American Academy of Child and Adolescent Psychiatry, 46*: 820–830.

Goldston, D. (1999). Impulsivity and suicide. (Reply to letter to the editor.) *Journal of the American Academy of Child and Adolescent Psychiatry, 38*: 940.

Goldston, D., Daniel, S., Reboussin, B., Reboussin, D., Kelley, A., & Frazier, P. (1998). Psychiatric diagnoses of previous suicide attempters, first-time attempters, and repeat attempters on an adolescent inpatient psychiatry unit. *Journal of the American Academy of Child and Adolescent Psychiatry, 37*: 924–932.

Goldston, D. B., Daniel, S. S., Reboussin, D. M., Reboussin, B. A., Frazier, P. H., & Kelley, A. E. (1999). Suicide attempts among formerly hospitalized adolescents: a prospective naturalistic study of risk during the first 5 years after discharge. *Journal of the American Academy of Child and Adolescent Psychiatry, 38*: 660–671.

Gothelf, D., Apter, A., Brand-Gothelf, A., Offer, N., Ofek, H., Tyano, S., & Pfeffer, C. R. (1998). Death concepts in suicidal adolescents. *Journal of the American Academy of Child and Adolescent Psychiatry, 37*: 1279–1286.

Gould, M., Fisher, P., Parides, M., Flory, M., & Shaffer, D. (1996). Psychosocial risk factors of child and adolescent completed suicide. *Archives of General Psychiatry, 53*: 1153–1162.

Gould, M., King, R., Greenwald, S., Fisher, P., Schwab-Stone, M., Kramer, R., Flisher, A., Goodman, S., Canino, G., & Shaffer, D. (1998). Psychopathology associated with suicidal ideation and attempts among children and adolescents. *Journal of the American Academy of Child and Adolescent Psychiatry, 37*: 915–923.

Gould, M. S., Shaffer, D., Fisher, P., & Garfinkel, R. (1998). Separation/ divorce and child and adolescent completed suicide. *Journal of the American Academy of Child and Adolescent Psychiatry, 37*: 155–162.

Green, R. (1987). *The "Sissy Boy" Syndrome and the Development of Homosexuality*. New Haven, CT: Yale University Press.

Grilo, C., Sanislow, C., Shea, M., Skodol, A., Stout, R., Pagano, M., Yen, S., & McGlashan, T. (2003). The natural course of bulimia nervosa and eating disorder not otherwise specified is not influenced by personality disorders. *International Journal of Eating Disorders, 34*: 319–330.

Grinfeld, M. J. (2006). Psychiatric drugs for kids: how many is too many? *Psychiatric Times, 23*(11): 1 ff. October 2006.

Grøholt, B., Ekeberg, Ø., Wichstrom, L., & Haldorsen, T. (1998). Suicide among children and younger and older adolescents in Norway: a comparative study. *Journal of the American Academy of Child and Adolescent Psychiatry, 37*: 473–481.

Grøholt, B., Ekeberg, Ø., Wichstrom, L., & Haldorsen, T. (2000). Young suicide attempters: a comparison between a clinical and an epidemiological sample. *Journal of the American Academy of Child and Adolescent Psychiatry, 39*: 868–875.

Group for the Advancement of Psychiatry (1996). *Adolescent Suicide. GAP Report 140*. Washington DC: American Psychiatric Association Press.

Gupta, M. (2004). Evidence-based medicine: ethically obligatory or ethically suspect? *Evidenced-Based Mental Health, 7*: 96–97.

Haliburn, J. (2000). Reasons for adolescent suicide attempts. [Letter to the editor]. *Journal of the American Academy of Child and Adolescent Psychiatry, 39*: 13–14.

Hamburg, D. A. (1995). President's Essay—1995 Annual Report. Carnegie Corporation. New York. Based on: Carnegie council on adolescent development (1995), *Great Transitions: Preparing Adolescents for a New Century*. Concluding report on adolescent development. New York: Carnegie Corporation of NY, and Carnegie task force on meeting the needs of young children (1994). *Starting Points: Meeting the Needs of Our Youngest Children*. Report of the Carnegie task force on meeting the needs of young children. New York: Carnegie Corporation of NY.

Harris, G. (2006). Proof is scant on psychiatric drug mix for young. *The New York Times*, Health section, 23 November.

Harris, G. (2008). Half of doctors routinely prescribe placebos. *The New York Times*, Health section, 24 October.

Harris, G., Carey, B., & Roberts, J. (2007). Psychiatrists, troubled children and drug industry's role. *New York Times*, 10 May, p. A1.

Harris, J. (2005). The increased diagnosis of "juvenile bipolar disorder": what are we treating? *Psychiatric Services*, 56: 529–531.

Harry, J. (1990). A probability sample of gay males. *Journal of Homosexuality*, 19: 89–104.

Hawton, K., Cole, D., O'Grady, J., & Osborn, M. (1982). Motivational aspects of deliberate self-poisoning in adolescents. *British Journal of Psychiatry*, 141: 286–291.

Hawton, K., Fagg, J., Platt, S., & Hawkins, M. (1993). Factors associated with suicide after parasuicide in young people. *British Medical Journal*, 306: 1641–1644.

Hay, P. (2002). Integrating treatment in eating disorders. *Psychiatric Times*, July: 31–33.

Heatherton, T. F., & Baumeister, R. F. (1991). Binge eating as escape from self-awareness. *Psychological Bulletin*, 110: 86–108.

Heatherton, T. F., & Polivy, J. (1992). Chronic dieting and eating disorders: a spiral model. In: J. H. Crowther, D. L. Tennenbaum, S. E. Hobfoll, & M. A. P. Stephens (Eds.), *The Etiology of Bulimia Nervosa: The Individual and Familial Context* (pp. 133–155). Washington, DC: Hemisphere.

Heatherton, T. F., Mahamedi, F., Striepe, M., Field, A. M., & Keel, P. (1997). A 10-year longitudinal study of body weight, dieting, and eating disorder symptoms. *Journal of Abnormal Psychology*, 106: 117–125.

Heebink, D. M., Sunday, S. R., & Halmi, K. A. (1995). Anorexia nervosa and bulimia nervosa in adolescence: effects of age and menstrual status on psychological variables. *Journal of the American Academy of Child and Adolescent Psychiatry*, 34: 378–382.

Herzog, D., Dorer, D., Keel, P., Selwyn, S., Ekeblad, E., Flores, A., Greenwood, D., Burwell, R., & Keller, M. (1999). Recovery and relapse in anorexia and bulimia nervosa: a 7.5-year follow-up study. *Journal of the American Academy of Child and Adolescent Psychiatry*, 38: 829–837.

Herzog, D. B., Keller, M. B., Sacks, N. R., Yeh, C. J., & Lavori, P. W. (1992). Psychiatric comorbidity in treatment-seeking anorexics and bulimics. *Journal of the American Academy of Child and Adolescent Psychiatry*, 31: 810–818.

Hetherington, E., & Kelly, J. (2002). *For Better Or For Worse: Divorce Reconsidered*. New York: W. W. Norton.

Hoberman, H., & Garfinkel, B. (1988). Completed suicide in children and adolescents. *Journal of the American Academy of Child and Adolescent Psychiatry*, 27: 689–695.

Hoffman, L. (2009). Evidence-based psychodynamic psychotherapy. Book essay reviewing: R. A. Levy & J. S. Ablon (Eds.), *Handbook of Evidence-based Psychodynamic Psychotherapy: Bridging the Gap Between Science and Practice*. Totowa, NJ: Humana Press. *Journal of the American Psychoanalytic Association*, 57(6): 1481–1488.

Hoffman, L. (2014). Ever evolving approaches to exploring the human mind. Book essay reviewing: *Diagnostic and Statistical Manual of Mental Disorders, 5th Edition*. Washington, DC: American Psychiatric Association, 2013. *Journal of the American Psychoanalytic Association*, 62: 125–147.

Hofman, S., Barlow, D., Papp, L., Detwiler, M., Ray, S., Shear, M., Woods, S., & Gorman, J. (1998). Pretreatment attrition in a comparative treatment outcome study on panic disorder. *American Journal of Psychiatry*, 155: 43–47.

Hollis, C. (1996). Depression, family environment, and adolescent suicidal behavior. *Journal of the American Academy of Child and Adolescent Psychiatry*, 35: 622–630.

Hollon, S., & Wilson, G. T. (2014). Psychoanalysis or cognitive–behavioral therapy for bulimia nervosa: the specificity of psychological treatments (Editorial). *American Journal of Psychiatry*, 171: 13–16.

Hooker, E. (1957). The adjustment of the male overt homosexual. *Journal of Projective Techniques*, 21: 18–31.

Hooker, E. (1972). Homosexuality. In: J. M. Livingood (Ed.), *National Institute of Mental Health Task Force on Homosexuality: Final Report and Background Papers*. DHEW Publication No. (ADM) 76–357 [reprinted 1976].

Hopkins, H., & Gelenberg, A. (2001). Treating bipolar disorder: toward the third millenium. *Psychiatric Times*, February: 83–85.

Hsu, L. K. G., Chesler, B. E., & Santhouse, R. (1990). Bulimia nervosa in eleven sets of twins: a clinical report. *International Journal of Eating Disorders*, 9: 275–282.

Hutchings, J., Bywater, T., Daley, D., Gardner, F., Whitaker, C., Jones, K., Eames, C., & Edwards, R. T. (2007). Parenting intervention in sure start services for children at risk of developing conduct disorder: pragmatic randomized controlled trial. *British Medical Journal*, 334(7597): 678.

Huth-Bocks, A. C., Kerr, D. C. R., Ivey, A. Z., Kramer, A. C., & King, C. A. (2007). Assessment of psychiatrically hospitalized suicidal adolescents: self-report instruments as predictors of suicidal thoughts and behavior. *Journal of the American Academy of Child and Adolescent Psychiatry*, 46: 387–395.

Hyman, S., & Lieberman, J. (2013). Change, challenge, and opportunity: psychiatry through the looking glass of research. *Psychiatric News*, *48*(20), 18 October, p. 5.

Insel, T. R. (2010). Psychiatrists' relationships with pharmaceutical companies: part of the problem or part of the solution? [Commentary] *Journal of the American Medical Association*, *303*(12): 1192–1193.

Ioannidis, J. (2013). How many contemporary medical practices are worse than doing nothing or doing less? [Editorial] *Mayo Clinic Proceedings*, *88*(8): 779–781.

Ipser, J. C., Stein, D. J., Hawkridge, S., & Hoppe, L. (2009). Pharmacotherapy for anxiety disorders in children and adolescents. *Cochrane Database of Systematic Reviews*, *3*: CD005170 (ISSN: 1469–493X).

Isay, R. (1989). *Being Homosexual*. New York: Farrar, Straus, and Giroux.

Janus, S., & Janus, C. (1993). *The Janus Report on Sexual Behavior*. New York: Wiley.

Jensen, P. S. (2006). After TADS, can we measure up, catch up, and ante up? *Journal of the American Academy of Child and Adolescent Psychiatry*, *45*: 1456–1460.

Jensen, P. S., Youngstrom, E. A., Steiner, H., Findling, R. L., Meyer, R. E., Malone, R. P., Carlson, G. A., Coccaro, E. F., Aman, M. G., Blair, J., Dougherty, D., Ferris, C., Flynn, L., Green, E., Hoagwood, K., Hutchinson, J., Laughren, T., Leve, L. D., Novins, D. K., & Vitiello, B. (2007). Consensus report on impulsive aggression as a symptom across diagnostic categories in child psychiatry: implications for medication studies. *Journal of the American Academy of Child and Adolescent Psychiatry*, *46*: 309–322.

Johnson, C., & Wonderlich, S. (1992). Personality characteristics as a risk factor in the development of eating disorders. In: J. H. Crowther, D. L. Tennenbaum, S. E. Hobfoll, & M. A. P. Stephens (Eds.), *The Etiology of Bulimia Nervosa: the Individual and Familial Context* (pp. 179–196). Washington, DC: Hemisphere.

Johnson, J. G., Cohen, P., Kasen, S., & Brook, J. S. (2002). Childhood adversities associated with risk for eating disorders or weight problems during adolescence or early adulthood. *American Journal of Psychiatry*, *159*: 394–400.

Johnston, L. D., Bachman, J. G., & O'Malley, P. M. (1997). *Monitoring the Future: Questionnaire Responses from the Nation's High School Seniors, 1995*. Ann Arbor, MI: Institute for Social Research, University of Michigan (cited in Whitehead & Popenoe, 1999).

Johnston, L. D., Bachman, J. G., & O'Malley, P. M. (2006). *Monitoring the Future: Questionnaire Responses from the Nation's High School Seniors,*

2005. Ann Arbor, MI: Institute for Social Research, University of Michigan.

Joiner, T. E. Jr., Heatherton, T. F., & Keel, P. K. (1997). Ten-year stability and predictive validity of five bulimia-related indicators. *American Journal of Psychiatry, 154*: 1133–1138.

Joiner, T. E., Rudd, M. D., Rouleau, M. R., & Wagner, K. D. (2000). Parameters of suicidal crises vary as a function of previous suicide attempts in youth inpatients. *Journal of the American Academy of Child and Adolescent Psychiatry, 39*: 876–880.

Jones, E. (1922). Some problems of adolescence. In: *Papers on Psychoanalysis* (5th edn) (pp. 389–406). London: Balliére, Tindall & Cox, 1948.

Kafantaris, V. (1995). Treatment of bipolar disorder in children and adolescents. *Journal of the American Academy of Child and Adolescent Psychiatry, 34*: 732–741.

Kafantaris, V., Coletti, D. J., Dicker, R., Padula, G., & Kane, J. M. (2001). Adjunctive antipsychotic treatment of adolescents with bipolar psychosis. *Journal of the American Academy of Child and Adolescent Psychiatry, 40*: 1448–1456.

Kafantaris, V., Coletti, D. J., Dicker, R., Padula, G., & Kane, J. M. (2003). Lithium treatment of acute mania in adolescents: a large open trial. *Journal of the American Academy of Child and Adolescent Psychiatry, 42*: 1038–1045.

Kafantaris, V., Coletti, D. J., Dicker, R., Padula, G., Pleak, R. R., Alvir, J. M. J., & Kane, J. M. (2004). Lithium treatment of acute mania in adolescents: a placebo-controlled discontinuation study. *Journal of the American Academy of Child and Adolescent Psychiatry, 43*: 984–993.

Kandel, E. (1998). A new intellectual framework for psychiatry. *American Journal of Psychiatry, 155*: 467–469.

Kaplan, S., Pelcovitz, D., Salzinger, S., Mandel, F., & Weiner, M. (1997). Adolescent physical abuse and suicide attempts. *Journal of the American Academy of Child and Adolescent Psychiatry, 36*: 799–808.

Karlen, A. (1980). Homosexuality in history. In: J. Marmor (Ed.), *Homosexual Behavior: A Modern Reappraisal* (pp. 75–79). New York: Basic Books.

Kashani, J. H., Goddard, P., & Reid, J. C. (1989). Correlates of suicidal ideation in a community sample of children and adolescents. *Journal of the American Academy of Child and Adolescent Psychiatry, 28*: 912–917.

Kaye, D. (2007). Personal communication (Director of Training in Child/ Adolescent Psychiatry, University at Buffalo School of Medicine; Executive Council, American Association of Directors of Psychiatry Residency Training).

Kaye, W. (2009). Eating disorders: hope despite mortal risk (Editorial). *American Journal of Psychiatry, 166*: 1309–1311.

Keel, P., Mitchell, J., Miller, K., Davis, T., & Crow, S. (1999). Long-term outcome of bulimia nervosa. *Archives of General Psychiatry, 56*: 63–69.

Keel, P. K., & Mitchell, J. E. (1997). Outcome in bulimia nervosa. *American Journal of Psychiatry, 154*: 313–321.

Keel, P. K., Dorer, D. J., Eddy, K. T., Delinsky, S. S., Franko, D. L., Blais, M. A., Keller, M. B., & Herzog, D. B. (2002). Predictors of treatment utilization among women with anorexia and bulimia nervosa. *American Journal of Psychiatry, 159*: 140–142.

Keller, M. B., Ryan, N. D., Strober, M., Klein, R. G., Kutcher, S. P., Birmaher, B., Hagino, O. R., Koplewicz, H., Carlson, G. A., Clarke, G. N., Emslie, G. J., Feinberg, D., Geller, B., Kusumakar, V., Papatheodorou, G., Sack, W. H., Sweeney, M., Wagner, K. D., Weller, E. B., Winters, N. C., Oakes, R., & McCafferty, J. P. (2001). Efficacy of paroxetine in the treatment of adolescent major depression: a randomized, controlled trial. *Journal of the American Academy of Child and Adolescent Psychiatry, 40*: 762–772.

Kendall-Tackett, K. A., Meyer Williams, L., & Finkelhof, D. (1993). Impact of sexual abuse on children: a review and synthesis of recent empirical studies. *Psychololigical Bulletin, 113*: 164–180.

Kendler, K. S., MacLean, C., Neale, M., Kessler, R., Heath, A., & Eaves, L. (1991). The genetic epidemiology of bulimia nervosa. *American Journal of Psychiatry, 148*: 1627–1637.

Kennard, B., Silva, S., Vitiello, B., Curry, J., Kratochvil, C., Simons, A., Hughes, J., Feeny, N., Weller, E., Sweeney, M., Reinecke, M., Pathak, S., Ginsburg, G., Emslie, G., March, J., & the TADS Team (2006). Remission and residual symptoms after short-term treatment in the Treatment of Adolescents with Depression Study (TADS). *Journal of the American Academy of Child and Adolescent Psychiatry, 45*: 1404–1411.

Ketter, T. A. (2006). Understanding the complexity of patients and treatment in bipolar disorder: a case based approach. Presentation at Continuing Medical Education LLC-sponsored symposium, San Francisco, CA, 14 October, 2006.

Khan, A. (1987). Heterogeneity of suicidal adolescents. *Journal of the American Academy of Child and Adolescent Psychiatry, 26*: 92–96.

King, C. A., Hovey, J. D., Brand, E., Wilson, R., & Ghaziuddin, N. (1997). Suicidal adolescents after hospitalization: parent and family impacts on treatment follow-through. *Journal of the American Academy of Child and Adolescent Psychiatry, 36*: 85–93.

King, M., & McDonald, E. (1992). Homosexuals who are twins: a study of 46 probands. *British Journal of Psychiatry, 160*: 407–409.

King, R. A. (2010). Personal communication (Professor of Child Psychiatry, Yale University Medical School, and Medical Director, Tourette's and OCD Specialty Clinic, Yale Child Study Center).

Kinsey, A. C., Pomeroy, W. B., & Martin, C. E. (1948). *Sexual Behavior in the Human Male*. Philadelphia, PA: W. B. Saunders.

Kinsey, A. C., Pomeroy, W. B., Martin, C. E., & Gebhard, P. H. (1953). *Sexual Behavior in the Human Female*. Philadelphia, PA: W. B. Saunders.

Kinsey Institute (1999). Online at http://kinseyinstitute.org/resources/bib-homoprev.html.

Kinzl, J. H., Traweger, C., Guenther, V., & Biebl, W. (1994). Family background and sexual abuse associated with eating disorders. *American Journal of Psychiatry, 151*: 1127–1131.

Kirkpatrick, M. (1989). Women in love in the 1980s. *Journal of the American Academy of Psychoanalysis, 17*: 535–542.

Kirkpatrick, M., & Morgan, C. (1980). Psychodynamic psychotherapy of female homosexuality. In: J. Marmor (Ed.) *Homosexual Behavior: A Modern Reappraisal* (pp. 357–375). New York: Basic Books.

Kirsch, I., & Antonuccio, D. (2002). Antidepressants versus placebos: meaningful advantages are lacking. Point/Counterpoint. *Psychiatric Times*, September, pp. 6–9.

Kirsch, I., Moore, T. J., Scoboria, A., & Nicholls, S. S. (2002). The emperor's new drugs: an analysis of antidepressant medication data submitted to the U.S. Food and Drug Administration. *Prevention & Treatment, 5*: Article 23. Available at: www.journals.apa.org/prevention/volume5/toc-jul15–02.html.

Klein, R., Pine, D., & Klein, D. (1998). Resolved: mania is mistaken for ADHD in prepubertal children. Debate Forum. *Journal of the American Academy of Child and Adolescent Psychiatry, 37*: 1091–1099.

Klimes-Dougan, B., & Radke-Yarrow, M. (2000). Children of depressed mothers (Reply to letter to the editor). *Journal of the American Academy of Child and Adolescent Psychiatry, 39*: 137.

Klimes-Dougan, B., Free, K., Ronsaville, D., Stilwell, J., Welsh, C. J., & Radke-Yarrow, M. (1999). Suicidal ideation and attempts: a longitudinal investigation of children of depressed and well mothers. *Journal of the American Academy of Child and Adolescent Psychiatry, 38*: 651–659.

Kohn, R., Levav, I., Chang, B., Halperin, B., & Zadka, P. (1997). Epidemiology of youth suicide in Israel. *Journal of the American Academy of Child and Adolescent Psychiatry, 36*: 1537–1542.

Kotler, L. A., Cohen, P., Davies, M., Pine, D. S., & Walsh, B. T. (2001). Longitudinal relationships between childhood, adolescent, and adult eating disorders. *Journal of the American Academy of Child and Adolescent Psychiatry, 40*: 1434–1440.

Kovacs, M., & Pollock, M. (1995). Bipolar disorder and comorbid conduct disorder in childhood and adolescence. *Journal of the American Academy of Child and Adolescent Psychiatry, 34*: 715–723.

Kowatch, R. A., Fristad, M., Birmaher, B., Wagner, K. D., Findling, R. L., Hellander, M., & The Child Psychiatric Work Group on Bipolar Disorder (2005). Treatment guidelines for children and adolescents with bipolar disorder. *Journal of the American Academy of Child and Adolescent Psychiatry, 44*: 213–235.

Kowatch, R. A., Suppes, T., Carmody, T. J., Bucci, J. P., Hume, J. H., Kromelis, M., Emslie, G. J., Weinberg, W. A., & Rush, A. J. (2000). Effect size of lithium, divalproex sodium, and carbamazepine in children and adolescents with bipolar disorder. *Journal of the American Academy of Child and Adolescent Psychiatry, 39*: 713–720.

Kroeber, A. (1940). Psychosis or social sanction. *Character and Personality, 8*: 204–215. Reprinted in *The Nature of Culture* (p. 313). Chicago, IL: University of Chicago Press.

Krowchuck, D., Kreiter, S., Woods, C., Sinal, S., & DuRant, R. (1998). Problem dieting behaviors among young adolescents. *Archives of Pediatric and Adolescent Medicine, 152*: 884–888.

Kye, C., Waterman, G. S., Ryan, N., Birmaher, B., Williamson, D., Iyengar, S., & Dachille, S. (1996). A randomized, controlled trial of amitriptyline in the acute treatment of adolescent major depression. *Journal of the American Academy of Child and Adolescent Psychiatry, 35*: 1139–1144.

LaBarbera, P. (2002). The gay youth suicide myth. *Journal of Human Sexuality*. Online at www.leaderu.com/jhs/labarbera.html.

Lam, D. H., Hayward, P., Watkins, E. R., Wright, K., & Sham, P. (2005). Relapse prevention in patients with bipolar disorder: cognitive therapy outcome after 2 years. *American Journal of Psychiatry, 162*: 324–329.

Lam, D. H., Watkins, E. R., Hayward, P., Bright, J., Wright, K., Kerr, N., Parr-Davis, G., & Sham, P. (2003). A randomized controlled study of cognitive therapy for relapse prevention for bipolar affective disorder: outcome of the first year. *Archives of General Psychiatry, 60*: 145–152.

Lam, R. L., Goldner, E. M., Solyom, L., & Remick, R. A. (1994). A controlled study of light therapy for bulimia nervosa. *American Journal of Psychiatry, 151*: 744–750.

Larzelere, R. E., Smith, G. L., Batenhorst, L. M., & Kelly, D. B. (1996). Predictive validity of the suicide probability scale among adolescents in group home treatment *Journal of the American Academy of Child and Adolescent Psychiatry*, *35*: 166–172.

Laumann, E., Gagnon, J. H., Michael, R. T., & Michaels, S. (1994). *The Social Organization of Sexuality: Sexual Practices in the United States*. Chicago, IL: University of Chicago Press.

Leckman, J. F., & King, R. A. (2007). A developmental perspective on the controversy surrounding the use of SSRIs to treat pediatric depression (Editorial). *American Journal of Psychiatry*, *164*: 1304–1306.

LeGrange, D., Crosby, R. D., Rathouz, P. J., & Leventhal, B. L. (2007). A randomized controlled comparison of family-based treatment and supportive psychotherapy for adolescent bulimia nervosa. *Archives of General Psychiatry*, *64*: 1049–1056.

Leichsenring, F., & Rabung, S. (2008). Effectiveness of long-term psychodynamic psychotherapy: a meta-analysis. *Journal of the American Medical Association*, *300*: 1551–1565.

Leichsenring, F., Salzer, S., Jaeger, U, Kächele, H., Kreische, R., Leweke, F., Rüger, U., Winkelbach, C., & Leibing, E. (2009). Short-term psychodynamic psychotherapy and cognitive-behavioral therapy in generalized anxiety disorder: a randomized, controlled trial. *American Journal of Psychiatry*, *166*: 875–881.

Levine, M. P., & Smolak, L. (1992). Toward a model of the developmental psychopathology of eating disorders: the example of early adolescence. In: J. H. Crowther, D. L. Tennenbaum, S. E. Hobfoll, & M. A. P. Stephens (Eds.), *The Etiology of Bulimia Nervosa: the Individual and Familial Context* (pp. 59–80). Washington, DC: Hemisphere.

Lewinsohn, P. M., Klein, D. N., & Seeley, J. R. (2000). Bipolar disorder during adolescence and young adulthood in a community sample. *Bipolar Disorders*, *2*: 281–293.

Lewinsohn, P. M., Rohde, P., & Seeley, J. (1993). Psychosocial characteristics of adolescents with a history of suicide attempts. *Journal of the American Academy of Child and Adolescent Psychiatry*, *32*: 60–68.

Lewinsohn, P. M., Rohde, P., Seeley, J., Klein, D., & Gotlib, I. (2000). Natural course of adolescent major depressive disorder in a community sample: predictors of recurrence in young adults. *American Journal of Psychiatry*, *157*: 1584–1591.

Lewinsohn, P. M., Striegel-Moore, R. H., & Seeley, J. R. (2000). Epidemiology and natural course of eating disorders in young women from adolescence to young adulthood. *Journal of the American Academy of Child and Adolescent Psychiatry*, *39*: 1284–1292.

Libby, A. M., Brent, D. A., Morrato, E. H., Orton, H. D., Allen, R., & Valuck, R. J. (2007). Decline in treatment of pediatric depression after FDA advisory on risk of suicidality with SSRIs. *American Journal of Psychiatry, 164*: 884–891.

Lieberman, A., Ippen, C. G., & Van Horn, P. (2006). Child–parent psychotherapy: 6-month follow-up of a randomized controlled trial. *Journal of the American Academy of Child and Adolescent Psychiatry, 45*: 913–918.

Lipton, L. (2000). Take gains from placebo effect more seriously, psychiatrists urged. *Psychiatric News* (Newspaper of the American Psychiatric Association) 5 May, pp. 36–37.

Livingood, J. M. (1972). Introduction. In: J. M. Livingood (Ed.), *National Institute of Mental Health Task Force on Homosexuality: Final Report and Background Papers* (pp. 2–7). DHEW Publication No. (ADM) 76–357 [reprinted 1976].

Lock, J., Garrett, A., Beenhakker, J., & Reiss, A. (2011). Aberrant brain activation during a response inhibition task in adolescent eating disorder subtypes. *American Journal of Psychiatry, 168*: 55–64.

Lubell, K. M., Kegler, S. R., Crosby, A. E., & Kach, D. (2007). Suicide trends among youths and young adults aged 10–24—United States, 1990–2004. Centers for Disease Control and Prevention *Morbidity & Mortality Weekly Report, 56*(35): 912–915.

Mahler, M., Pine, F., & Bergman, A. (1975). *The Psychological Birth of the Human Infant: Symbiosis and Individuation.* New York: Basic Books.

Mann, M. (2005). Clinical case discussion. Child Psychoanalytic Colloquium, San Francisco Center for Psychoanalysis, 17 September.

March, J. S., & Vitiello, B. (2009). Clinical messages from the treatment for adolescents with depression study (TADS). *American Journal of Psychiatry, 166*: 1118–1123.

March, J. S., Silva, S., Vitiello, B., & the TADS Team (2006). The Treatment of Adolescents with Depression Study (TADS): methods and message at 12 weeks. *Journal of the American Academy of Child and Adolescent Psychiatry, 45*: 1393–1403.

March, J. S., Szatmari, P., Bukstein, O., Chrisman, A., Kondo, D., Hamilton, J. D., Kremer, C. M. E., & Kratochvil, C. J. (2007). AACAP 2005 research forum: speeding the adoption of evidence-based practice in pediatric psychiatry. *Journal of the American Academy of Child and Adolescent Psychiatry, 46*: 1098–1110.

Marchi, M., & Cohen, P. (1990). Early childhood eating behaviors and adolescent eating disorders. *Journal of the American Academy of Child and Adolescent Psychiatry, 29*: 112–117.

Marmor, J. (1980). Clinical aspects of male homosexuality. In: J. Marmor (Ed.), Homosexual Behavior: A Modern Reappraisal (pp. 267–279). New York: Basic Books.

Marsh, R., Horga, G., Wang, Z., Wang, P., Klahr, K., Berner, L., Walsh, B. T., & Peterson, B. (2011). An fMRI study of self-regulatory control and conflict resolution in adolescents with bulimia nervosa. *American Journal of Psychiatry, 168*: 1210–1220.

Martin, G., Clarke, M., & Pearce, C. (1993). Adolescent suicide: music preference as an indicator of vulnerability. *Journal of the American Academy of Child and Adolescent Psychiatry, 32*: 530–535.

Marttunen, M. J., Aro, H. M., & Lönnqvist, J. K. (1992). Adolescent suicide: endpoint of long-term difficulties. *Journal of the American Academy of Child and Adolescent Psychiatry, 31*: 649–654.

Marttunen, M., Aro, J., Henriksson, M., & Lönnqvist, J. (1991). Mental disorders in adolescent suicide: DSM-III-R axes I and II diagnoses in suicides among 13- to 19-year-olds in Finland. *Archives of General Psychiatry, 48*: 834–839.

Massie, H., & Szajnberg, N. (2006). My life is a longing: child abuse and its adult sequelae. Results of the Brody longitudinal study from birth to age 30. *International Journal of Psychoanalysis, 87*: 471–496.

Masterson, J. (1967). *The Psychiatric Dilemma of Adolescence.* Boston: Little, Brown.

McClellan, J. (2005). Commentary: treatment gidelines for child and adolescent bipolar disorder. *Journal of the American Academy of Child and Adolescent Psychiatry, 44*: 236–239.

McElroy, S. (2000). Are impulse control disorders bipolar? Symposium 29: The coming of age of the bipolar spectrum. Presented at the 153rd annual meeting of the American Psychiatric Association, Chicago, IL, 16 May.

McElroy, S., Strakowski, S., West, S., Keck, P., & McConville, B. (1997). Phenomenology of adolescent and adult mania in hospitalized patients with bipolar disorder. *American Journal of Psychiatry, 154*: 44–49.

McGlashan, T. (1988). Adolescent versus adult onset of mania. *American Journal of Psychiatry, 145*: 221–223.

McHugh, R., Whitton, S., Peckham, A., Welge, J., & Otto, M. (2013). Patient preference for psychological vs pharmacologic treatment of psychiatric disorders: a meta-analytic review. *Journal of Clinical Psychiatry, 74*(Jun): 595–602 (summarized in *The Brown University Psychopharmacology Update, 24*(10): 8, October).

McKeown, R. E., Garrison, C. G., Cuffe, S. P., Waller, J. I., Jackson, K. L., & Addy, C. L. (1998). Incidence and predictors of suicidal behaviors in a longitudinal sample of young adolescents. *Journal of the American Academy of Child and Adolescent Psychiatry, 37*: 612–619.

McMain, S., Links, P., Gnam, W., Guimond, T., Cardish, R., Korman, L., & Streiner, E. (2009). A randomized trial of dialectical behavior therapy versus general psychiatric management for borderline personality disorder. *American Journal of Psychiatry, 166*: 1365–1374.

Melander, H., Ahlqvist-Rastad, J., Meijer, G., & Beermann, B. (2003). Evidence b(i)ased medicine—selective reporting from studies sponsored by pharmaceutical industry: review of studies in new drug applications. *British Medical Journal, 326*: 1171–1173.

Melvin, G. A., Tonge, B. J., King, N. J., Heyne, D., Gordon, M. S., & Klimkeit, E. (2006). A comparison of cognitive-behavioral therapy, sertraline, and their combination for adolescent depression. *Journal of the American Academy of Child and Adolescent Psychiatry, 45*: 1151–1161.

Menvielle, E. (2003). A changing clinical paradigm on childhood gender variance. *AACAP (American Academy of Child and Adolescent Psychiatry) News*, October, pp. 274–276.

Menza, M. (2001). Advances in the acute and long-term management of schizophrenia. Continuing Medical Education, Inc. presentation, San Mateo, CA, 10 February.

Michels, R. (2009). 2009 in review: systematic studies in psychotherapy (Editorial). *American Journal of Psychiatry, 166*(12): 1318–1319.

Miklowitz, D., George, E., Axelson, D. A., Kim, E. Y., Birmaher, B., Schneck, C., Beresford, C., Craighead, W. E., & Brent, D. A. (2004). Family-focused treatment for adolescents with bipolar disorder. *Journal of Affective Disorders, 82*(Suppl. l): S113–S128.

Miklowitz, D. J., George, E. L., Richards, J. A., Simoneau, T. L., & Suddath, R. L. (2003). A randomized study of family-focused psychoeducation and pharmacotherapy in the outpatient management of bipolar disorder. *Archives of General Psychiatry, 60*: 904–912.

Milne, D. (2005). Turns out placebo effect is all in your head. *Psychiatric News*, 7 October, pp. 26–27.

Milrod, B. (2009). Psychodynamic psychotherapy outcome for generalized anxiety disorder (Editorial). *American Journal of Psychiatry, 166*(8): 841–844.

Milrod, B., Leon, A. C., Busch, F., Rudden, M., Schwalberg, M., Clarkin, J., Aronson, A., Singer, M., Turchin, W., Klass, E. T., Graf, E., Teres, J. J., & Shear, M. K. (2007). A randomized controlled clinical trial of psychoanalytic psychotherapy for panic disorder. *American Journal of Psychiatry, 164*: 265–272.

Modell, A. (1965). On having the right to a life: An aspect of the super-ego's development. *International Journal of Psycho-Analysis*, 46: 323–331.

Modell, A. (1971). The origin of certain forms of pre-oedipal guilt and the implications for a psychoanalytic theory of affects. *International Journal of Psychoanalysis*, 52: 337–346.

Mojtabai, R. (2007). Americans' attitudes toward mental health treatment seeking: 1990–2003. *Psychiatric Services*, 58: 642–651.

Moore, T. (1975). Exclusive early mothering and its alternative: the outcome to adolescence. *Scandinavian Journal of Psychology*, 16: 255–272.

Moran, G., Fonagy, P., Kurtz, A., Bolton, A., Brook, C. (1991). A controlled study of the psychoanalytic treatment of brittle diabetes. *Journal of the American Academy of Child and Adolescent Psychiatry*, 30: 926–935.

Moran, M. (2007). Psychotherapy for BPD [borderline personality disorder] gets growing evidence base. *Psychiatric News*, 42(2): 26 ff. 19 January.

Motto, J. (1965). Suicide attempts—a longitudinal view. *Archives of General Psychiatry*, 13: 516–520.

Motto, J. (1979). The psychopathology of suicide: a clinical model approach. *American Journal of Psychiatry*, 136: 516–520.

Mufson, L., & Fairbanks, J. (1996). Interpersonal psychotherapy for depressed adolescents: a one-year naturalistic follow-up study. *Journal of the American Academy of Child and Adolescent Psychiatry*, 35: 1145–1155.

Mufson, L., & Velting, D. M. (2002). Psychotherapy for depression and suicidal behavior in children and adolescents. In: D. Shaffer & B. D. Waslick (Eds.), *The Many Faces of Depression in Children and Adolescents* (pp. 37–52). *Review of Psychiatry*, 21. Washington, DC: American Psychiatric Association.

Muratori, F., Picchi, L., Bruni, G., Patarnello, M., & Romagnoli, G. (2003). A two-year follow up of psychodynamic psychotherapy for internalizing disorders in children. *Journal of the American Academy of Child and Adolescent Psychiatry*, 42: 331–339.

Murphy, G. (1985). On suicide prediction and prevention. *Archives of General Psychiatry*, 40: 343–344.

Myers, K., McCauley, E., Calderon, R., Mitchell, J., Burke, P., & Schloredt, K. (1991). Risks for suicidality in major depressive disorder. *Journal of the American Academy of Child and Adolescent Psychiatry*, 30: 86–94.

National Center for Health Statistics (2001). Centers for Disease Control and Prevention: Deaths: final data for 1999. *National Vital Statistics Report*, 49(8).

Negron, R., Piacentini, J., Graae, F., Davies, M., & Shaffer, D. (1997). Microanalysis of adolescent suicide attempters and ideators during the acute suicidal episode. *Journal of the American Academy of Child and Adolescent Psychiatry, 36*: 1512–1519.

New America Media (2007). "California Dreamers", April 2007. Reported in San Francisco *Chronicle*, 25 April, p. A1.

Nottelmann, E., & Jensen, P. (1995). Bipolar affective disorder in children and adolescents. *Journal of the American Academy of Child and Adolescent Psychiatry, 34*: 705–708.

Noveck, J. (2007). Can moms really have it all with work and children? New Pew study suggests no, but options may be lacking. *Marin Independent Journal*, p. C3, 17 July.

Oberndorfer, T., Frank, G., Simmons, A., Wagner, A., McCurdy, D., Fudge, J., Yang, T., Paulus, M., & Kaye, W. (2013). Altered insula response to sweet taste processing after recovery from anorexia and bulimia nervosa. *American Journal of Psychiatry, 170*: 1143–1151.

Offer, D. (1969). *The Psychological World of the Teenager: A Study of Normal Adolescent Boys*. New York: Basic Books.

Offer, D., & Offer, J. (1975). *From Teenage to Young Manhood: A Psychological Study*. New York: Basic Books.

Ohring, R., Apter, A., Ratzoni, G., Weizman, R., Tyano, S., & Plutchik, R. (1996). State and trait anxiety in adolescent suicide attempters. *Journal of the American Academy of Child and Adolescent Psychiatry, 35*: 154–157.

Olmsted, M. P., Kaplan, A. S., & Rockert, W. (1994). Rate and prediction of relapse in bulimia nervosa. *American Journal of Psychiatry, 151*: 738–743.

Ostroff, R. B., Giller, E., Harkness, L., & Mason. J. (1985). The norepinephrine-to-epinephrine ratio in patients with a history of suicide attempts. *American Journal of Psychiatry, 142*: 224–227.

Overholser, J. C., Adams, D. A., Lehnert, K. L., & Brinkman, D. C. (1995). Self-esteem deficits and suicidal tendencies among adolescents. *Journal of the American Academy of Child and Adolescent Psychiatry, 34*: 919–928.

Pandey, G. N., Dwivedi, Y., Rizavi, H. S., Ren, X., Pandey, S. C., Pesold, C., Roberts, R. C., Conley, R. R., & Tamminga, C. A. (2002). Higher expression of serotonin 5-HT2A receptors in the postmortem brains of teenage suicide victims. *American Journal of Psychiatry, 159*: 419–429.

Parent, S. (2007). The mommy dilemma. *The Ark* [Tiburon, CA newspaper], 17 January, p. 5.

Pat-Horenczyk, R., Peled, O., Miron, T., Brom, D., Villa, Y., & Chemtob, C. M. (2007). Risk-taking behaviors among Israeli adolescents exposed to recurrent terrorism: provoking danger under continuous threat? *American Journal of Psychiatry, 164*: 66–72.

Pate, J. E., Pumariega, A. J., Hester, C., & Garner, D. M. (1992). Cross-cultural patterns in eating disorders: a review. *Journal of the American Academy of Child and Adolescent Psychiatry, 31*: 802–809.

Patel, N. C., DelBello, M. P., Bryan, H. S., Adler, C. M., Kowatach, R. A., Stanford, K., & Strakowski, S. M. (2006). Open-label lithium for the treatment of adolescents with bipolar depression. *Journal of the American Academy of Child and Adolescent Psychiatry, 45*: 289–297.

Pavuluri, M. N., Birmaher, B., & Naylor, M. W. (2005). Pediatric bipolar disorder: a review of the past 10 years. *Journal of the American Academy of Child and Adolescent Psychiatry, 44*: 846–871.

Pavuluri, M. N., Graczyk, P. A., Henry, D. B., Carbray, J. A., Heidenreich, J., & Miklowitz, D. J. (2004). Child- and family-focused cognitive-behavioral therapy for pediatric bipolar disorder: development and preliminary results. *Journal of the American Academy of Child and Adolescent Psychiatry, 43*: 528–537.

Perlis, R. H., Ostacher, M. J., Patel, J. K., Marangell, L. B., Zhang, H., Wisniewski, S. R., Ketter, T. A., Miklowitz, D. J., Otto, M. W., Gyulai, L., Reilly-Harrington, N. A., Nierenberg, A. A., Sachs, G. S., & Thase, M. T. (2006). Predictors of recurrence in bipolar disorder: primary outcomes from the systematic treatment enhancement program for bipolar disorder (STEP-BD). *American Journal of Psychiatry, 163*: 217–224.

Perlis, R. H., Perlis, C. S., Wu, Y., Hwang, C., Joseph, M., & Nierenberg, A. A. (2005). Industry sponsorship and financial conflict of interest in the reporting of clinical trials in psychiatry. *American Journal of Psychiatry, 162*(10): 1957–1960.

Petanjek, Z., & Kostovic, I. (2012). Epigenetic regulation of fetal brain development and neurocognitive outcome. *Proceedings of the National Academy of Sciences of the USA, 109*: 11062–11063.

Petty, R. G. (2006). Overcoming pitfalls in the diagnosis of bipolar disorder. In: Confronting the Diagnostic Challenges in Bipolar Disorder: Examining Stigma and Cultural Barriers. Presentation at Continuing Medical Education LLC-sponsored symposium, San Francisco, CA, 5 August.

Pfeffer, C., Hurt, S., Peskin, J., & Siefker, C. (1995). Suicidal children grow up: ego functions associated with suicide attempts. *Journal of the American Academy of Child and Adolescent Psychiatry, 34*: 1318–1325.

Pfeffer, C. R. (2007). The FDA pediatric advisories and changes in diagnosis and treatment of pediatric depression (Editorial). *American Journal of Psychiatry, 164*: 843–846.

Pfeffer, C. R., Peskin, J. R., & Siefker, C. A. (1992). Suicidal children grow up: psychiatric treatment during follow-up period. *Journal of the American Academy of Child and Adolescent Psychiatry, 31*: 679–685.

Pies, R. (2004). The twin prejudices that divide psychiatry. *Psychiatric Times*, February, p. 106.

Pigott, H. E., Leventhal, A. M., Alter, G. S., & Boren, J. J. (2010). Efficacy and effectiveness of antidepressants: current status of research. *Psychotherapy and Psychosomatics, 79*: 267–279.

Pillard, R., & Weinrich, J. (1986). Evidence of familiar nature of male homosexuality. *Archives of General Psychiatry, 43*: 808–812.

Pinto, A., & Whisman, M. (1996). Negative affect and cognitive biases in suicidal and nonsuicidal hospitalized adolescents. *Journal of the American Academy of Child and Adolescent Psychiatry, 35*: 158–165.

Placidi, G., Oquendo, M., Malone, K., Brodsky, B., Ellis, S., & Mann, J. J. (2000). Anxiety in major depression: relationship to suicide attempts. *American Journal of Psychiatry, 157*: 1614–1618.

Pokorny, A. (1983). Prediction of suicide in psychiatric patients: report of a prospective study. *Archives of General Psychiatry, 40*: 249–257.

Polanczyk, G., Silva de Lima, M., Horta, B. L., Biederman, J., & Rohde, L. A. (2007). The worldwide prevalence of ADHD: a systematic review and metaregression analysis. *American Journal of Psychiatry, 164*: 942–948.

Policy Statement of the American Academy of Pediatrics (1993). Homosexuality and adolescence. *Pediatrics, 92*: 631–634.

Polivy, J., & Herman, C. P. (1999). Distress and eating: why do dieters overeat? *International Journal of Eating Disorders, 23*: 153–164. Abstracted in *Journal of the American Academy of Child and Adolescent Psychiatry, 39*: 1031 (2000).

Pomeroy, W. B. (1972). *Dr. Kinsey and the Institute for Sex Research*. New York: Harper and Row.

Pope, H. G. Jr., & Hudson, J. I. (1992). Is childhood sexual abuse a risk factor for bulimia nervosa? *American Journal of Psychiatry, 149*: 455–463.

Pope, H. G. Jr., Lalonde, J. K., Pindyck, L. J., Walsh, T., Bulik, C. M., Crow, S. J., McElroy, S. L., Rosenthal, N., & Hudson, J. I. (2006). Binge eating disorder: a stable syndrome. *American Journal of Psychiatry, 163*: 2181–2183.

Porter, E. (2006). Gender equality revolution in workforce might be over: more women staying at home with family. *Marin Independent Journal* (p. D2), 2 March [from *New York Times*].

Position Statement on Homosexuality and Human Rights (1974). *American Journal of Psychiatry*, 131: 497.

Potter, L., Rosenberg, M., & Hammond, W. R. (1998). Discussion: suicide in youth: a public health framework. *Journal of the American Academy of Child and Adolescent Psychiatry*, 37: 484–487.

Poulsen, S., & Lunn, S. (2014). Response to Tasca et al. (Letters to the Editor). *American Journal of Psychiatry*, 171: 584.

Poulsen, S., Lunn, S., Daniel, S., Folke, S., Mathiesen, B., Katznelson, H., & Fairburn, C. (2014). A randomized controlled trial of psychoanalytic psychotherapy or cognitive-behavioral therapy for bulimia nervosa. *American Journal of Psychiatry*, 171: 109–116.

Prasad, V., Vandross, A., Toomey, C., Cheung, M., Rho, J., Quinn, S., Chacko, S., Borkar, D., Gall, V., Selvarai, S., Ho, N., & Cifu, A. (2013). A decade of reversal: an analysis of 146 contradicted medical practices. *Mayo Clinic Proceedings*, 88: 790–798.

Raznahan, A., Greenstein, D., Lee, N., Classen, L., & Giedd, J. (2012). Prenatal growth in humans and postnatal brain maturation into late adolescence. *Proceedings of the National Academy of Sciences of the USA*, 109: 11366–11371.

Regnerus, M. (2012). How different are the adult children of parents who have same-sex relationships? Findings from the new family structures study. *Social Science Research*, 41: 752–770.

Reinherz, H. Z., Giaconia, R. M., Silverman, A. B., Friedman, A., Pakiz, B., Frost, A. K., & Cohen, E. (1995). Early psychosocial risks for adolescent suicidal ideation and attempts. *Journal of the American Academy of Child and Adolescent Psychiatry*, 34: 599–611.

Reisman, J. (2000). *Kinsey, Crimes & Consequences*. Crestwood, KY: The Institute for Media Education.

Remafedi, G. (1990). Fundamental issues in the care of homosexual youth. *Medical Clinics of North America*, 74: 1169–1179.

Remafedi, G., Resnick, M., Blum, R., & Harris, L. (1992). Demography of sexual orientation in adolescents. *Pediatrics*, 89: 712–721.

Rende, R., Birmaher, B., Axelson, D., Strober, M., Gill, M. K., Valeri, S., Chiappetta, L., Ryan, N., Leonard, H., Hunt, J., Iyengar, S., & Keller, M. (2007). Childhood-onset bipolar disorder: evidence for increased familial loading of psychiatric illness. *Journal of the American Academy of Child and Adolescent Psychiatry*, 46: 197–204.

Resnick, M. D., Bearman, P. S., Blum, R. W., Bauman, K. E., Harris, K. M., Jones, J., Tabor, J., Beuhring, T., Sieving, R. E., Shew, M., Ireland, M., Bearinger, L. H., & Udry, J. R. (1997). Protecting adolescents from harm: findings from the national longitudinal study on adolescent health. *Journal of the American Medical Association, 278*: 823–832.

Riess, B. F. (1980). Psychological tests in homosexuality. In: J. Marmor (Ed.), *Homosexual Behavior: A Modern Reappraisal* (pp. 296–311). New York: Basic Books.

Ritvo, R. (2006a). Is there research to support psychodynamic psychotherapy? Part I. *AACAP (American Academy of Child and Adolescent Psychiatry) News, 37*(4): 200–201. July/August.

Ritvo, R. (2006b). Is there research to support psychodynamic psychotherapy? Part II. *AACAP (American Academy of Child and Adolescent Psychiatry) News, 37*(5): 262–263. September/October.

Ritvo, R. (2007). Is there research to support psychodynamic psychotherapy? Part III. *AACAP (American Academy of Child and Adolescent Psychiatry) News, 38*(1): 14–15. January/February.

Robbins, D., & Alessi, N. (1985). Depressive symptoms and suicidal behavior in adolescents. *American Journal of Psychiatry, 142*: 588–592.

Roberts, R. E., & Chen, Y.-W. (1995). Depressive symptoms and suicidal ideation among Mexican-origin and anglo adolescents. *Journal of the American Academy of Child and Adolescent Psychiatry, 34*: 81–90.

Roberts, R. E., Roberts, C. R., & Chen, Y. R. (1998). Suicidal thinking among adolescents with a history of attempted suicide. *Journal of the American Academy of Child and Adolescent Psychiatry, 37*: 1294–1300.

Roberts, S. (2007). Hubby-free ... and loving it? Reported in *Marin Independent Journal*, 16 January, pp. A1 & 7.

Robinson, P. H., & Holden, N. L. (1986). Bulimia nervosa in the male: a report of nine cases. *Psychological Medicine, 16*: 795–803.

Rodham, K., Hawton, K., & Evans, E. (2005). Deliberate self-harm in adolescents: the importance of gender. *Psychiatric Times*, January, pp. 36–41.

Romano, S. F., Halmi, K. A., Sarkar, N. P., Koke, S. C., & Lee, J. S. (2002). A placebo-controlled study of fluoxetine in continued treatment of bulimia nervosa after successful acute fluoxetine treatment. *American Journal of Psychiatry, 159*: 96–102.

Rorty, M., Yager, J., & Rossotto, E. (1994). Childhood sexual, physical, and psychological abuse in bulimia nervosa. *American Journal of Psychiatry, 151*: 1122–1126.

Rosack, J. (2005). New data show declines in antidepressant prescribing. *Psychiatric News* (Newspaper of the American Psychiatric Association) 40(17), 2 September, p. 1.

Rose, J. (2000). "Faced with guilt": a suicide risk education tool [Letter to the Editor]. *Journal of the American Academy of Child and Adolescent Psychiatry, 39*: 273–274.

Rosen, J. C. (1992). Body-image disorder: definition, development, and contribution to eating disorders. In: J. H. Crowther, D. L. Tennenbaum, S. E. Hobfoll, & M. A. P. Stephens (Eds.), *The Etiology of Bulimia Nervosa: the Individual and Familial Context* (pp. 157–177). Washington, DC: Hemisphere.

Rosenberg, D., & Wingret, P. (2006). First comes junior in a baby carriage. *Newsweek*, 4 December, pp. 56–57.

Rosenberg, M. (2002). Children with gender identity issues and their parents in individual and group treatment. *Journal of the American Academy of Child and Adolescent Psychiatry, 41*: 619–621.

Rotheram-Borus, M. J., & Trautman, P. D. (1988). Hopelesness, depression, and suicidal intent among adolescent suicide attempters. *Journal of the American Academy of Child and Adolescent Psychiatry, 27*: 700–704.

Rotheram-Borus, M. J., Piacentini, J., Van Rossem, R., Graae, F., Cantwell, C., Castro-Blanco, D., Miller, S., & Feldman, J. (1996). Enhancing treatment adherence with a specialized emergency room program for adolescent suicide attempters. *Journal of the American Academy of Child and Adolescent Psychiatry, 35*: 654–663.

Ruhm, C. J. (2006). Maternal employment and adolescent development. National Bureau of Economic Research Working Papers Series. Accessed online at: www.uncg.edu/eco/cjruhm/papers/maternal on 27 October, 2007. *Labour Economics* [in press at that time].

Russell, G. F. M. (1979). Bulimia nervosa: an ominous variant of anorexia nervosa. *Psychological Medicine, 9*: 429–448.

Sackheim, H. (2001). Commentary: functional brain circuits in major depression and remission. *Archives of General Psychiatry, 58*: 649–650.

Safer, D. J. (2006). Should selective serotonin reuptake inhibitors be prescribed for children with major depressive and anxiety disorders? [Commentary]. *Pediatrics, 118*: 1248–1251. Also reported in *Child & Adolescent Psychiatry Alerts, VIII*(10): 55–56, October 2006.

Saghir, M., & Robins, E. (1973). *Homosexuality*. Baltimore: Williams & Wilkins.

Saghir, M., & Robins, E. (1980). Clinical aspects of female homosexuality. In: J. Marmor (Ed.), *Homosexual Behavior: A Modern Reappraisal* (pp. 280–295). New York: Basic Books.

Samuelson, R. (2006). The end of motherhood? *Newsweek*, 29 May, p. 39.

San Francisco Chronicle (1999). Only 26% married with children. 24 November, p. A3.

Schmidt, U., Lee, S., Beecham, J., Perkins, S., Treasure, J., Yi, I., Winn, S., Robinson, P., Murphy, R., Keville, S., Johnson-Sabine, E., Jenkins, M., Frost, S., Dodge, L., Berelowitz, M., & Eisler, I. (2007). A randomized controlled trial of family therapy and cognitive behavior therapy guided self-care for adolescents with bulimia nervosa and related disorders. *American Journal of Psychiatry, 164*: 591–598.

Schuker, E. (2001). Book review of T. Dean & C. Lane (Eds.), *Homosexuality and Psychoanalysis*. Chicago: University of Chicago Press, 2001. *Journal of the American Psychoanalytic Association, 49*: 1462–1466.

Seiden, R. H. (1971). *Suicide Among Youth—A Review of the Literature, 1900–1967*. Public Health Service Publication. Washington, DC: U.S. Government Printing Office, 1969.

Seidman, S. N., & Rieder, R. O. (1994). A review of sexual behavior in the United States. *American Journal of Psychiatry, 151*: 330–341.

Sell, R. L., Wells, J. A., & Wypij, D. (1995). The prevalence of homosexual behavior and attraction in the United States, the United Kingdom and France: results of national population-based samples. *Archives of Sexual Behavior, 24*: 253–248.

Settlage, C. (1974). The technique of defense analysis in the psychoanalysis of an early adolescent. In: M. Harley (Ed.), *The Analyst and the Adolescent at Work* (pp. 3–39). Chicago, IL: Quadrangle.

Shaffer, D. (1996). Discussion of: Predictive validity of the suicide probability scale among adolescents in group home treatment. *Journal of the American Academy of Child and Adolescent Psychiatry, 35*: 172–174.

Shaffer, D., & Greenberg, T. (2002). Suicide and suicidal behavior in children and adolescents. In: D. Shaffer & B. D. Waslick (Eds.), *The Many Faces of Depression in Children and Adolescents. Review of Psychiatry, 21*: 129–178. Washington, DC: American Psychiatric Association Press.

Shaffer, D., Fisher, P., Hicks, R. H., Parides, M., & Gould, M. (1995). Sexual orientation in adolescents who commit suicide. *Suicide and Life Threatening Behavior, 25*: 64S–71S.

Shaffer, D., Garland, A., Gould, M., Fisher, P., & Trautman, P. (1988). Preventing teenage suicide: a critical review. *Journal of the American Academy of Child and Adolescent Psychiatry, 27*: 675–687.

Shaffer, D., Gould, M., Fisher, P., Trautman, P., Moreau, D., Kleinman, M., & Floroy, M. (1996). Psychiatric diagnosis in child and adolescent suicide. *Archives of General Psychiatry, 53*: 339–348.

Shafii, M., Carrigan, S., Whittinghill, J. R., & Derrick, A. (1985). Psychological autopsy of completed suicide in children and adolescents. *American Journal of Psychiatry, 142*: 1061–1064.

Shane, M., Shane, E., & Gales, M. (1997). *Intimate Attachments: Towards a New Self Psychology*. New York: Guilford Press.

Shedler, J. (2010). The efficacy of psychodynamic therapy. *American Psychologist, 65*: 98–109.

Sikich, L., Frazier, J., McClellan, J., Findling, R., Vitiello, B., Ritz, L., Ambler, D., Puglia, M., Maloney, A., Michael, E., DeJong, S., Slifka, K., Noyes, N., Hlastala, S., Pierson, L., McNamara, N., Delporto-Bedoya, D., Anderson, R., Hamer, R., Lieberman, J. (2008). Double-blind comparison of first-and second-generation antipsychotics in early-onset schizophrenia and schizo-affective disorder: findings from the treatment of early-onset schizophrenia spectrum disorders (TEOSS) study. *American Journal of Psychiatry, 165*:1420–1431. doi:10.1176/appi.ajp.2008.08050756.

Simeon, J. G., Dinicola, V. F., Ferguson, H. B., & Copping, W. (1990). Adolescent depression: a placebo-controlled fluoxetine treatment study and follow-up. *Progress in Neuro-Psychopharmacology & Biological Psychiatry, 14*: 791–795.

Simon, G. E. (2006). How can we know whether antidepressants increase suicide risk? (Editorial). *American Journal of Psychiatry, 163*: 1861–1863.

Simon, T. R., & Crosby, A. E. (2000). Suicide planning among high-school students who report attempting suicide. *Suicide and Life Threatening Behavior, 30*: 213–221.

Sloan, D., & Stancavish, D. (2005). Managing treatment failure: a pharmacologic basis for switch strategies. *Q & A: Depression & Anxiety with Michael E. Thase, M.D.* Supplement to *Psychiatric Times*, 2, June.

Smith, T. W. (1991). Adult sexual behavior in 1989: number of partners, frequency of intercourse and risk of AIDS. *Family Planning Perspectives, 23*: 102–107.

Sobo, S. (1999). Mood stabilizers and mood swings: in search of a definition. *Psychiatric Times*, October, pp. 36ff.

Socarides, C. W. (1989). *Homosexuality: Psychoanalytic Therapy*. Northvale, NJ: Jason Aronson Inc.

Spirito, A., Brown, L., Overholser, J., & Fritz, G. (1989). Attempted suicide in adolescence: a review and critique of the literature. *Clinical Psychology Review, 9*: 335–363.

Spirito, A., Overholser, J., & Hart, K. (1991). Cognitive characteristics of adolescent suicide attempters. *Journal of the American Academy of Child and Adolescent Psychiatry, 30*: 604–608.

Spittler, K. (2005). Endogenous opioid activity may cause "placebo effect". *NeuroPsychiatry Reviews*, October 2005, p. 6.

Stein, D., Apter, A., Ratzoni, G., Har-Even, D., & Avidan, G. (1998). Associations between multiple suicide attempts and negative affects in adolescents. *Journal of the American Academy of Child and Adolescent Psychiatry, 37*: 488–494.

Steinberg, L. (1990). Autonomy, conflict, and harmony in the family relationship. In: S. Feldman & G. Elliott (Eds.), *At the Threshold: The Developing Adolescent* (pp. 255–276). Cambridge, MA: Harvard University Press.

Steinberg, L. (2005). *Adolescence.* New York: McGraw-Hill.

Steiner, H., & Lock, J. (1998). Anorexia nervosa and bulimia nervosa in children and adolescents: a review of the past 10 years. *Journal of the American Academy of Child and Adolescent Psychiatry, 37:* 352–359.

Steinhausen, H.-C., & Weber, S. (2009). The outcome of bulimia nervosa: findings from one-quarter century of research. *American Journal of Psychiatry, 166:* 1331–1341.

Stone, K. (2006). The placebo response. *NeuroPsychiatry Reviews, 7*(10): 10–11, October.

Striegel-Moore, R. H. (1992). Prevention of bulimia nervosa: questions and challenges. In: J. H. Crowther, D. L. Tennenbaum, S. E. Hobfoll, & M. A. P. Stephens (Eds.), *The Etiology of Bulimia Nervosa: the Individual and Familial Context* (pp. 203–223). Washington, DC: Hemisphere.

Strober, M., & Humphrey, L. L. (1987). Familial contributions to the etiology and course of anorexia nervosa and bulimia nervosa. *Journal of Consulting and Clinical Psychology, 55:* 654–659.

Strober, M., Schmidt-Lackner, S., Freeman, R., Bower, S., Lampert, C., & DeAntonio, M. (1995). Recovery and relapse in adolescents with bipolar affective illness: a five-year naturalistic, prospective follow-up. *Journal of the American Academy of Child and Adolescent Psychiatry, 34:* 724–731.

Stronski Huwiler, S. M., & Remafedi, G. (1998). Adolescent homosexuality. *Advances in Pediatrics, 45:* 107–144.

Summerville, M. B., Abbate, M. F., Siegel, A. M., Serravezza, J., & Kaslow, N. J. (1992). Psychopathology in urban female minority adolescents with suicide attempts. *Journal of the American Academy of Child and Adolescent Psychiatry, 31:* 663–668.

Sylvester, K. (2001). Caring for our youngest: pubic attitudes in the United States. *Future Child, 11*(1): 52–61.

Szatmari, P. (2003). The art of evidence-based child psychiatry. *Evidence-Based Mental Health, 6:* 99–100.

Szatmari, P. (2004). Response to Dr. Gupta. *Evidence-Based Mental Health, 7:* 97–98.

Target, M., & Fonagy, P. (1994a). Efficacy of psychoanalysis for children with emotional disorders. *Journal of the American Academy of Child and Adolescent Psychiatry, 33:* 361–371.

Target, M., & Fonagy, P. (1994b). The efficacy of psychoanalysis for children: prediction of outcome in a developmental context. *Journal of the American Academy of Child and Adolescent Psychiatry, 33*: 1134–1144.

Tasca, G. A., Hilsenroth, M., & Thompson-Brenner, H. (2014). Psychoanalytic psychotherapy or cognitive-behavioral therapy for bulimia nervosa (Letters to the Editor). *American Journal of Psychiatry, 171*: 583–584.

Thase, M. (2001). Commentary: neuroimaging profiles and the differential therapies of depression. *Archives of General Psychiatry, 58*: 651–653.

Thase, M. (2013). Comparative effectiveness of psychodynamic psychotherapy and cognitive–behavioral therapy: it's about time, and what's next? (Editorial). *American Journal of Psychiatry, 170*(9): 953–956.

The Carlat Psychiatry Report (2006). *Bipolar II Disorder: A Useful Concept?* 4(8): 2 ff. August.

Thelen, M. H., Lawrence, C. M., & Powell, A. L. (1992). Body image, weight control, and eating disorders among children. In: J. H. Crowther, D. L. Tennenbaum, S. E. Hobfoll, & M. A. P. Stephens (Eds.), *The Etiology of Bulimia Nervosa: the Individual and Familial Context* (pp. 81–101). Washington, DC: Hemisphere.

Thompson, E., & Eggert, L. (1999). Using the suicide risk screen to identify suicidal adolescents among potential high school dropouts. *Journal of the American Academy of Child and Adolescent Psychiatry, 38*: 1506–1514.

Time (2004). What makes teens tick. Science section, 10 May, pp. 56–65.

Toth, S. L., Maughan, A., Manly, J. T., Spagnola, M., & Cicchetti, D. (2002). The relative efficacy of two interventions in altering maltreated preschool children's representational models: implications for attachment theory. *Development and Psychopathology, 14*: 877–908.

Townsley, J. (2001). Homosexuality and science: biology and the social sciences. Presentation at the Midwestern Bisexual Lesbian Gay Transgender Allies College Conference. Online at: www.jeramyt.org/gay/gayscience.html.

Trautman, P. D., Levin, M. A., & Krauskopf, M. A. (1987). Home visits with non-compliant adolescent suicide attempters. *Proceedings of the 34th Annual Meeting of the American Academy of Child and Adolescent Psychiatry*, Washington, DC.

Trautman, P. D., Stewart, N., & Morishima, A. (1993). Are adolescent suicide attempters noncompliant with out-patient care? *Journal of the American Academy of Child and Adolescent Psychiatry, 32*: 89–94.

Trowell, J., Kolvin, I., Weeramanthri, T., Sadowski, H., Berelowitz, M., Glasser, D., & Leitch, I. (2002). Psychotherapy for sexually abused girls: psychopathological outcome findings and patterns of change. *British Journal of Psychiatry, 180*: 234–247.

Trowell, J., Rhode, M., Miles, G., & Sherwood, I. (2003). Childhood depression: work in progress. *Journal of Child Psychotherapy, 29*: 147–169.

Tuller, D. (2002). Gay teen studies called flawed. *San Francisco Chronicle*, 25 December, p. A2.

Turner, E. H., Matthews, A. M., Linardatos, E., Tell, R. A., & Rosenthal, R. (2008). Selective publication of antidepressant trials and its influence on apparent efficacy. *New England Journal of Medicine, 358*: 252–260.

Tynan, W. D., & Pendley, J. (2013). Making the case for case studies (Editorial). *Clinical Practice in Pediatric Psychology, 1*(2): 106–107.

U.S. Food and Drug Administration (2005). Antidepressant use in children, adolescents, and adults. Available at http://www.fda.gov/cdr/drug/antidepressants/default.htm. Originally created 22 March, 2004, revised 12 July, 2005.

U.S. Food and Drug Administration (Office of Adolescent Health) (2014). Sexually transmitted diseases. Accessed at http://www.hhs.gov/ash/oah/adolescent-health-topics/reproductive-health/stds.html   (last visited October 2014).

Van Furth, E., van Strien, D., Martina, L., van Son, M., Hendrickx, J., & van Engeland, H. (1996). Expressed emotion and the prediction of outcome in adolescent eating disorders. *International Journal of Eating Disorders, 20*: 19–31. Cited in Steiner and Lock (1998).

Velting, D. M., Shaffer, D., Gould, M. S., Garfinkel, R., Fisher, P., & Davies, M. (1998). Parent–victim agreement in adolescent suicide research. *Journal of the American Academy of Child and Adolescent Psychiatry, 37*: 1161–1166.

Viinamäki, H., Kuikka, J., Tiihonen, J., Lehtonen, J. (1998). Change in monoamine transporter density related to clinical recovery: a case-control study. *Nordic Journal of Psychiatry, 52*: 39–44.

Vitiello, B., Rohde, P., Silva, S., Wells, K., Casat, C., Waslick, B., Simons, A., Reinecke, M., Weller, E., Kratochvil, C., Walkup, J., Pathak, S., Robins, M., March, J., & the TADS Team (2006). Functioning and quality of life in the Treatment for Adolescents with Depression Study (TADS). *Journal of the American Academy of Child and Adolescent Psychiatry, 45*: 1419–1426.

Waddell, C., & Godderis, R. (2005). Rethinking evidence-based practice for children's mental health. *Evidence-Based Mental Health, 8*: 60–62.

Wagner, K., Rouleau, M., & Joiner, T. (2000). Cognitive factors related to suicidal ideation and resolution in psychiatrically hospitalized children and adolescents. *American Journal of Psychiatry, 157*: 2017–2021.

Wallerstein, J. (1991). The long-term effects of divorce on children: a review. *Journal of the American Academy of Child and Adolescent Psychiatry, 30*: 349–360.

Wallerstein, J. S., Lewis, J. M., & Blakeslee, S. (2000). *The Unexpected Legacy of Divorce: A 25-year Landmark Study.* New York: Hyperion.

Walter, H. J., Vaughan, R. D., Armstrong, B., Krakoff, R. Y., Maldonado, L. M., Tiezze, L., & McCarthy, J. F. (1995). Sexual, assaultive, and suicidal behaviors among urban minority junior high school students. *Journal of the American Academy of Child and Adolescent Psychiatry, 34*: 73–80.

Watts, V. (2014). Expert hopeful about future of treatment for eating disorders. *Psychiatric News (Clinical and Research News), 49*: 18, 21 March.

Weiss, J. (1993). *How Psychotherapy Works: Process and Technique.* New York: Guilford Press.

Weiss, J., Sampson, H., & the Mount Zion Psychotherapy Research Group (1986). *The Psychoanalytic Process: Theory, Clinical Observation & Empirical Research.* New York: Guilford Press.

Weller, E., Weller, R., & Fristad, M. (1995). Bipolar disorder in children: misdiagnosis, underdiagnosis, and future directions. *Journal of the American Academy of Child and Adolescent Psychiatry, 34*: 709–714.

Werry, J. S. (2007). Predicting completed suicide [Letter to the editor]. *Journal of the American Academy of Child and Adolescent Psychiatry, 46*: 1097.

West, A. E., Henry, D. B., & Pavuluri, M. N. (2007). Maintenance model of integrated psychosocial treatment in pediatric bipoloar disorder: a pilot feasibility study. *Journal of the American Academy of Child and Adolescent Psychiatry, 46*: 205–212.

Whitehead, B. D., & Popenoe, D. (1999). Changes in teen attitudes toward marriage, cohabitation and children 1975–1995. The National Marriage Project. Accessed online at: http://marriage.rutgers.edu/Publications/pubteena.htm on 2 April, 2006.

Whittington, C. J., Kendall, T., Fonagy, P., Cottrell, D., Cotgrove, A., & Boddington, E. (2004a). Selective serotonin reuptake inhibitors in childhood depression: systematic review of published versus unpublished data. *Lancet, 363*: 1342–1345.

Whittington, C. J., Kendall, T., Fonagy, P., Cottrell, D., Cotgrove, A., & Boddington, E. (2004b). [Reply/Letters to Editor]. *Lancet, 364*: 661.

Wichstrøm, L. (2000). Predictors of adolescent suicide attempts: a nationally representative longitudinal study of Norwegian adolescents. *Journal of the American Academy of Child and Adolescent Psychiatry*, 39: 603–610.

Wieseler, B., McGuaran, N., & Kaiser, T. (2010). Finding studies on reboxetine: a tale of hide and seek. *British Medical Journal*, 341: c4942. Published online 21 October, 2010.

Wilens, T. E., & Spencer, T. J. (2000). The stimulants revisited. *Child and Adolescent Psychiatric Clinics of North America*, 9(3): 573–603. Cited in Sallee, F. R. (2008). The role of alpha 2 antagonists in the attention deficit/hyperactive disorder treatment paradigm. Medscape Psychiatry & Mental Health ADHD Expert Column Series, posted 24 July, 2008.

Wilson, E. O. (1975). *Sociobiology: The New Synthesis*. Cambridge, MA: Harvard University Press.

Wilson, R. S., Krueger, K. R., Arnold, S. E., Schneider, J. A., Kelly, J. F., Barnes, L. L., Tang, Y., & Bennett, D. A. (2007). Loneliness and risk of Alzheimer disease. *Archives of General Psychiatry*, 64: 234–240.

Winters, N. C., Myers, K., & Proud, L. (2002). Ten-year review of rating scales. II: scales assessing suicidality, cognitive style, and self-esteem. *Journal of the American Academy of Child and Adolescent Psychiatry*, 41: 1150–1181.

Withrow, E. (2007). Global trade in human eggs is thriving. *Marin Independent Journal*, 28 January, p. A12.

Wohlfarth, T., Lekkerkerker, F., & van Zwieten, B. (2004). [Letter to Editor]. *Lancet*, 364: 659–660.

Wonderlich, S., Ukestad, L., & Perzacki, R. (1994). Perceptions of nonshared childhood environment in bulimia nervosa. *Journal of the American Academy of Child and Adolescent Psychiatry*, 33: 740–747.

Wonderlich, S. A. (1992). Relationship of family and personality factors in bulimia. In: J. H. Crowther, D. L. Tennenbaum, S. E. Hobfoll, & M. A. P. Stephens (Eds.), *The Etiology of Bulimia Nervosa: the Individual and Familial Context* (pp. 103–126). Washington, DC: Hemisphere.

Wonderlich, S. A., Crosby, R. D., Mitchell, J. E., Roberts, J. A., Haseltine, B., DeMuth, G., & Thompson, K. M. (2000). Relationship of childhood sexual abuse and eating disturbance in children. *Journal of the American Academy of Child and Adolescent Psychiatry*, 39: 1277–1283.

Wood, S., & Lowes, R. (2010). Psychiatrists dominate "doctor-dollars" database listing big pharma payments. *Medscape Medical News*, 22 October. Accessed at http://www.medscape.com/viewarticle/731028?src=mpnews&spon=12&uac=98285PV

Yan, J. (2008). Spike in youth suicides spurs search for causes. *Psychiatric News: Newspaper of the American Psychiatric Association, 43*(19). 3 October, 2009, p. 1ff.

Yan, J. (2009). Depressed teens sustain gains from long-term treatment. *Psychiatric News: Newspaper of the American Psychiatric Association, 44*(20). 16 October, p. 17ff.

Yan, J. (2013). Genome analysis quantifies risk across psychiatric disorders. *Psychiatric News: Newspaper of the American Psychiatric Association 48*(18). 20 September, p. 14ff. re: (2013), Genetic relationship between five psychiatric disorders estimated from genome-wide SNPs. *Nature Genetics, 45*: 984–994. Abstract posted at www.nature.com/ng/journal/vaop/ncurrent/full/ng.2711.html

Yuen, N., Nahulu, L., Hishinuma, E., & Miyamoto, R. (2000). Cultural identification and attempted suicide in native Hawaiian adolescents. *Journal of the American Academy of Child and Adolescent Psychiatry, 39*: 360–367.

Zalsman, G., Netanel, R., Fischel, T., Freudenstein, O., Landau, E., Orbach, I., Weizman, A., Pfeffer, C. R., & Apter, A. (2000). Human figure drawings in the evaluation of severe adolescent suicidal behavior. *Journal of the American Academy of Child and Adolescent Psychiatry, 39*: 1024–1031.

Zlotnick, C., Donaldson, D., Spirito, A., & Pearlstein, T. (1997). Affect regulation and suicide attempts in adolescent inpatients. *Journal of the American Academy of Child and Adolescent Psychiatry, 36*: 793–798.

Zubieta, J.-K., Bueller, J. A., Jackson, L. R., Scott, D. J., Xu, Y., Koeppe, R. A., Nichols, T. E., & Stohler, C. S. (2005). Placebo effects mediated by endogenous opioid activity on μ-opioid receptors. *Journal of Neuroscience, 25*: 7754–7762.

Zuger, B. (1984). Early effeminate behavior in boys: outcome and significance for homosexuality. *Journal of Nervous and Mental Disease, 172*: 90–97.

INDEX